THE ART
OF THE FILM

by Ernest Lindgren

COLLIER BOOKS
A Division of Macmillan Publishing Co., Inc.
NEW YORK

To Rose, my wife

whose encouragement
and criticism have con-
tributed so much to this
book

THE ART
OF THE FILM

Contents

Illustrations

Preface

The success of the first edition of this book has been most gratifying. Designed as a modest introduction to the principles of film technique, the steady sales of the first edition have necessitated reprinting, it has been translated into several foreign languages, and it appears to have become a standard textbook for organized film courses in America and elsewhere. Encouraged by this undiminished demand, the publishers asked me to "bring it up to date" by the addition of new material for a second edition. A work of this kind, however, which is essentially a statement of fundamental principles, should not require being brought up to date in the same way as a history that has fallen behind its time. If the principles were valid when first presented, they will continue to be so.

It remains as true as ever that any film that is more than a mechanical recording, whether of actuality or a theatrical presentation, depends on its use of editing, and it is still necessary to understand clearly what this means in terms of joining lengths of film together, or combining elements of sound in a re-recording, before one can extend the principle (as Eisenstein himself eventually did) to include the montage of elements within a single shot, or to see in montage the creative mechanism of all forms of art.

It might be thought that one could have added to such a book as this a good deal on the subject of television, which has spread so rapidly since the first edition appeared, but I have not felt strongly tempted to do so, first, because television considered as a subject in itself requires a full and independent treatment, and secondly, because television considered as an extension of the film has not yet, apart from differences of style imposed by its own technical characteristics, developed any new basic principles, and it is not easy to see how it could do so. Both film and television as art forms have in common that they achieve their effects by a succession of moving images and of sounds, and there is no effect obtainable in television that cannot be obtained in the film, although the contrary is not always true; film is still the more comprehensive medium and allows the producer more calculation and precision in obtaining his effects. Television will influence the film in greater or lesser degree, but it is too soon to assess what forms this influence will take; for the moment television is not so much a new and distinctive medium of artistic expression as a window to the world through which one may be shown a horse race, a riot, a religious service, a juggling act, a theater play, a ballet, a new cathedral, a concert pianist or—a film.

I have, however, taken this opportunity slightly to recast the form of the book, and to complete it (as it always seemed to me it needed completing) by the addition of a new section on film criticism, by a revision of the factual references where they had become outdated, by additions to the glossary and by the inclusion of many new stills. In the new section on criticism it has been my aim rather to indicate a fundamental approach than to suggest particular precepts, on the premise that if one's basic attitude is well founded, the precepts, if needed, will suggest themselves.

The acknowledgments made in the first edition I am happy to reaffirm. In addition I must thank Mrs. Margarita Fry for her help in preparing the additional material for this edition and Mr. John Gillett for his kind assistance in selecting the new stills. Most of the stills were supplied by the National Film Archive in the British Film Institute.

The purpose of this book is if anything even more timely in 1962 than when it first appeared; I can only hope it will continue to make its modest contribution toward creating that climate of public sympathy and understanding without which no serious and dedicated film-maker can hope to survive.

For the human mind is capable of being excited without the application of gross and violent stimulants; and he must have a very faint perception of its beauty and dignity who does not know this, and who does not further know, that one being is elevated above another, in proportion as he possesses this capability. It has therefore appeared to me, that to endeavour to produce or enlarge this capability is one of the best services in which, at any period, a Writer can be engaged; but this service, excellent at all times, is especially so at the present day. For a multitude of causes, unknown to former times, are now acting with a combined force to blunt the discriminating powers of the mind, and, unfitting it for all voluntary exertion, to reduce it to a state of almost savage torpor.

WORDSWORTH
Preface to the Second Edition of "Lyrical Ballads," 1800

PART ONE
MECHANICS

1 · The Division of Talent

*The cost of a film ranges between the
price of a hospital and the estimated cost
of clearing the slums of Southwark.*
JOHN GRIERSON

In its methods of production the film differs radically from
the other representative arts. A play, a poem, a novel, a
piece of sculpture, a musical composition or a painting all
have in common that each is normally the work of a single
person, the individual creative artist. George Bernard Shaw,
for example, in the preface to *Immaturity*, describes how
he served his literary apprenticeship: "I bought supplies
of white paper, demy size, by sixpennorths at a time; folded
it in quarto; and condemned myself to fill five pages of it a
day, rain or shine, dull or inspired. I had so much of the
school-boy or clerk still in me, that if my five pages ended in
the middle of a sentence, I did not finish it until the next
day. On the other hand, if I missed a day, I made up for it
by doing a double task on the morrow. On this plan, I produced five novels in five years." Again, Benedict records that
when he visited Beethoven in 1822, he found him at work on
his Ninth Symphony, composing in a room "in the most ap-
palling disorder—music, money, clothing on the floor, the
bed unmade, broken coffee-cups upon the table, the open
pianoforte with scarcely any strings left and thickly covered
with dust, while he himself was wrapped in a shabby old
dressing-gown."

Given the barest necessities of food, shelter and the
modest materials of their craft, nothing stands between
such men and the creation of what is in them to create except their own personal limitations; and the value of the

best that they produce depends essentially on the fact that it is the unfettered expression of an individual mind.

The normal method of film production, on the other hand, requires the cooperation of many craftsmen and technicians working together as a team, as a production unit. To point the contrast, let us set beside the glimpse of Shaw and Beethoven at work a glimpse of Walt Disney at work. He is engaged in a story conference on one of the sequences of *Fantasia,* Moussorgsky's *Night on Bald Mountain.* The music has been played through while the outline story-sketches have been projected one by one onto a screen at the appropriate moments. The conference then proceeds as follows:

B: I think it seems all right.

J: It seems a little incongruous.

Walt: We have to have a little more chance for the audience to understand what this whole thing is about on Bald Mountain. The result now is confusing.

D: If you stuck to a simple theme like having the graveyard spirits come out instead of going to the town, that might simplify it.

Walt: You mean you worry about the town?

D: Yes:

Walt: It sort of symbolizes something. The forces of good on one side and of evil on the other is what I'm trying to see in the thing. What other reason can there be for it?

D: Well, the devil convokes all these spirits in the air and also brings them from the ground.

Walt: Everything comes from the town, doesn't it? The same as the good comes from the town?

D: The music seems too strong for just what there is here on the town. It seems to me it would be more appropriate if you stayed on the mountain and showed wild things rushing about and stormy skies—instead of cutting into a placid town with all this racket going on.

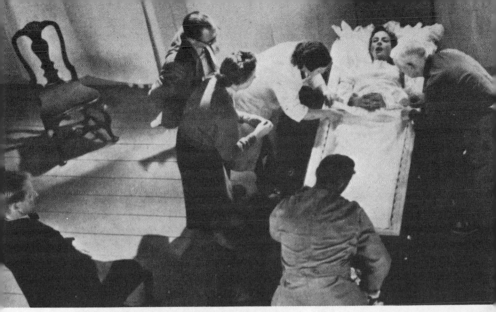

1. *The director in the act of creation.* (Above): *Carl Dreyer (extreme right) arranging a scene for* ORDET *(Denmark, 1955).* (Below): *Tony Richardson working out movements for a scene in* A TASTE OF HONEY *(Great Britain, 1961).*

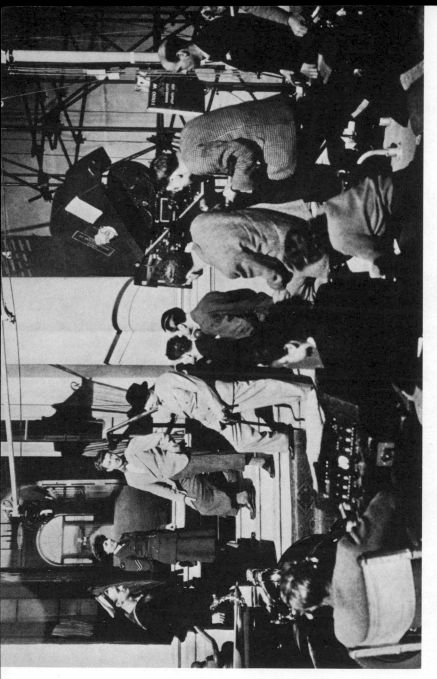

2. *Shooting in the studio. Anthony Asquith (fifth standing figure from the left) directing a shot for* WHILE THE SUN SHINES *(Great Britain, 1947).*

B: You can get a lot of interest out of the town.

J: I don't think the town will be placid when the spirits come down from the mountain. Everything is active. The shutters on the windows and everything will be alive as though bewitched. Then when you come to the end of the town, here is the graveyard, and you follow up with those spirits. I think that will be cleared up as soon as it is properly represented.

B: I was just thinking of a simplification of it.

J: I think it's swell.

Walt: I think you should do more with the spirits retreating, too. The devil pulling all the stuff out of the mountain doesn't seem to mean anything to me now.

At this point in the conference a silence ensues. . . . Suddenly—

Walt: If anybody has any thoughts, speak out. If you think it stinks, say so. If you think it needs something, well what about it? [1]

There have been films in the history of the cinema that have been so far conceived and brought to completion by single individuals as to be properly regarded as one-man productions; but they are the exception, not the rule. Normally a film is made by a cooperative group—the production unit. Film publicists of Hollywood, searching for impressive statistics, have computed that 246 different trades, crafts and professions are brought into the making of a single American film.

It is in America, of course, that the organization of production is most highly standardized, and a brief sketch of the American system, which has become the accepted pattern for studio organization elsewhere, will help to make clear the duties and responsibilities of the principal tech-

[1] Quoted by Professor Robert D. Feild in *The Art of Walt Disney* (Collins, London, 1944). A stenographer is present at all story conferences in the Disney Studio to record the proceedings, so that a report can be circulated to all concerned on the following day.

nicians concerned. It is important that at the outset of a survey that will involve frequent reference to producer, director, editor, shooting-script, and the like, we should understand as precisely as possible what these terms mean.

The head of the film studio is known as the producer. He is responsible for the efficient running of the studio and for the commercial success of its productions: responsible, that is to say, to the board of directors, which controls the company's finances. The producer has a certain sum of money to spend during the year, and it rests with him to plan a program of production within the limits of that expenditure that will show a sound financial return. The film producer is not the equivalent of the theatrical producer. Primarily he is a businessman with a specialized knowledge of public tastes and fashions in film entertainment, an impresario rather than an artist.

The producer's first task in making a film is to find a suitable story. To assist him, the studio employs a number of readers and scouts, under the supervision of a story editor, to comb through books and magazines and to watch new plays for material that might lend itself to film adaptation. Plays and novels that have already achieved a wide popularity lending itself to further commercial exploitation will be considered even when their subjects are not particularly suitable to the film medium.

Although a studio draws much of its story material from such outside sources, a certain amount may be original material drafted by writers inside the studio. They may be commissioned to write, or may themselves submit, stories designed to suit certain stars, or to repeat former successes, or to exploit subjects of topical interest. Original work by free-lance writers unknown to the studio stands little chance of acceptance. At this stage the story is normally presented in the form of a synopsis of a page or two in which the bare outline of the action is set out in the briefest possible form to enable its character and merits to be judged.

When a story has been chosen, its production is entrusted

to an assistant known as an associate producer, who then becomes responsible, under the producer, for coping with all the problems—financial, technical, artistic and personal —the making of the film may involve. In a large studio there may be as many as eight or ten associate producers, and each one will be recognized as having a special aptitude for certain types of film.

The associate producer begins his work by selecting a writer who can be trusted to take the story in its original synopsis form and follow it through the various drafts that will be necessary before it is ready for shooting. He may appoint one of the studio writers, or a free-lance; the one necessary requirement is that the writer's talents should suit the character of the story. In the course of work on the story the associate producer may also call in other specialist writers, one to contribute new situations, another to add some light dialogue, a third to tighten up the continuity, and so on. This is why several people are frequently mentioned in the credit titles of a film as being responsible for the script.

It is probable that a director for the film will have been chosen by the producer; if not, one must now be appointed by the associate producer. The main function of the director is to take charge of the shooting of the picture on the studio floor, that is, to direct and rehearse the actors and to decide how each shot is to be taken. Of all the technicians engaged on the production he is the most important, since it is he who is responsible for the way in which the suggestions contained in the shooting script are translated into moving pictures and sound. In order that he should be able to fulfill this central function most competently, his influence should extend both backward and forward: before shooting it is not only desirable that he should consult at every stage with such immediate colleagues as the art director, the composer, and the cameraman, but he should also work in the closest sympathy with the writer; after shooting there should likewise be the closest cooperation between him and the editor, since the way in which the director has planned each shot should have been conditioned by the function he foresees it playing in the final assembly. Writer, director and editor are the three main contributors to a single craft, the craft of narration or exposition in the medium of moving pictures and sounds. If their work is to have the unity of style and purpose that characterizes the best kind of exposition, and certainly all art, then it is essential either that they should work together in the closest harmony or that one of the three minds (and it is usually the director's) should dominate the labors of the other two. There have even been notable cases where the director has taken on himself the responsibility for all three functions. There are likewise other cases where writer, director or editor has been at variance with, or even indifferent to, the ideas of his colleagues, and the consequence is all too apparent in the finished film.

Most directors have a preference and a special aptitude for making certain kinds of film, and the best of them develop a marked personal style that is as recognizable as the style of an author. The producer will, therefore, endeavor to choose a director whose talents and style are appropriate to the type of story he has in hand.

The director begins his work by discussing the first draft of the story with the writer. When this first draft is completed to the satisfaction of producer, director and writer, it goes to the production office, which supervises the budgets and coordinates the activities of all the specialist departments in their work on the various studio productions. The task of the production office is to translate the story draft into terms of manpower and materials so that an estimate of its cost can be prepared. To supervise this work, the production office appoints a unit manager to look after each production.

The director, in the meantime, will have chosen his assistant director. The designation is a little misleading, since this person does not, in the strict sense, assist in the direction of the picture, nor is he necessarily on the verge of developing into a full-fledged director. He is the director's factotum, his slave-of-the-lamp, and would more accurately be described as "director's assistant." When the director decides that certain properties must be obtained, that certain locations must be explored, that certain types must be secured for a crowd scene, it is normally the assistant director's job to obtain, to explore, to secure. His function is to relieve the director as far as possible of material worries so that he can have freedom to concentrate on ideas and effects without too close a regard to the details of their realization.

It is in consultation with the assistant director that the unit manager analyzes the script and prepares a breakdown showing exactly what each department will be required to contribute to the production. The erection of a given set, for example, will not only concern the art department, but also the carpentry, paint, upholstery, property and electrical departments. When each department has submitted its own estimate of cost, the production office is in a position to estimate the cost of the complete production. If this exceeds the amount the producer originally allotted to it, the writer and director must either justify the increase of expenditure or make revisions in the story that will bring it within the limits of the producer's budget figure.

During the preparatory work on the film, which may take three or four months, the director also has frequent consultations with his art director and cameraman. The art director is responsible for designing the studio sets, including both backgrounds and furnishings, and in some cases the actors' costumes as well. He must be at once artist and architect and practical film technician. In designing his sets he has to bear in mind not only the needs of the director, but also those of the cameraman, who has to light and photograph the sets, and the sound engineer, who has to record in them. Frequent discussions with these colleagues will be necessary and small models are often made so that everyone concerned can see what the finished sets will be like and make suggestions for their improvement. The art director must also have a detailed knowledge of the technical possibilities of the special-effects department. By the use of technical tricks and special printing processes, of models and backgrounds, he can create the illusion of settings that would be far more expensive, or even perhaps impossible, to build full size on the studio floor.

If the director wishes to have music for his film, he will call upon the studio's music department. Usually one composer is assigned to a production, but in the case of a musical, songwriters may also be engaged. At this early stage, when the film still has to undergo many alterations, the composer does no more than sketch in his themes for the various scenes, working to the director's requirements. He will not write the complete score until the shooting and editing have been completed and he can fit his music exactly to the length of the scenes.

The final draft of the story, known as the shooting script, is eventually completed to everyone's satisfaction, and the picture is then described as ready for shooting, or ready to go on the floor. Since it is neither economical nor convenient, however, to shoot the scenes in the order in which they appear in the story, the assistant director works through the shooting script and makes out a shooting schedule, which is a day-by-day timetable for the shooting, with the scenes regrouped so that as far as possible those with the same set or location or requiring the same group of actors can be shot together.

The opening scene of the film, for example, may take place on the deck of a liner, the main part of the action in the port at which it docks, and the final scene on board again as the liner once more puts out to sea. In such a case the two scenes on the liner's deck will be shot one immediately after the other, although in the finished film one is to appear at the beginning and the other at the end; the editor will put them in their proper place when he assembles the film. In the meantime the liner set can be dismantled and valuable studio space cleared for a new set.

This method of shooting is not without its difficulties. It requires the film actor to make adjustments that the stage actor, playing his part straight through from beginning to end, never needs to make. It also demands a most careful attention to detail if clumsy breaks in continuity are to be avoided. In bringing together shots that are widely separated in the film story, the shooting schedule also, of course, separates shots that in the finished film will follow one another. A man may be shown stepping from a drawing room in one shot into a garden in the next, but the shooting of the action in the garden may have taken place a fortnight before that in the drawing room. If the actor has chosen in the interim to discard his brilliantly striped tie for a brilliantly spotted one, the result will be disastrous; as he is shown stepping from drawing room into garden, his tie will appear to undergo a magical change. To guard against errors of this kind is the task of the continuity or script girl, who sits at the director's side making detailed notes of every shot as it is taken.

Because of the importance attached to the star in commercial entertainment films it is highly probable that when the producer first chose the story and decided to entrust it to a particular associate producer and director, he chose the stars at the same time. He may even have set out by looking for a story to suit a particular star. At any rate, the starring players will have been decided on at a very early stage in the production. Thereafter the studio's casting director is called on to select the supporting players, subject to the approval of associate producer and director.

As the time for shooting approaches, the leisureliness of the earlier preparations gradually disappears and the production unit works itself into a frenzy of activity. The studio sets are built and decorated; the stars are tested for makeup and wardrobe; last-minute changes of all kinds have to be made; plans that have gone wrong have to be put right; tempers that have become ruffled have to be smoothed.

The process of shooting a film in the studio normally takes about two months, although for some films, especially where there is a good deal of shooting on location, the time taken may be longer. The taking of a single shot involves a great amount of preparation. In order to light the set effectively, the cameraman will need a considerable number of lamps, and these have to be fixed in position and cables run to them; many minor adjustments may have to be made before the cameraman is satisfied with his lighting. The recording engineer also gets to work placing his microphone and making adjustments to secure the best sound effects. The set is dressed with the necessary props, last-minute minor alterations may be made to the set itself, and any special effects that may be required, such as the production of fog effects or the like, are tested. It is at this stage that the stand-ins appointed for the principal players are brought in to enable the technicians to make their tests for position, viewpoint and lighting. Then the players, who have been kept waiting while all this preparation takes place, come onto the set to rehearse their words and actions under the supervision of the director.

When the director feels that everything is as good as it can be, the shot is taken. If he is not entirely satisfied, or if he wants to make doubly sure, he may order one or more retakes to be made before going on to the next shot; it is much more economical to expose some extra film than to be compelled to construct the setup all over again later on. Working in this way, a unit will on the average shoot, during the course of an eight-hour day, a quantity of film that will account for only three to six minutes' running time of the finished picture. At the end of the day, the film is sent to the laboratories, where the negative of each shot is processed and a print taken from it. These prints, known as "rushes" or "dailies," are seen the next day by the director, editor and other principal technicians in the studio's viewing theater. The set is not dismantled until the "rushes" have been approved.

When the shooting has been finished, it becomes the job of the editor to cut and assemble the various shots. He begins by making what is known as a "rough cut," which is a first rough-and-ready joining together of the shots in their proper order. This is viewed by the producer and director, retakes or additional connecting shots that may seem desirable are made, and then the actors and technical crews are finally dismissed and the sets demolished.

The editor then sets to work to improve his rough cut. He pays the very closest attention to the exact length of each shot and to the precise point at which he will make the transition from one shot to the next. Sometimes he finds he can improve on the original by omitting certain shots altogether or by rearranging the order of the shots. It might appear that the work of the editor would be largely mechanical, especially where the shooting script has been exactly worked out, since he has the script to follow. A good editor, however, can play a part in the creative work of a film. A script is never conceived to perfection, if only because a film is so largely concerned with movement, which cannot be exactly foreseen or controlled; not until the movement is permanently fixed in the cinematograph shot does it become possible to deal with it in exact terms. Obviously the editor cannot achieve miracles when he is given bad cinematographic material; but given good material, he can give its assembly a unity, a tempo, a dramatic force, which, deriving its origin from the script, nevertheless goes beyond what the script alone could provide for.

When the editing of the picture print has been completed, such devices as dissolves, wipes and fades are added by the processing laboratory; the composer writes the full score for the music, timing it to fit the scenes exactly; and the music and any other additional sound effects required are recorded. Finally, all the recorded sound (dialogue, music and sound effects), which will be on several different tracks, is re-recorded onto a single track and the picture negative is cut to match the edited picture print. From this final track and the picture negative, the first print, combining both picture and sound, can be struck.

Such a bald and abbreviated account as this, with each stage of the process neatly divided and labeled, must inevitably give to production the appearance of an altogether soulless and uninspiring routine; in fact, it is so far the contrary that those who work in the studio, from the director down to the merest prop hand who pulls the invisible wire that makes a studio palm tree sway gently as in the wind, are held by a magic from which they seldom find or desire release. In the well-run studio each technician is conscious of being a member of a creative team; there is an infectious air of enthusiasm that engenders a free and easy camaraderie between art director and cameraman, star and clapper boy. Clashes of opinion and temperament arise, of course, but they have to be reconciled in the interests of the production as a whole, and an ability to work well with others is indispensable.

It is evident that the large Hollywood studios are highly departmentalized and that this explains the standardized product that emerges from them, but there are numerous exceptions. Charlie Chaplin, who has ·borne the sole creative responsibility for all his later films, is one. Paul Muni, to judge by his own account, was another; instead of being assigned to a part in a film already chosen by the producer, he chose his own films. "My arrangement with the studio," he wrote in 1938, "gives me a choice of four stories at a time, which the studio submits to me three months before production. I select two of these for my year's work, or two from a second group if none of the first are satisfactory. The choice is made from a script which may vary from a ten-page synopsis to an elaborate treatment. . . . If a synopsis is submitted, the studio supervisor usually discusses it with me so that we may nail down the writer at the earliest stage in his work, and tell him hopefully what we want when he is called into conference. . . . When the writer is at work, the production supervisor confers with him frequently to bring his script closer to what we think it should be. At the end of this period the first rough draft appears. This reaches me, and I take it home, go through it, talk it over with my wife, and expose it to every critical spotlight I can find. Again the producer, writer and I confer. This time we reach a final decision on the script. Now the director comes into the conference. . . ." [2]

Outside Hollywood one finds more marked variations. In England, where production is on a smaller scale, and therefore less highly organized, there is certainly a much greater measure of freedom, and the same is true of France. The director Harry Watt once described how he was sent by his employers, Ealing Studios, to Australia to make a film, how he arrived there alone with only a suitcase, how he spent months exploring the country, looking for a subject and a story, and how he finally collected a team of technicians together and brought back the film *The Overlanders*. Thorold Dickinson, again, worked on the idea of his film, *Men of Two Worlds*, with his scriptwriter, associate producer, cameraman and art director, and this small group went to Tanganyıka to study the background, carry out research, and shoot material on location. Later they returned to Britain and the film was completed at Denham Studios with a full production staff. The production units of documentary films and short films generally are, of course, very much smaller, and in such cases it is even commoner for the director to follow a film through from beginning to end, writing the script, supervising the shooting and doing the cutting. Some of these films are made by selecting and assembling material that is already recorded on film, and in such cases the work of the director is entirely one of editing.

Although this account of production procedure is, therefore, an accurate one as far as it goes and has for us the merit that it indicates the functions of each of the principal

2 *We Make the Movies*, ed. Nancy Naumberg (Faber, London, 1938), p. 132.

technicians and no more, it must be accepted with these two important qualifications: that it is likely to be found in its entirety only in large, highly standardized studios of the Hollywood type and varies from one country to another, from one studio to another, from one type of film to another, and even from one production to another; and that because those concerned are all, in their own sphere, creative workers conscious of making a vital contribution to a work of the imagination, there is an all-pervading atmosphere of creative excitement and an eagerness and freedom of cooperation that the dissecting description entirely fails to convey.

This means, incidentally, that in order to read the credit titles of a film correctly, it may not always be sufficient to know what the titles signify in general; one may also have to take into account the particular circumstances of the production or the personalities of those engaged in it. For example, although two well-known directors, Frank Capra and David MacDonald, were responsible for the form of *Tunisian Victory,* they did not, of course, direct the film in the accepted sense; their work in this case consisted almost entirely of editing material that had already been shot on the battlefield by Army cameramen. Again, those qualified to judge have no doubt that Anthony Asquith was the real director of *Pygmalion,* although much publicity was given to the producer, Gabriel Pascal, and the direction was credited to Asquith and Leslie Howard jointly. A third example is the case of such a man as Erich Pommer, who was described as a producer but who always interested himself so actively in the creative work of his films that they were stamped more with the personality of Pommer than with that of the director working under him.[3]

3 Presumably the system of the Ufa Studios where Pommer first worked was responsible for this. The director Robert Stevenson, reading a paper to the British Kinematograph Society in 1933 on his experiences in German studios, said: "Nowadays in the German system, the director is dependent on the producer in the sense that the producer conceives the film from the outset and brings it to birth, while the director is a craftsman, just as much as the cameraman is. . . . A man like Pommer who, without being a director, chooses the subject, develops the script, guides the director on the floor, and supervises the cutting, can impress his personality and his

Because so many highly skilled technicians and craftsmen and elaborate technical resources are required, the making of a film is expensive in the extreme. Normal production costs for a black-and-white feature film today are about £200,000; a spectacle film in color may cost as much as £5,000,000 (the reputed cost of *Ben-Hur*). Such sums are made possible by the very low costs of distribution and the enormous size of the mass film audience. When a producer has spent (to take our more modest estimate) £200,000, he finds himself with perhaps twenty tins of film negative (ten for the picture and ten for the sound track). To make a positive projection print from this negative might cost no more than £100, and if one supposes that for distribution in Britain fifty such positive prints are made (which represents a fair average), this would give a total cost, for prints only, of £5,000. The huge cost of production is recovered by securing the widest possible exhibition of these cheaply made positive prints in cinemas that are inexpensive to maintain in relation to the many hundreds or thousands of people they can hold. Moreover, after the production cost has been recovered, all additional income, owing to the cheapness of distribution, is mainly profit. If out of four million people (and the weekly cinema attendance in Britain is in the neighborhood of seven million a week) two million want to see one kind of film and two million another, two different films have to be made, each with a circulation of only two million; but if all four million can be persuaded to accept the same kind of film, a producer can get a circulation twice as large for a single film and the additional circulation will produce a maximum of profit for a minimum of expenditure. That is what gives the film industry a constant incentive to provide for the widest possible levels of public taste and to ignore minority preferences.

In no other art is the artist so completely dependent on

---

imagination upon a group of pictures in a way that is quite impossible either for a head office committee, or a director working unsupported." (*Proceedings of the British Kinematograph Society*, No. 20; 1933.)

public approbation. A man who is determined to succeed as a writer can buy his paper, "sixpennorths at a time," and write; his other main requirement, as Anthony Trollope put it, is a piece of cobbler's wax to keep him fastened in his chair. But a nascent Bernard Shaw of the screen, however convinced he may be of his own ability, will have no chance of making a film unless he can command large capital resources. If he has none of his own, he must either work in some subordinate capacity for those who have and help to put *their* ideas on the screen, or else he must borrow, and this he will only be able to do if he can produce convincing assurance not only that the money will not be lost, but also that it will yield handsome dividends proportionate to the heavy risks the lenders will be incurring; that is to say, he must convince his backers that the film will be well distributed and that it will have the widest possible appeal.

Whatever we say or believe about the art of the film will finally have to be measured against these hard facts. It is true that they are severely discouraging to original experimental work and may even prevent the emergence of real talent; as John Grierson has said, "in the practical issue nothing is quite so diffident as a million dollars." On the other hand, they ensure that the cinema will remain an art of the people, and thus protect it against that loss of vitality that overtakes an art whenever it becomes the obscure cult of a precious élite. It behoves the common people, however, to recognize that their position as the true patrons of the cinema confers on them responsibilities as well as privileges; for when we say that the film-maker is dependent on substantial financial backing, this means that in the long run he is dependent on those from whom the financiers expect their profits to come. Alfred Hitchcock once said: "The art of directing for the commercial market is to know just how far you can go. In many ways I am freer now to do what I want to do than I was a few years ago. I hope in time to have more freedom still—if audiences will give it to me." [4]

4 *Footnotes to the Film*, ed. Charles Davy (Lovat Dickson, London, 1937), p. 15.

Film technicians want to make good films, but they cannot make them without the support of the public. It is sometimes said that the members of the public do not realize their power. What is more to the point is that even when they realize it, they have no means of exercising it consciously and collectively. The power of the public in such matters as these can only be exercised unconsciously by individuals being drawn in sufficiently large numbers, for their individual enjoyment, to good films made by sensitive artists and shunning mediocre and bad films like the plague because they know them to be mediocre and bad. It is the intention of this book to indicate the immense resources of the film as an artistic medium and to draw the reader's interest to the exciting preoccupation of watching and encouraging their development, not as a social duty, but for the rich pleasure of it.

The omens for the future of film art were never so propitious as they are today. Until recently the sheer immensity of the vast mass audience, which was the source of the film industry's prosperity as a purveyor of amusement, has been a heavy drag on its development as an art. Members of this audience have been accustomed to go to the cinema week in and week out, because it was somewhere to go, because it was near at hand, cheap and comfortable, because it offered an attractive escape especially from the drab dullness of city life, and because it was a place in which to enjoy a cosy community feeling without any of the social obligations that community life normally imposes. Some films they found entertaining, others boring, but week after week they went, led on by habit and the persuasion of the trailers, not understanding that every time they paid to see a film and sat undemonstratively through it they were casting a vote for more films of the same kind and helping to build up in the film distribution offices the legend of "What the public wants," which has dominated nine tenths of film production for the last forty years or more.

Today this is changing. Television has arrived and is spreading through the world like wildfire, particularly in the highly industrialized countries where the cinemas have been most densely concentrated. Television is the first competitor the cinema has had to face in its own field of screen entertainment. It is cheaper and more accessible than the film; we do not even have to step outside our doors to it, for it brings its mesmeric power to our own hearthsides. The result is that large numbers of the old audience who went to the cinema from habit and because there was nowhere else to go have now deserted it and stay at home to gaze at what is vulgarly but affectionately called (in England) "the telly." In every country where this has happened, the film industry has had to face a serious crisis in its affairs; some cinemas have been forced to close, and those that remain open are often emptier than they were; Jeremiahs prepared to write off the film as a thing of the past have not been lacking.

A slimmer film industry, however, is not necessarily a less healthy one, and it may prove in the end that television has come as a blessing in disguise. In 1929 the German film experimentalist, Hans Richter, wrote a book called *Filmgegner von Heute—Filmfreunde von Morgen* ("Film Enemies of Today—Film Friends of Tomorrow"). By this he meant, as he explained in his foreword, that all those who attacked the popular and ephemeral film-making of the time were the true friends of the better film of the future. Today the screen addicts whose attitude toward the films they saw was either indifferent or complacent are now deserting the cinema for television; the audience that remains contains a correspondingly higher proportion of viewers who have a more positive, although perhaps more discriminating, love for it. The surprising thing is that in such a country as Great Britain, which was the first to have a public television service and where there are today ten million television sets in use, the weekly cinema attendance should still be as high as twelve million a week; that the audience today exercises discrimination may be seen from the fact that although the cinemas are emptier than they were formerly for poor films, exceptionally good films still draw large audiences and are brought back for reshowing.

As an art form the film is developed far beyond the level that has so far been reached by television; those concerned in film-making have the opportunity to build on that advantage and to carry the film, which already has such a rich and varied heritage, to new heights. To do this they will need the support of a devoted and discriminating public, and this public will have to be sustained and informed by criticism and discussion at a new level, such as has only been found until now within the small coteries of film society and specialized cinema.

This is the justification of the study on which we are about to embark.

2 · The Film-Maker's Tools

Although the motion picture medium more than any other calls for the imaginative mind, more than any other, too, it calls for the practical mind.
ERIC ELLIOTT

The invention of the cinematograph, which was completed by 1895, was the result of combining the principles of three previous inventions, the magic lantern, photography and that species of optical toy that gives the appearance of movement to a rapid succession of static images.

One of the best known of optical toys was the Zoetrope or Wheel of Life, the earliest reference to which is the following description by W. G. Horner in an issue of *The Philosophical Magazine* for 1834: "The apparatus is merely a hollow cylinder, of a moderately high margin, with apertures at equal distances, and placed cylindrically round the edge of a revolving disc. Any drawings which are made on the interior surface in the intervals of the apertures will be visible through the opposite apertures and, if executed on the same principle of graduated action, will produce the same surprising play of relative motions as the common *magic disk*[1] does when spun before a mirror. . . . I have given this instrument the name of *Daedalum*,[2] as imitating the practice which the celebrated artist of antiquity was fabled to have invented, of creating figures of men and animals endued with motion."[3]

[1] A reference to another optical toy, the Phenakistoscope, invented a year earlier.
[2] The name Zoetrope was given to the toy in the United States by William E. Lincoln, who took out a patent for it in 1867.
[3] Quoted on p. 23 of Hopwood and Foster's *Living Pictures* (Longman's, London, 1915), to which the reader is referred for a detailed account of these optical toys and their history.

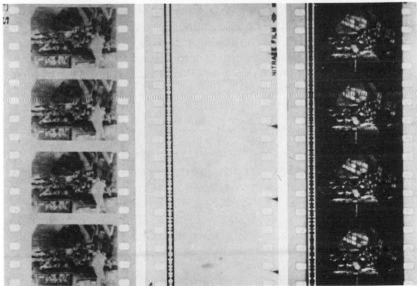

3. (Above): *A Zoetrope (reproduced by courtesy of The Science Museum, London).*
(Below): *35-mm. picture negative, sound-track negative and projection print, shown
actual size (reproduced by courtesy of Ealing Studios from the film* NICHOLAS
NICKLEBY, *Great Britain, 1947).*

In another well-known toy of this kind a number of pictures, each showing a slightly different stage in some continuous action, are printed on the leaves of a flexible book. The bound edge is held firmly in one hand and the book is bent back by the thumb of the other, so that as the thumb is slowly withdrawn the leaves fly past the eye in rapid succession and produce the illusion of a moving picture. It is a more elaborate form of this toy, known as the Mutoscope, that provides the mechanism of the moving peepshow machines still to be found on seaside piers and in amusement arcades.[4]

All these devices are dependent on a characteristic of the eye known as *persistence of vision*. If, while one is looking at an object, it suddenly disappears, the image of it will remain on the retina of the eye for a brief space of time (approximately one tenth of a second) and during that time one will continue to "see" the object although it is no longer before the eye. This can be demonstrated by means of another simple and easily made optical toy of the nineteenth century, the Thaumatrope. A small cardboard disc, an inch or two in diameter, has a drawing of perhaps a bird on one surface and a birdcage on the other. The disc is suspended between two lengths of string fastened into holes pierced at each side of it. When the strings are held taut between the thumb and forefinger of each hand and rapidly twirled the disc spins around, presenting a single picture of the bird inside the cage. What happens here is that the eye sees repeated views of each picture in such rapid succession that the persistence of vision bridges the gaps between them and they appear as a continuous picture. Since two such continuous pictures are being presented simultaneously in the same position, they merge into one.[5]

---

[4] A considerable collection of optical toys, as well as early cinematograph apparatus, may be found on display at the Science Museum, London.

[5] An even simpler form of this illusion is the subject of the following story told by Charles Babbage in his autobiography, *Passages from the Life of a Philosopher:*

"One day Herschel (Sir John), sitting with me after dinner, amusing himself by spinning a pear upon the table, suddenly asked whether I could show him the two

Much the same thing happens with optical toys designed to create the illusion of movement. Whatever their form, they are all designed to present a series of static pictures in rapid succession to the eye. It is essential that each picture in the series should be stationary, or approximately so, at the moment it is observed, and that the observer's vision should be momentarily interrupted while each picture moves away from his line of sight and the next one comes into it. Herein lies the reason for the slits in the Zoetrope. As it spins round, the slits pass before the observer's eye, each slit in turn revealing the image opposite to it within the cylinder. If the band of images in the Zoetrope were run continuously past the eye (an effect that can be obtained by looking at them over the rim of the cylinder instead of through the slits), the result would be merely an indistinct blur. Given a succession of stationary pictures, however, the persistence of vision bridges the gap between them and creates the illusion, not only of an unbroken visual impression, but also, if the pictures represent successive stages in a piece of movement, the illusion of seeing that movement re-created.

The vogue of the optical toy began in the early 1830s. The earliest photographs of unquestionable date are those made by Niepce and Daguerre in 1829. After that it was clearly only a matter of time before ingenious inventors, faced with such a confluence of possibilities, began to search for some means of taking photographs in rapid succession so that they could afterwards be merged again, by a device incorporating the principles of the optical toy, into a continuous visual image with all the movement of the original scene exactly reproduced; this once achieved, it was a short step to add the third element, the principle of the magic lantern, and project these moving pictures onto a screen.

---

sides of a shilling at the same moment. I took out of my pocket a shilling, and, holding it up before the looking-glass, pointed out my method. "No," said my friend, "that won't do"; then, spinning my shilling upon the table, he pointed out his method of seeing both sides at once."

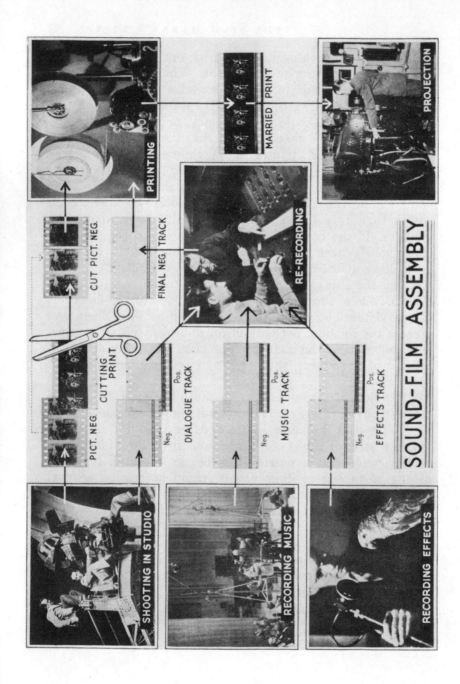

SOUND-FILM ASSEMBLY

PRINTING

MARRIED PRINT

PROJECTION

CUT PICT. NEG.

FINAL NEG. TRACK

RE-RECORDING

PICT. NEG. CUTTING PRINT

DIALOGUE TRACK

Neg. Pos.

MUSIC TRACK

Neg. Pos.

EFFECTS TRACK

Neg. Pos.

SHOOTING IN STUDIO

RECORDING MUSIC

RECORDING EFFECTS

A major obstacle to this development was the difficulty of finding a photographic support that would enable a sufficient quantity of photographs to be taken in regular succession at a sufficient speed, which, as we have seen, means a speed of more than ten a second. The normal support used at the time was the glass plate, and although at least one camera that would allow a series of glass plates to fall rapidly into position was devised, glass was obviously too clumsy for the purpose. Friese-Greene, the English inventor, experimented with oiled paper, and on June 21, 1887, took out a provisional patent for a rapid-action camera made to take perforated strips of "paper or other suitable material." [6] The solution was eventually found in the use of a thin flexible ribbon of transparent celluloid coated with photographic emulsion. The earliest apparatus in which such a celluloid film was certainly used was the Edison Kinetoscope, patented in 1889. This was a form of peepshow machine for showing photographic moving pictures to one viewer at a time; the photographs were carried on an endless band of perforated film, fifty feet in length. It was from the Kinetoscope that the early film projectors of the brothers Lumière in France and R. W. Paul in England, and indeed the whole commercial development of cinematography, derived.[7] A model of the Kinetoscope came into the hands of Auguste and Louis Lumière and suggested to them the idea of projecting the pictures onto a screen. They called their projector "Le Cinématographe," a name that has now fallen into common parlance. Their first public cinematograph show was given on December 28, 1895, in Paris. In the following year they came to London and gave the first public film show in this country on February 21, 1896, at the Polytechnic, Regent Street, London. R. W. Paul

6 Friese-Greene's champions have taken this comprehensive phrase to include celluloid film, with which he also experimented, and claim that the priority of his patent entitles him to be regarded as the true inventor of cinematography.

7 Perhaps the most striking evidence of the fact is that the standard film in use today is almost exactly the same in its dimensions as that which Edison devised for his Kinetoscope; the only important difference is that a sound track has been added.

also adapted the Kinetoscope independently, calling his projector the Theatrograph (subsequently the Animatograph). It is said that Edison rejected the idea of projecting the Kinetoscope pictures, on the grounds that this would exhaust its commercial possibilities too rapidly.

Anyone who has the opportunity to go into the projection box of a modern cinema showing a normal black-and-white picture and to examine the film being projected will find that it consists of a ribbon of flexible, transparent plastic, 35 mm. wide,[8] coated on one side with a photographic emulsion. Both edges of the film are perforated by a line of regularly spaced, square-looking holes (sprocket holes); these are designed to engage with sprocket teeth in the rollers (sprocket wheels) over which the film is drawn in its passage through the projector. Along the middle of the film, and covering most of the width between the two lines of sprocket holes, is printed a series of translucent still photographs (technically known as frames); the remainder of the width is occupied by the sound track. Each frame corresponds to a single picture in the optical toy, and successive frames show, step by step, successive stages in some continuous movement or action. The sound track, which runs along the length of the film in the form of a narrow continuous band, may consist either of a number of transverse lines of various densities (a variable density track) or of a series of black-and-white corrugations or "mountains" and "valleys" (a variable area track); the differences between the two are purely technical and do not concern us here.

In order that this inert ribbon of film can come to life as movement and sound, it has to be run through the projector. This consists of two main parts, technically known as the picture head and the sound head. The picture head (which in the days of the silent film, of course, constituted the

8 35-mm. film is most common and is known as standard film. Narrower widths, of 16 mm. and 8 mm., known as substandard film, are made for amateur film-makers and for nontheatrical projection; and wider film (e.g., 70 mm.) is manufactured for certain forms of wide-screen picture and other special purposes.

whole of the projector) is nothing more than a kind of magic lantern through which the film passes; as it does so, the frames are projected onto the screen one after another so rapidly that the persistence of vision is able to bridge the gap between them and they merge into a smoothly moving picture. As we have already seen (p. 26), the illusion of movement will only arise from the intermittent observation of *stationary* pictures. This is secured in the projector by two devices: the first is an intermittent movement of the mechanism that draws the film through the projection gate in a regular series of jerks and stops; [9] the second is some kind of rotational shutter that cuts off the projection beam at regular intervals. As each frame is projected onto the screen, it is held still for an instant; the shutter then passes across the beam, and during this moment of darkness the film is jerked down so that the next frame comes into precisely the same position as the first occupied; the shutter moves away and this frame is in turn projected. In the case of silent film this cycle of operations was repeated at the rate of sixteen times a second, although this speed, never strictly adhered to, was habitually exceeded toward the end of the silent period; for sound film the projection speed was standardized at twenty-four frames per second.

After passing through the picture head, the film passes through the sound head. Here a thin beam of light is projected through the sound track onto a photoelectric cell and the variations of density or area in the track produce oscillations of intensity in the light beam that are converted into electrical impulses; these impulses are amplified and then carried to loudspeakers behind the screen, where they are converted into vibrations of sound. The movement of the film through the picture head, as we have already seen, is intermittent; its movement through the sound head, however, must be continuous, for any interruption or variation of speed would be audible.

9 So that this jerky movement shall not strain and tear the film, the projectionist in threading it through the mechanism leaves a loose loop of film above and below the picture gate.

Technically, the length of film is measured in feet and (where a smaller unit is required) in frames. There are sixteen frames in every foot of film, so that at the standard projection speed of twenty-four frames per second, one and a half feet pass through the projector every second, or ninety feet a minute. A film lasting eighty minutes, the average length of the present-day feature film, is, therefore, 7,200 feet long. For convenience of handling, such a film is divided into a number of smaller rolls called reels. A reel is commonly understood to be of the order of 1,000 feet, which until recent years was the length of film carried by the spools used in a standard projector. Usually a reel is between 700 and 1,000 feet, but it may occasionally be as much as 1,200 feet. Sometimes the length of film is given in reels, but obviously, because of the indeterminate length of the reel, this can be no more than a very rough-and-ready guide.[10]

It should perhaps be added, for the sake of completeness, that a cinema projection box is fitted with at least two projectors. While the first reel of a film or program is being run on projector one, the second reel is put onto projector two and threaded up so that as the first reel comes to an end, the second reel can be started immediately. The first reel is then taken off projector one and the third reel put on, in order that it can be started as soon as the second reel comes to an end. Using the projectors in this way, and aided by leads and changeover cues [11] of standard design, the projectionist is able to maintain a continuous run that leaves the audience oblivious of the switch from reel to reel.

Although, as we have seen, picture and sound appear together on the finished projection print, they are originally recorded by two quite separate pieces of mechanism. The picture is taken by a camera that has all the essential parts of the ordinary still camera, but in addition is fitted, like

10 For many years now, projectors have been made to take 2,000-foot spools and a 2,000-foot reel is in common use in America and now seems to be becoming standard in Great Britain.
11 See Glossary.

the projector, with a mechanism for running film past the camera aperture in a series of jerks and stops at the rate of twenty-four frames a second. In the early days of the silent film, camera and projector were both cranked by hand and the correct speed was a matter of individual judgment; today they are motor driven and the speed can be regulated exactly.

The film used in the camera is a negative film, and when it has been processed its pictures look like the negatives taken by an ordinary snapshot camera, the darkest parts of the original scene being clear, and the lightest parts dark. Along one side of the picture a path of clear transparent film is left for the sound track. This negative film is never used for projection, of course; for that purpose a positive copy is printed off the negative, and in fact, as we shall see, a mute positive (so called because it is the picture only without the sound track) is made at this stage for use in editing. Apart from the fact that tone values are reversed, and that there is a slight difference in the shape of the sprocket holes, negative and positive film look exactly alike to the nonexpert. Just as in still photography, a large number of positive prints can be made from one original negative.

Where sound is recorded during shooting, as in the case of a dialogue scene, the words of the actors are picked up by a microphone placed as near them as possible (usually it is suspended just over their heads) but outside the camera's field of view. The sound of their voices is converted by the microphone into electrical impulses that are carried along wires to the sound camera. This is entirely independent of the picture camera and is housed in a soundproof recording room cut off from the rest of the studio. Through the sound camera runs a length of negative film at a constant speed of ninety feet per minute. A lamp shining through a narrow aperture throws a small beam of light onto one side of the film as it runs past, and this is photographed as the narrow path that constitutes the sound track. The electrical impulses carried from the microphone cause corresponding variations in either the brightness of the lamp or the size of the aperture through which it shines, the effect in either case being to vary the amount of light reaching the film. When this negative film is taken from the sound camera and developed, it appears as a perfectly blank and transparent cellulose strip, except that along one side there runs a narrow band of photographic emulsion in varying portions of light and dark (the variation being either in area or density, according to the method used).

We now have two lengths of negative film, one known as the mute negative (or picture negative or action negative) and the other known as the sound negative. The projection print is made by printing these two negatives onto a single positive film, where picture and sound will be found to fit exactly one alongside the other; such a positive film is sometimes described as a "married print."

In the case of our dialogue scene great care must be taken in making the married print to ensure that picture and sound are correctly synchronized, so that at precisely the moment we hear one of the actors say a word we see his lips form that word. If picture and sound track are printed even two or three frames out of step, the difference can be disturbing. It is to facilitate synchronization of sound and picture in such scenes that studios employ a clapper boy. At the beginning of each take he stands in front of the actors with a board on which is chalked the title or number of the production, the number of the scene [12] and the number of the take; these data will enable the editor to identify the shot among the many hundreds of others taken in the course of shooting. At the top of the board is a pair of conspicuously striped clappers, the lower half being a part of the board and the upper half an extension of it hinged to it at one end, so that this upper half can be opened and closed with a bang. As soon as the picture and sound cameras have

[12] In studio jargon a shot is called a *scene*, which is a shortened form of the term *script scene* (see p. 60).

begun to turn, the clapper boy bangs the clappers smartly together and then walks away, leaving the actors to play their parts. The loud report of the clappers makes a very well-defined impression on the sound track; the point in the picture negative corresponding to this will be the frame that shows the clappers on the point of coming together. If these two are placed in correct relationship to each other,[13] then sound and picture will be in correct relationship throughout the whole of the take. When they have served their purpose, of course, these lengths of film showing the clapper boy are cut out by the editor.

All cinematograph film, whether positive or negative, sound track or picture, can be cut with a pair of scissors as easily as a strip of paper, and one length of film can be easily and permanently joined to another by the use of film cement. The ends of film to be joined are trimmed square, a little of the photographic emulsion is scraped from one of the ends in order to bare the cellulose base, film cement is applied and then both ends are pressed together for half a minute. The cement (for its composition, see Glossary) momentarily dissolves the two cellulose surfaces with which it comes into contact and creates a cellulose weld that is extremely strong. The process is simple enough, and yet, as we shall come to see, the fact that it can be done at all has been of major importance in determining the character of film technique.

If one shot is joined to another in the way just described and the whole length of film so made is projected, the second shot will displace the first on the screen instantaneously. This change is known as the *cut*. It is the commonest form of transition from one shot to another. It is not, of course, the only form. If while taking a shot the cameraman grad-

---

13 This somewhat involved phrase is used deliberately, since the correct relationship of sound and picture in the married print is not obtained simply by arranging that each picture frame is *side by side* with its corresponding portion of the sound track. Since the film has to travel an appreciable distance in the projector from the picture head to the sound head, it will be clear upon reflection that the two negatives must be so arranged in printing that the sound is a little *ahead* of its corresponding picture. The standard interval is 19½ frames.

ually closes the aperture of his camera so as to reduce to zero the light reaching the film, the effect on the screen will be that of a *fade-out;* that is to say, the shot will gradually fade away until the screen is quite dark. Contrariwise, in beginning a shot by gradually opening the camera aperture, he can produce a *fade-in.* A fade-out or fade-in can be long or short according to the speed with which the aperture is closed or opened. If a fade-out at the end of one shot is superimposed on a fade-in of equal length at the beginning of another shot, the result is the form of transition known as the *dissolve* or *mix:* as the first shot slowly disappears the second gradually appears, and for a short space of time the two are merged together on the screen.

At one time all fades and dissolves were made in the camera. The dissolve was made by ending a shot with a fade-out of a certain length, two feet perhaps, then winding the film in the camera back for two feet, and taking the next shot with a fade-in of two feet. This was an intricate business and was possible only where the second shot could be taken immediately after the first; it is not surprising, therefore, that the dissolve was rarely used. Today, however, all fades and dissolves are made optically in the processing laboratory after the film has been shot, and the cameraman is not bothered with them; when the editor has joined all the shots of the film together in their final assembly, he indicates to the laboratory by marks on the cutting print where he wants such optical effects. The development of laboratory technique has also made possible the introduction of an additional form of transition known as the *wipe.* The simplest form of wipe consists of a horizontal, vertical or diagonal line of division, sharp or blurred, that passes across the screen, eliminating the first shot and revealing the second. There are, however, hundreds of different forms it can take. The line can rotate fan-wise on a fixed point; it can take the form of a star bursting in the middle of the first shot to reveal the second; or the shot can suddenly be made to appear to rotate, like a picture postcard, to reveal the second shot on its reverse side. These more intricate and showy wipes, which enjoyed a brief heyday, are now rarely found outside publicity trailers, where they appear in profusion.

A purely practical consequence of the fact that film can be cut and joined is that a film does not have to be shot in one continuous process, but can be built up from many lengths of film shot at different times and in different places.[14] One result, as we have seen,[15] is to simplify the business of shooting by enabling all the shots that require a given set or location or group of actors to be photographed together; they will be arranged and joined together in their correct sequence when the editor comes to assemble the film. Again, if a director wishes to make it clear that a certain scene is set in Bombay, he does not have to transport all his cast and technicians there; he obtains a number of shots of Bombay from the studio film library or from a stock-shot library specializing in such material (or at the very most he may send a small camera unit to India if that is the only solution) and then inserts these shots into his scene in such a way as to suggest that the whole action was photographed in India.[16] These, however, are purely devices of practical convenience.

The freedom with which film can be cut and joined, together with the independent existence of picture and sound on two separate negatives, makes possible all kinds of arrangement of the film-maker's material that go far beyond considerations of convenience and that have the most vital consequences for the film as a medium of expression. The simplest way for a director to reproduce our dialogue scene would be by means of a single shot showing the two actors

---

14 With this may be contrasted the direct televising of a dramatic production (as distinct from the televising of a film) where the action is given a single continuous performance in the broadcasting studio and the television cameras, working to a prearranged plan designed to ensure smooth continuity, move from one position to another to pick up their various parts of the action as it proceeds.

15 Pp. 12-13.

16 Exactly how such an impression can be obtained will be made clearer by the chapters on film editing.

at once (known to the technician as a *two-shot*) and synchronized with its sound track, so that we both saw the lip
movements and heard the sound of every word they spoke.
The conversation itself might be interesting, but filmically
such a shot would lack interest. The director might add to
its interest by taking a number of close-ups of each actor in
addition to the two-shot and cutting them into it, so that
after a brief glimpse of the two characters together to establish their relationship, we might see first a close-up of Miss
A as she spoke, then a close-up of Mr. B as he replied, and
so on. In this way the picture would gain in variety, but it
would still be bound by an artless synchronization with the
sound track. In listening to a conversation in ordinary life
we do not always look at the person speaking; sometimes we
look at the person spoken to in order to see his reaction to
what is being said. If in the picture negative one of the
close-ups of Mr. B speaking is replaced by a close-up of Miss
A listening to him, precisely this effect can be obtained. In
the married print the close-up of Miss A will be combined
with the sound of Mr. B's voice and on the screen we shall
see the first while we are listening to the second.

Just as the picture negative can be manipulated in this
way independently of the sound track, so can the sound
track be manipulated independently of the picture. Sound-
track film, as we have seen, can also be cut and joined, and
in the earliest days of the sound film some technicians and
critics, recognizing the primitive crudity of the "hundred-
per-cent talkie" then in vogue, maintained that lengths of
sound track should be cut and edited in exactly the same
way as the picture.[17] Since then, however, a quite different

---

[17] Compare Pudovkin, writing in 1929 of the methods employed in his first sound
film, *Deserter:* "I took sound-strips and cut, for example, for a word of a speaker
broken in half by an interruption, for the interrupter in turn overswept by the tide
of noise coming from the crowd, for the speaker audible again, and so on. . . . I
maintain that directors lose all reason to be afraid of cutting the sound-strip if they
accept the principle of arranging it in a distinctive composition. Provided that they
are linked by a clear idea of the course to be pursued, various sounds can, *exactly
like images,* be set side by side in montage." (*Film Technique,* Newnes, London,
1933, p. 170. The italics are mine.)

technique, involving the re-recording of several component tracks onto a final track, has been developed, and is now universally employed where it is desired to combine several sound recordings taken at different times and in different places.

Normally, in a film that has dialogue, natural sound effects and music, only the dialogue is recorded during the shooting on the studio floor. The music is recorded later on a second track, and the various sound effects are also recorded on lengths of film that are joined together to make up the effects tracks. The three tracks, dialogue, music and effects, are then run simultaneously through a re-recording apparatus and re-recorded in combination onto a fourth sound track, which thus becomes the final negative sound track for the finished film. Each of the component tracks is controlled by an individual volume control in re-recording, so that the recording engineer can mix them in any way he wishes; his position is precisely similar to that of a sound engineer in broadcasting, controlling and mixing the sounds coming from several different studios.[18]

19 The flexibility of sound-recording methods is well illustrated by the device known as prescoring, which has frequently been used to record the performances of stars in musical films. Bernard Brown describes it as follows: "[First both orchestra and soloist rehearse.] Next we record the orchestra alone, the soloist mouthing the words silently and the musical director following her. . . . If this is a good 'take' the orchestra is dismissed. The procedure is very economical, as we finish with the musicians in one-half of the time that used to be required to record both voice and orchestra at the same time. . . . Next we play back the orchestral record we have just made, using headphones to listen to it. . . . The soloist has only one earphone, so that she is able to hear the music played back with one ear and her own voice with the other. In order to pronounce her words clearly and get the proper tone placement in her throat, it is sometimes necessary for the singer to make peculiar faces, which she can do without embarrassment as she is among friends and *not* being photographed. In recording the songs it is not necessary to make many takes, as we are able to take the best parts of two or three and assemble them into one good take, which saves a lot of time in addition to the soloist's voice. When his assembly has been done, we make a combined record of voice and orchestra which we use as a play back on the set when photographing the scene. . . . [This is done as follows: The record of the song is placed upon a reproducing machine, which is interlocked with the camera so that the camera and the playback run at the same speed. As the camera turns and photographs the actor, the record is produced over a loud-speaker and the singer mouths the words of the song again . . . she can now think about the scene and look her best, without having to worry about the quality of her singing.]" ("Pre-scoring for Song Sequences" in the *Journal of the Society of Mo-*

Thus sounds may be "assembled" as shots are assembled in editing, but there is a fundamental difference between the methods used in each case. As we shall come to see later, the difference is not merely technical, but arises from the difference between the mechanism of seeing and the mechanism of hearing. It remains true, however, that different though the methods are, in the medium of film both images and sounds, even from the most diverse sources, may be combined, and that any kind of relationship between the two is possible. The significance of this will become apparent as we proceed.

---

tion Picture Engineers, October 1937, p. 356). In recent years the recording and mixing of sound has been simplified and made more flexible by the use of magnetic tape.

PART TWO
TECHNIQUE

3 · The Anatomy of the Fiction Film

People in the know maintain that the true origin of a film is money; in short, that in the first place somebody has to be found who is willing to put money into the affair, so that a story can be bought and worked upon, agreements drawn up with the director, actors and cameraman, a stage hired, and so on. This is all very true; but in order to find that somebody, as a rule you have to pester him persistently, that there is, sir, a magnificent and attractive theme for the most successful popular film of the season, and that you can guarantee him a profit of at least a hundred per cent. And willy-nilly, we have to begin with the story, even if it strikes us as strange that at the beginning of an enterprise so modern, grandiose and technically advanced as a film stands something so old-fashioned and technically primitive as a mere idea, or a literary fiction.
KAREL CAPEK

Having now a broad idea of the way in which a film is made, and of the tools used in its production and reproduction, the way is clear for us to embark on a study of film technique in some detail. Let us then begin by examining the film in its general outline, as a shape, as a whole; and in setting ourselves such an aim, it will be observed, we are presupposing that a film is, in fact, a complete whole and does have a shape. This is the first thing we are entitled to expect of any work of art—that it shall have unity and be a thing complete in itself that we can appreciate for its own sake, every part falling into place to create a satisfying pattern unmarred by redundancies, irrelevances or omissions.

We are entitled to expect this of a film of any kind although the degree of unity may vary as between one kind and another. A newsreel, for example, or a cine-magazine, in which an assortment of different topics is brought together, has very little unity beyond what can be imposed upon it by a uniformity of style and treatment. An educational film derives a greater unity from the fact that it is normally devoted to a single subject, such as the life cycle of a frog or the principle of the lever. A documentary film, again, goes much further because it is usually concerned not merely with a single subject, but also with presenting a point of view or advancing an argument. Harry Watt's *North Sea*, for example, was made to demonstrate that the safety of ships at sea owes much to a highly organized system of radio communications; Paul Rotha's *World of Plenty* argues that the measure for national control and international cooperation among the allies that were essential for the distribution of food supplies amid the scarcities and rigors of war are equally necessary if the world's food supply is to be fairly distributed in time of peace. In such a case, the field of relevant material offered to the director is wide and varied, but the necessity of presenting his argument in the most economical and cogent manner compels him to select only those things that will effectively advance it and rigorously to reject anything that is likely to confuse it. The unity of such a film, in short, derives from the necessity of presenting the argument clearly and concisely; insofar as it fails to do this it will be confused and rambling and lacking in unity.

When we pass, however, from the educational or documentary film to the fiction film, from the realm of exposition to the realm of dramatic representation, we find that is by no means so easy to define the source from which unity springs. We are faced at the outset by the difficulty that a subject or an argument is not essential to fiction. It is true that some stories have a moral: "The story of Eric," says the author of *Eric or Little by Little*, "was written with but one single object—the vivid inculcation of inward purity and moral purpose, by the history of a boy who, in spite of the inherent nobleness of his disposition, falls into all folly and wickedness, until he has learnt to seek help from above." The moral story, however, is a special type of fiction; it is not typical of fiction in general. The great majority of works of fiction, and the best of them, have no explicit moral at all.

Before we attempt to establish the source from which the fiction film must derive its unity, it will be useful to have a tolerably clear idea of what we mean by a fiction film, and what we mean, indeed, by the term *fiction* in general, as applied also to the short story, the novel and the play. A work of fiction is a representation of the behavior of people regarded as individual persons. In *The Poetics* Aristotle described it as an imitation of men in action, and as Professor Lascelles Abercrombie has pointed out, "by *men in action* he does not necessarily mean *men doing things;* he means *things happening in terms of human nature,* events embodied in human lives." [1]

As it stands, such a definition would also include history, and we must, therefore, add the further qualification that the actions with which fiction is concerned must be such as have been conceived primarily in the author's imagination. Just what is involved in this distinction has been aptly underlined by Mr. E. M. Forster in his study of the novel, where he says:

> The historian deals with actions, and with the characters of men only so far as he can deduce them from their actions. He is quite as much concerned with character as the novelist, but he can only know of its existence when it shows on the surface. If Queen Victoria had not said, "We are not amused," her neighbours at table would not have known she was not amused, and her ennui could never have been announced to the public. She might have frowned, so that they would have deduced her state from that—looks and gestures are also historical evidence. But if she remained impassive—what would anyone know? The hidden life is, by definition, hidden. . . . And it is the function of the novelist to reveal the hidden life at its source; to tell us more about Queen Victoria than could

[1] *Principles of Literary Criticism* (Gollancz, London, 1932).

be known, and thus to produce a character who is not the Queen Victoria of history.[2]

The function of fiction in general then, and of the fiction film in particular, is to present an imaginary story of the thoughts and actions of individual human beings. It should be observed, incidentally, that stories that have animals as characters are not excluded by this definition; all of them, from the tales of Aesop to those of Disney, qualify as fiction only insofar as they involve some humanization of their characters. We must, therefore, expect to find the unity of a work of fiction deriving not from a subject or an idea or argument, but from the human activities that are its characteristic material; one should be able to summarize the essence of a work of fiction, in other words, in some statement about its action.

When, however, we compare various forms of fiction, we find our problem complicated by the fact that there are wide differences between the kinds of action they can successfully represent. Comparing the novel with the drama, for example, we find that whereas the story of a novel can be highly complicated, the story of a play must be relatively simple. The reason for this is clear. The play, using the medium of dialogue, represents its story as actually taking place before us while we sit and watch it, and the events with which it is concerned must be such as we can absorb at a single sitting, which in practice means within the space of a little over two hours. The novel, on the other hand, presenting its narrative in the form of a written description in the past tense, is designed to be read over a considerable period of time; the reader may return to it again and again according to his own inclination and convenience.

In *The Poetics* Aristotle draws attention to this difference between the two forms, or rather between tragedy, the particular form of drama with which he was concerned, and epic, the prototype of the modern novel. He suggests that

2 *Aspects of the Novel* (Arnold, London, 1927), p. 65.

whereas the epic can be composed of several interwoven threads of action with many characters and extend over a long passage of time, the conditions of dramatic performance restrict tragedy to the treatment of a single action only. He emphasizes the importance of the singleness of the action to the unity of the drama by saying "epic imitation has less unity; as is shown by this, that any epic poem will furnish subjects for several tragedies."

Although, as we shall discover, there are very great differences between the medium of stage drama and the medium of the film, and although in many respects the film is much more akin to the novel, nevertheless the conditions of exhibition of the film are almost exactly the same as those of the play. The film, too, represents its action as taking place before us while we sit and watch it, and it requires to be viewed in a single sitting; the only difference, indeed, is that most films run for a shorter time than most plays. It follows, therefore, that the story of the most successful kind of film, like that of the best drama, will confine itself to the representation of a single action. In the shape of its main outline, the film has the same kind of simplicity as the play.

To speak of a play or a film being restricted to the representation of a single action, however, is of little use unless we have some idea of what is meant here by the term "a single action." Searching for an illustration, I open a newspaper and my eyes fall upon the words MAN JUMPS INTO CANAL. Here, with a vengeance, is action, the very essence of action crystallized into a headline. As it stands, however, it is incomplete; the editor meant it to be incomplete, so that having shocked me into attention, it would then tease me to read the paragraph below it. In the first place, I want to know why the man jumped in. Did he want to end his life, for example? As I read, this question is answered for me. "Walking along the towpath of the canal at Buckland early this morning, a farm labourer named George Smith noticed a boy in difficulties. . . ." The man, then, jumped in to save the life of the boy. But at once the second question begins to form itself in my mind. What was the result of his action? Was the boy saved? As soon as I have the answer to this, I have the notion of a complete whole: cause, action and result, corresponding to what Aristotle describes as "a beginning, a middle and an end."

The story of the man jumping into the canal to save the boy is hardly, of itself, important enough to make a play. Nevertheless, it is a complete action of this kind to which the form of the drama lends itself. A central character is presented in a set of circumstances that either immediately, or as the result of some development, compel him to take some action or make some decision, and as a result certain consequences ensue.

In the case of any well-constructed play it is possible to summarize this central action in the form of a brief statement. The essence of Shakespeare's *Julius Caesar,* for example, might be described as follows: A high-minded Roman, Brutus, believing the welfare of his state to be imperiled by the personal ambitions of its ruler, Julius Caesar, is persuaded to join a group of political intriguers in their plot to assassinate Caesar and shares in the retribution that overtakes them. Unfortunately there is not, as far as I am aware, a generally accepted term that can be used unambiguously to denote such a concise summary of the central action. Sometimes the word *theme* is used (as when James Agate, groping for the elusive word, says, "I know of no great drama, however difficult, whose gist, purport, central theme cannot be outlined upon half a sheet of notepaper" [3]) ; but *theme* normally means "topic" or "subject," and it may well obscure, therefore, precisely the distinction we are trying to make. The only solution would appear to be the adoption of some such expression as *action-theme* (used, I believe, in Hollywood story departments) or *plot-theme.*

If we analyze any good examples of the fiction film in the same way, we shall find that their actions too are of the kind that can be summarized in a concise statement. Here, by

[3] *The Sunday Times* (London), March 24, 1946.

5. *Conflict and spectacle in the Western.* (Above): *Ricky Nelson and John Wayne in Howard Hawks'* RIO BRAVO *(USA, 1958).* (Below): *John Ford's* WAGONMASTER *(USA, 1950).*

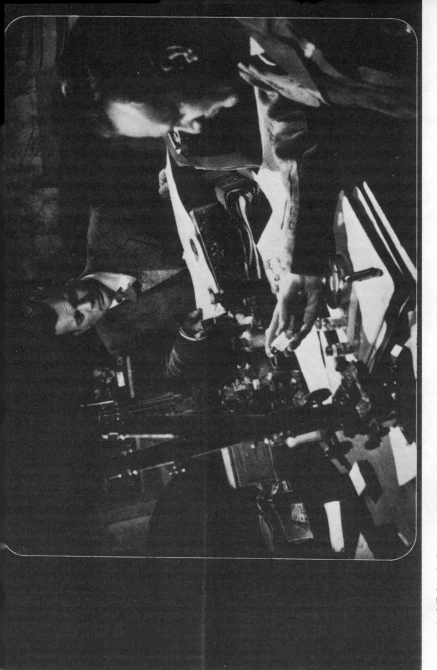

6. A skilled and observant assembly of objects from the studio property department create the atmosphere of this scene from Sir Carol Reed's THE THIRD MAN (Great Britain, 1949). The actors are Joseph Cotten and Trevor Howard.

way of example, are the plot-themes of four films of acknowledged distinction:

Kameradschaft (produced in Germany in 1931; directed by G. W. Pabst) : When the French part of a coal mine on the Franco–German frontier is flooded and men are entrapped, miners on the German side voluntarily cross the frontier and go to their aid.

L'Atalante (produced in France in 1934; directed by Jean Vigo) : The young skipper of a barge on the Seine brings his bride to live on the boat. As the first flush of marital happiness fades, she frets at her confined life and leaves the barge after a momentary quarrel. Piqued, the husband puts off without her, and lost to each other they suffer the anguish of separation until a chance meeting enables them to come together again, reconciled.

The Informer (produced in the United States in 1935; directed by John Ford) : To obtain money to emigrate to America with his girl, a man turns informer against a member of the Sinn Fein, who is shot in resisting capture. The informer's tormented conscience at first prevents him from carrying out his original intention, and then leads him step by step to self-betrayal until, by the rough justice of the Sinn Fein, he is executed.

Brief Encounter (produced in England in 1945; directed by Noel Coward and David Lean) : A middle-aged and happily married woman, the mother of two children, falls in love with a doctor who is also married; realizing that to pursue their infatuation involves deceiving or injuring others whom they love, they decided to part and never to meet again.

Professor Lascelles Abercrombie points out that this completeness of action has no counterpart in real life: "for such is not the process of natural events. In nature nothing at any assignable point begins, and nothing at any assignable point comes to an end: all is perfect continuity." [4] To return for a moment to our newspaper headline, a curious person might go on asking questions indefinitely. How did the boy come to be in the water? Why was the laborer walking along at that particular time? Was he subsequently rewarded for his heroism? Did the reward make him conceited? And so on. Undoubtedly there are answers to all these questions, but as far as the central event goes they are irrelevant and serve only to lead us away from it and on to other events. The completeness and the unity of the action is established by a process of selection, in which all incidents not strictly germane to its development as a logical sequence of cause and effect are rigorously excluded. Such a process of selection is of the greatest importance in all the arts, and not least in the film, as we shall have many occasions to observe. From the very first planning of the action to the final assembly of the completed shots and sound tracks, the film-maker is engaged in selection at every stage.

Thus we find, as we expected, that the unity of a fiction film derives not from the presentation of a subject or an idea or an argument, but from its action; it is dependent on the representation of a single action, the elaboration of a single plot-theme. It is important to understand precisely the sense in which the word *plot-theme* is used here and not to confuse it with subject or idea or moral purpose. *Kameradschaft*, for example, was obviously made with the intention of securing sympathy for the cause of international cooperation and friendship, but it is not from a concept of such a general kind that its unity springs.

An apt illustration of the importance of this distinction is provided by Pudovkin's analysis of the film *Intolerance*. This film, the most ambitious of Griffith's works, failed to achieve the effect its director intended. Despite its undeniable sincerity and great technical virtuosity, audiences have always found it too long and too discursive. In order to represent intolerance as one of the major causes through-

[4] *Principles of Literary Criticism.*

out history of anguish and misery, Griffith employed four stories—the fall of ancient Babylon, the crucifixion of Jesus, the massacre of St. Bartholomew and a modern tale of social injustice. These stories were interlaced throughout the film, so that one sees first a part of one, and then a part of another, the leaps in time being covered by the motif of a mother rocking a cradle.[5] Pudovkin explains the failure of the film saying that its theme is too vast for filmic representation:

> First of all must be mentioned the scale of theme. Formerly there ruled a tendency . . . to select such themes as embrace material spreading extraordinarily widely over time and space. As example may be quoted the American film *Intolerance,* the theme of which may be represented as follows: "Throughout all ages and among all peoples, from the earliest times to the present day, stalks intolerance, dragging in its wake murder and blood." This is a theme of monstrous extent; the very fact that it spreads "throughout all ages and among all peoples" already conditions an extraordinary breadth of material. The result is extremely characteristic. In the first place, scarcely compressed into twelve reels, the film became so ponderous that the tiredness it created largely effaced its effect. In the second place, the abundance of matter forced the director to work the theme out quite generally, without touching upon details, and consequently there was a strong discrepancy between the depth of the motif and the superficiality of its form.[6]

It seems to me that Pudovkin is misled here by a failure to distinguish theme from plot-theme. A page or two later he says "Note as rule: formulate the theme clearly and exactly,

5 The descriptive title in the film reads: "A golden thread binds the four stories—a fairy girl with sunlit hair—her hand on the cradle of humanity—eternally rocking." Terry Ramsaye in *A Million and One Nights* (p. 756) gives the source of the device as the following from Walt Whitman's *Leaves of Grass:*

. . . endlessly rocks the cradle,
Uniter of here and hereafter.

6 *Film Technique,* pp. 7-8.

otherwise the work will not acquire that essential meaning and *unity* that conditions every work of art"; yet the theme of *Intolerance* as he describes it is merely the subject of the film, the idea behind it, and as we have already seen, it is not on this that the unity of a work of fiction is based. The real weakness of *Intolerance* does not lie in the excessive magnitude of its theme, but in the fact that Griffith did not embody that theme in a single clearly articulated course of action. What he chose to do instead was to compose his film of four separate stories, all dealing with the same subject, and to that extent related, but each with its own plot-theme. The interlacing of the stories during their presentation could not disguise the underlying disunity, which sprang from his absence of a plot-theme for the film as a whole.

It should perhaps be made clear at this point that although the source of unity in a fiction lies in its central action and not in the theme underlying it, this is not to say that the theme can be dismissed as unimportant. Not all films have an explicit moral purpose, but they all have an implicit one. Because the author of a story is concerned with human behavior he inevitably expresses certain social attitudes. Sometimes he does so deliberately and consciously as his main object, sometimes he does so only by implication or even by omission, but he cannot escape from the necessity and neither can his audience. A complete appraisal of any film must at some point take into account its underlying purpose and must attempt to assess its value. When all that can be said of its structure and craftsmanship has been said, we still have to relate it to the life it mirrors and of which it is a part. This is something we shall return to more fully in the third part of this book.

It is important that the writer of a film script should attempt to formulate his plot-theme as early as possible. It is necessary to say "as early as possible" because in practice it usually happens that the writer does not begin his work with a plot-theme at all; at any rate, not with the one that finally emerges. He may begin with a much more general idea, such as that of writing a film on Lord Nelson or on life in the mining area of South Wales, or he may work outward from some point of deail. But as soon as the work begins to assume shape, a central action begins to suggest itself, and the writer must then work to develop his narrative in subordination to his unifying concept.

Logically, the next step after the formulation of the plot-theme is the working out of the plot itself in some detail. The main action has to be conceived in a series of minor actions that, as they follow each other in due sequence, serve to introduce the characters, to establish their relationship to each other, to develop the story to its climax, and finally, to round it off suitably at its conclusion. As the work on the plot progresses, the writer begins to visualize his story in terms of scenes and sequences and the contents of each scene begin to assume a definite shape.

Immediately after the writer embarks on this process of planning the action, however, he is compelled to think in terms of the medium in which he is working. If it is the medium of drama, he must take account of the fact that virtually the whole of his action must be represented in dialogue. There are many things that cannot be shown on the stage and that, if important to his story, must be described as having taken place offstage: a horse race, for example, or an earthquake. Moreover, he cannot suddenly leave one scene and change to another except by a fall of the curtain, a valuable device when used in moderation, but one that cannot be employed too frequently without marring the flow of the action; he must, therefore, arrange for one group of characters to move off the stage and another to move on easily and naturally. He may even be influenced in his planning of the action by considerations that are not essential but desirable, such as the desirability, for reasons of economy, of using one set for all the scenes.

I should perhaps interpolate here that the competent artist will regard the natural limitations of his medium rather as sources of opportunity than as irksome restraints. In the

play *Ladies in Retirement,* for example, which evolves round
the murder of a woman, one stage set was used throughout
and it included the bricked-up oven in which the body had
been hidden. The constant presence of this silent accuser
throughout the play added considerably to its suspense. In
the film of this play, however, the producers naturally took
advantage of the greater mobility of the film medium to follow the action from one room to another, with the result
that the oven lost much of its dramatic force. In this case a
gain in freedom resulted in a loss of effect.

The writer of a novel or short story is not bound by the
playwright's limitation. There is no event he is not free to
describe; he can even explore the dim recesses of the unconscious mind, as James Joyce did in *Finnegans Wake.*
The novelist's medium has its own problems, nevertheless.
There is the question, for example, of what point of view he
is to maintain. If the story is to be told in the first person by
one of the characters, this will impose certain limitations
that must be overcome without undue strain on credibility;
if, on the other hand, it is to be told in the third person by
an omniscient narrator, the author must avoid being so explicit as to lose all sense of suspense.

The scriptwriter of a film likewise must elaborate his plot
with a full sense of the possibilities and limitations of the
film medium. It is obvious, for example, that apart from the
restriction to a single action the film-maker is free from
most of the limitations of the dramatist. There is no event,
however vast or however minute, that he cannot show. "The
essence of the theatre," wrote Mr. James Agate,[7] "is that
everything is happening in a small artificially lighted box;
the essence of the cinema is that it has the whole daylight
world to play about in." The film-maker can move easily
and rapidly from one scene to another; he can move backward and forward in time, he can compress or extend time,
he can show actions developing simultaneously. He therefore has greater freedom than the stage dramatist, in the

[7] *The Sunday Times* (London), November 19, 1944.

sense that he is able to control and present more easily a wider variety of dramatic incidents. Even the magical, the fantastic and the supernatural are not beyond his grasp. But he cannot rely so extensively as the novelist on description, at least of the verbal kind. He has to create a representation of something actually happening; it is not enough for him to describe character, he must reveal it in action.

All these, however, are the merest generalities, obvious to everyone, and it is clear that we must explore the nature of the film medium a good deal further before we can fully appreciate the limitations that the scriptwriter must reckon with and before we can judge whether he has made the fullest use of his possibilities.

4 · Editing: Basic Principles

"That's exactly it," I answered gravely. *"If I take people to pieces, I do it so as to put them together again better than they were before; I make them more real, so to speak, more significant, more essentially themselves, if you catch my meaning."*

LOGAN PEARSALL SMITH

"The foundation of film art is editing"; the statement with which Pudovkin begins his classic little manual *Film Technique* is as valid today as when it first appeared in 1928, and it seems likely to remain so as long as the cinema may last. It has survived the advent of sound and is equally unlikely to be weakened by the advent of color or television or stereoscopy.

The development of film technique, in fact, has been primarily the development of editing, for it was a device virtually unknown to the earliest film-makers. The inventors of the first cinematograph cameras began by setting up their apparatus in the open air and taking moving snapshots of anything that appealed to their fancy: workers leaving a factory, a train coming into a station, a baby at a dinner table, men playing cards—these were some of the subjects, for example, that appeared in the first program shown by the Lumière brothers. None of these "films" was longer than fifty feet (the length of the endless band used in the Kinetoscope). Very soon in these early films we find short prearranged and rehearsed pieces of action being shown. In one of the Lumière films the gardener is watering his plants when a small boy creeps up behind him and steps on the hosepipe; puzzled by the stoppage of water, the gardener looks down the nozzle, the boy takes his foot off, and the water gushes into the gardener's face; he chases the boy and gives him the drubbing he deserves. Again, in another film of the same period, a miller with a sack of flour and a sweep with a sack of soot accidentally jostle each other in passing; angry words quickly lead to blows and they belabor each other with their bags until the miller is as black as a crow and the sweep as white as a snowman. Later on (toward 1903) longer films of anything up to eight or nine hundred feet (and thus subsequently called "one-reelers") were produced by joining several such short scenes together to tell a simple story.

Here, for example, are the first three scenes of an early British story film of this kind, *The Life of Charles Peace*, made by Walter Haggar in Pembroke in 1905.

Title: PEACE'S FIRST BURGLARY

Scene I: (Interior: a room.) Peace and his accomplice climb in through a window and begin to lever open a chest. While they are at work, the occupants of the house come into the room and surprise them. Peace escapes through a window. His accomplice tries to follow him but he is shot and falls back into the room.

Title: PEACE AT DYSON'S HOUSE

Scene II: (Interior: a room in Dyson's house.) Peace is discovered playing his violin to Mr. and Mrs. Dyson, who beat time to the music. When Peace stops, Dyson suggests a drink and goes out to get the glasses. Peace sits beside Mrs. Dyson and begins to embrace her. Dyson returns suddenly, and realizing the situation, grabs hold of Peace and throws him down. Peace gets up and goes out, shaking his fist at Dyson.

Title: THE MURDER OF DYSON

Scene III: (Exterior: a corner of a field, close to a

hedge.) Peace enters with a note; he fastens it on a bush and then hides behind the hedge. Mrs. Dyson enters, sees the note, and takes hold of it to read it. At this moment her husband enters, and although she tries to conceal the note, he snatches it from her and reads. Looking into the hedge, he finds Peace hiding and drags him out. Peace then draws a revolver and shoots him. Mrs. Dyson throws herself on the body and Peace walks off in triumph.

All these early film scenes, however, whether complete in themselves or parts of a longer story film, were made in the simplest possible way; that is to say, they were taken in one continuous shot, in one uninterrupted turning of the camera.[1] This meant that where, in particular, the scene was a piece of dramatic action, the camera had to be far enough away for the whole of the action, and all the actors, to come within its field of view.

This is precisely what we find in *The Life of Charles Peace*. The effect is as though each scene had been acted on a theater stage and had been photographed by a camera set up in the auditorium at such a distance from the stage as to cause the margins of the frame to coincide with the stage proscenium. The whole of the setting is visible, but everything in it is detached and remote. The view is always a frontal one and all significant movement of the actors takes place horizontally across the screen, from right to left or left to right. The camera was used mechanically to record a piece of theatrical staging, much as the gramophone is used to record mechanically the performance of a piece of music.

Let us now compare this with a more modern film. In 1935 the French director René Clair came to England to di-

---

[1] It is doubtless as a survival of this early convention that even today in film scripts a shot is commonly described as a scene or script scene.

rect *The Ghost Goes West* for London Film Productions. The story, which was adapted from a sketch by Eric Keown published in *Punch,* concerned a young man named Donald Glourie who was compelled by poverty to sell the family castle to an American millionaire. The millionaire arranged to have the castle dismantled stone by stone, transported to America, and reerected there. In doing this, however, he unwittingly also took to America the family ghost. Murdoch Glourie.[2] It was decided that one sequence of the film should show the ghost landing. This was how the sequence appeared in the first treatment:

SEQUENCE 19
That same night the ghost lands while the stones of the castle are being piled up on the dockside. He finds the place strange, and realizes after contact with the workmen that his old Scottish tongue and modern American slang have very little in common.[3]

Subsequently it was decided to alter this idea slightly and to give action and heightened contrast to the sequence by showing the ghost landing in the middle of a gangsters' shooting affray. This is how the sequence finally appeared in the film, as it is described in the release script (each number in the left-hand margin denoting a shot or script scene):

DISSOLVE TO:
CHIMES
INT. WHARF. NIGHT. LONG SHOT. TRAVEL AND PAN LEFT TO RIGHT.
We see parts of the castle, packages and stones. STOP

2 The dual role of Donald and Murdoch Glourie was played by Robert Donat.
3 This and the next quotation come from the book *Successful Film Writing* by Seton Margrave (Methuen, London, 1936), which consists of an introductory essay on film writing, followed by Eric Keown's original story, and the first treatment and complete release script of *The Ghost Goes West.*

TRAVELING. Murdoch appears in LONG SHOT and walks toward the camera. He looks around.

248. EXT. WHARF. NIGHT. 5 ft. 8 frs. LONG SHOT.
An open car is waiting in front of the door of the wharf. Men are bringing barrels and cases and putting them into the car.

249. INT. WHARF. NIGHT. 6 ft. 2 frs. MEDIUM SHOT.
A man is carrying toward another man. The second sees that the first is going to run into a barrel and tries to warn him.
    SECOND MAN: Hey! Watch out!
CASE DROPS
But it is too late, and the first man drops the case. They look around furtively.

250. MEDIUM SHOT. 4 ft. 10 frs.
A watchman who was doing his rounds hears this noise and looks off-left in its direction. He brings his gun out.
    WATCHMAN: Hey! What are you doing in here? . . .

251. MEDIUM LONG SHOT. 4 ft.
The two gangsters. They hear (off-screen): . . . Hands up or I'll shoot! The second, then the first, fire off-left.
GUNSHOTS

253. MEDIUM CLOSE SHOT. 2 ft. 4 frs.
An iron door opens, a gangster enters and fires off-right.
GUNSHOTS

254. MEDIUM SHOT. 2 ft. 2 frs.
The watchman realizes someone is firing from the other side, ducks down behind boxes and starts firing off-right.
GUNSHOTS

255. MEDIUM LONG SHOT. 6 ft. 9 frs.
PAN RIGHT TO LEFT and show gangsters hiding behind cases of stones, firing away.
GUNSHOTS

256. CLOSE SHOT. 2 ft. 3 frs.
Showing one of the armors of the castle. PAN TO LEFT and
show a gangster emerging with a machine-gun, which he
brings up into position for firing.
GUNSHOTS
MACHINE-GUN FIRE

257. MEDIUM LONG SHOT. 4 ft. 14 frs.
Murdoch looking around bewildered. We see men firing be-
hind him, and we see the shots through him.
MACHINE-GUN FIRE

258. MEDIUM SHOT. 3 ft. 10 frs.
More policemen arrive and duck by the side of the watch-
man. They fire off-right.
MACHINE-GUN FIRE

259. MEDIUM SHOT. 3 ft. 11 frs.
Of Murdoch, looking around right and left.
NOISE LESSENS

260. MEDIUM LONG SHOT. 6 ft. 3 frs.
Three gangsters back in from right and fire off-right as
they back up and exit. Then three more gangsters run
through from right to left.
NOISE CEASES

There is obviously a great difference of technique between this and *The Life of Charles Peace*. In the modern
film a scene is not normally taken in one single shot but is
built up by the combination of a number of shots, each
showing only a fragment of the complete action. Some are
taken from one viewpoint, some from another; some are
taken with the camera a considerable distance away from
the subject (the long shot), others are taken with the
camera very near (the close shot). Such a technique is made
possible by the fact that, as we have already seen, cinematograph film can easily be cut and joined. But this alone does
not justify or explain it, since in any case it is clearly a

more laborious procedure to take several shots of a short piece of dramatic action than to take one. Nobody who looks at an early film and a modern film together on the screen can doubt that the modern film is much more interesting, lively and realistic. The question that arises is: Why should it be so? What is the essential, the fundamental difference between the old method and the new?

To find the answer to this question let us call into the witness box some well-known writers of prose fiction. The first witness shall be the nineteenth-century author Wilkie Collins. In one of his short stories, *The Terribly Strange Bed,* he describes how he went to a gaming house and won a lot of money at cards, and was then induced to spend the night in the house in a four-poster bed, the canopy of which, as he afterward discovered, could be silently screwed down to suffocate its sleeping occupant. Fortunately, he was unable to sleep, and so was saved from murder. This is how he describes his restlessness after he had got into bed:

I looked about the room at the different articles of furniture. . . . There was, first, the bed I was lying in; a four-poster bed, of all things in the world to meet with in Paris. . . . Then there was the marble-topped wash-hand stand, from which the water I had spilled, in my hurry to pour it out, was still dripping, slowly and more slowly, on the brick floor. Then two small chairs, with my coat, waistcoat, and trousers flung on them. Then a large elbow-chair, covered with dirty white dimity, with my cravat and shirt-collar thrown over the back. Then a chest of drawers with two of the brass handles off, and a tawdry, broken china inkstand placed on it by the way of ornament for the top. Then the dressing-table, adorned by a very small looking-glass, and a very large pincushion. Then the window—an unusually large window. Then a dark old picture, which the feeble candle dimly showed me. . . . This picture put a kind of constraint upon me to look upward too—at the top of the bed. It was a gloomy and not an interesting object, and I looked back at the picture. . . .

The second witness is Samuel Richardson, the eighteenth-century author of *Clarissa*. At one point in the novel Clarissa is abducted from her home by Robert Lovelace. To frighten her into running away with him Lovelace arranges for his servant to bang outside the door while they are talking, and he then tells Clarissa that it is her brother and uncles coming to attack him. Clarissa describes the scene afterward in a letter:

> Now behind me, now before me, now on this side, now on that, turned I my affrighted face, in the same moment; expecting a furious Brother here, armed servants there, an enraged Sister screaming, and a Father armed with terror in his countenance more dreadful than even the drawn sword which I saw, or those I apprehended.

And finally, here is an extract from the short detective story called "The Case of Oscar Brodski" [4] by an author of our own day, R. Austin Freeman:

> Thorndyke glanced at the rail with but slight attention: that question had ceased to interest him. But the light of his lantern flashed on to the ground at the side of the track—a loose, gravelly soil mixed with fragments of chalk—and from thence to the soles of the inspector's boots, which were displayed as he knelt by the rail.
>
> "You observe, Jervis?" he said in a low voice, and I nodded. The inspector's boot-soles were covered with adherent particles of gravel and conspicuously marked by the chalk on which he had trodden.

It is the business of the writer of fiction to observe life and to describe his characters and their reactions in life-like terms, and the evidence of all the three witnesses we have chosen testifies to one fact; namely, that it is a normal

4 In *The Singing Bone* (Hodder and Stoughton, London).

part of our behavior—so normal, indeed, that we never stop to remark on it—to look one moment at one thing, and the next moment at another, according to the direction in which our attention is attracted. Sometimes in order to alter our view a mere movement of the eyes is sufficient; sometimes we may turn our head round, or up or down; sometimes we may feel impelled to move our whole body, either to turn round, or to walk to a particular point.

The view of dramatic action that we get in a theater where we gaze from a distance at a room with its fourth wall removed so that only three walls are visible, and where the action takes place in an area of our field of vision so limited that we can follow the whole of it without the necessity of turning our head to one side or the other, up or down—such a view is in the highest degree artificial, and quite unlike our experience in real life. When I actually enter a room, I find it impossible to see the whole of the room at once. I must look to the left, to the right, before me, behind me, up to the ceiling, down to the floor. At each moment what I see will be no more than a fragment of the room; only in my memory can there ever be a complete picture of it, built up from the various fragments as I gaze at each in turn.

Similarly, if I am in the middle of a scene of action, I shall find my attention, and with it my glance, attracted now in this direction and now in that. I may suddenly turn a street corner to find a small boy, thinking himself unobserved, carefully aiming a stone at a tempting window. As he throws it, my eyes instinctively and instantly turn to the window to see if he hits it. Immediately after they turn back to the boy again to see what he does next. Perhaps he has just caught sight of me and gives a cheeky grin; then he looks past me, his expression changes, and he bolts away as fast as his short legs will carry him. I look behind me to discover the reason, and find that a policeman has just turned the corner.

So we find that Wilkie Collins *"looked about the room . . .*

there was *first* the bed ... *then* there was the marble-topped wash-hand stand ... *then* two small chairs" and so on, and finally, "the dark old picture, which the feeble candle dimly showed me. This picture," he continues, "put a kind of constraint upon me to *look upward,* too—at the top of the bed. It was a gloomy and not an interesting object, and I *looked back* at the picture." And Richardson's Clarissa, frantic with terror, writes of herself thus: "Now *behind* me, now *before* me, now on *this side,* now on *that, turned* I my affrighted face." And thirdly, the observant Thorndyke of Austin Freeman's story, patiently searching for clues to a murder beside a railway line, *"glanced at the rail* with but slight attention: that question had ceased to interest him. But the light of his lantern"—and with it, of course, his roving eyes—*"flashed on to the ground ... and *from thence to the soles of the inspector's boots."*

The fundamental psychological justification of editing as a method of representing the physical world around us lies in the fact that it reproduces this mental process in which one visual image follows another as our attention is drawn to this point and to that in our surroundings. Insofar as the film is photographic and reproduces movement, it can give us a lifelike semblance of what we see; insofar as it employs editing, it can reproduce the *manner* in which we normally see it. This explains why the modern film is so much more vivid and interesting and lifelike than the primitive film, which was limited to the artificial, unreal manner of the theater.[5] It also explains a great deal more. Indeed, as will be apparent before we have done, this very simple fact is the keystone not merely by the whole theory of film editing, but of the whole technique of filmic representation. But for the present we must confine ourselves to editing.

During all our waking hours our glance is being constantly and instinctively directed from one point of attention to another: even as you read this book it is traveling

---

5 In the theater itself this artificiality is not felt as a restriction because the art of the play is essentially an art of speech and dialogue, not *essentially* a visual art.

steadily from word to word, from line to line; but this movement of the eye does not always proceed at the same rate. When a man is in a calm and placid mood, it will take place in quite a slow and leisurely fashion. If one may judge from the calm deliberation of his description, it was in this way that Wilkie Collins, waiting in his bed for the sleep that would not come, eyed his surroundings:

> I looked about the room at the different articles of fur-niture. . . . There was, first, the bed I was lying in; a four-poster bed, of all things in the world to meet with in Paris. . . . Then there was the marble-topped wash-hand stand, from which the water I had spilled, in my hurry to pour it out, was still dripping, slowly and more slowly, on to the brick floor

and so on.

But when the same man becomes an observer of, or a participant in, a very exciting and quickly moving piece of action, the tempo of his reactions is generally accelerated: his inclination is to throw his glance rapidly from one detail to another as he endeavors, with an almost feverish intensity, to absorb every implication of the scene. So we find Clarissa, startled with terror, Lovelace beseeching her to fly against her will on the one hand, the banging on the door resounding in her ears on the other, describing her feelings thus:

> Now behind me, now before me, now on this side, now on that, turned I my affrighted face, in the same moment; expecting a furious Brother here, armed servants there, an enraged Sister screaming, and a Father armed with terror in his countenance. . . .

Clarissa emphasizes the speed of her reactions by the use of the phrase "in the same moment," just as Wilkie Collins emphasizes the casualness of his by the detail of the water dripping, "slowly and more slowly." [6]

The impressions of a tranquil observer can be reproduced

6 Those who have seen Pudovkin's film *Mother* may remember that in the scene in which the mother sits motionless in her sad, night-long vigil by the body of her husband, Pudovkin inserts a close-up of water dripping slowly into a bowl.

in the film by what is known as slow cutting; that is to say, by the use of lengthy shots, each of which will remain on the screen for some little time before it is replaced by the next. The movement from shot to shot may be retarded still further, where necessary, by the use of the dissolve instead of the cut to emphasize the passage of time, even within the scene.

Contrariwise, the impressions of a highly excited observer can be reproduced by quick cutting; that is to say, by the use of a series of very short shots that follow each other with great rapidity.

Part of the skill of the film-maker lies in carefully adjusting the tempo of his cutting to the emotional content of his scene and in securing the alternation of one tempo with another so as to secure the clearest articulation of the rhythm of the film as a whole. Quick cutting in a scene that is quiet and peaceful will appear jerky and abrupt and give the spectator an appreciable sense of discomfort. For an exciting scene, on the other hand, he will instinctively demand quick cutting; his mind will be impelled to leap from one detail to the next, and unless the film editor in his cutting has anticipated these impulses at the right moment, the scene will suffer from slowness and heaviness and the excitement will be to a large extent destroyed. In such a scene as this, indeed, by accelerating the cutting speed even to a supernormal degree, the film-maker can, if he wishes, exaggerate the intensity of the spectator's excitement.

It is quite a mistake to suppose, however, that the speed of the cutting alone is sufficient to influence the spectator's emotions, as some writers appear to suggest. The cutting speed must be determined entirely by the emotional content of the scene. That is to say, it has its source, in the last analysis, in the film script. It is the script that guides both director and editor, and the pattern of cutting tempos that they produce in the finished film can only be one that already exists in more or less clearly defined outline in the narrative embodied in the script.

A characteristic example of quick cutting may be found

in the extract from D. W. Griffith's film *Intolerance,* quoted in Lewis Jacobs's book, *The Rise of the American Film.* Factory workers have come out on strike against a wage cut: the militia are brought out to subdue the strikers and they fire on them; in consternation the factory manager telephones to the owner, Jenkins, but he remains adamantly determined to enforce the cut:

227. MEDIUM LONG SHOT. 2 ft. 11 frs.
Cannon firing.

228. MEDIUM LONG SHOT. 1 ft. 12 frs.
Strikers—man in foreground bares his chest, daring soldiers to shoot him.

229. LONG SHOT. 1 ft. 12 frs.
Inside factory fence: four strikers beyond—factory guards in foreground.

230. MEDIUM SHOT. 2 ft. 8 frs.
Manager and assistant agitated—manager runs forward.

231. MEDIUM SHOT. 2 ft. 2 frs.
Factory door—manager runs in.

232. THREE-QUARTER SHOT. 1 ft. 12 frs.
Office—manager runs forward to telephone. Calls Jenkins.

233. MEDIUM SHOT. 1 ft. 10 frs.
Bars of fence—strikers behind, shaking fists and sticks.

234. LONG SHOT. 2 ft. 3 frs.
Jenkins's office—he answers phone.

235. (As 232.) 1 ft. 13 frs.
Manager at telephone, excited.

236. MEDIUM SHOT. 1 ft.
Jenkins at telephone, answering calmly.

237. ANOTHER ANGLE. 14 frs.
Jenkins.

7. (Left): *Two frames from the Lumiere film* BABY'S BREAKFAST *(France, 1895) and two from* QUEEN VICTORIA'S FUNERAL *(Great Britain, 1901): each film has only one camera setup throughout.* (Right): *Two frames from each of two scenes in* THE LIFE OF CHARLES PEACE *(Great Britain, 1905): the scene changes, but for each scene there is still only one camera setup.*

8. *Frames from eight successive shots of the scene in David Lean's* BRIEF ENCOUNTER *(Great Britain, 1945) when Alex (Trevor Howard) takes his last leave of Laura (Celia Johnson). In the modern film a single scene may include many variations of camera setup.*

9. *Two successive close-ups of Mae Marsh from D. W. Griffith's* INTOLERANCE *(see p. 76).*

10. This could be a detail of a painting, but is in fact a shot from Carl Dreyer's film THE PASSION OF JOAN OF ARC (France, 1928). It is from a succession of such details that the film-maker creates his picture in the dimension of time, as the painter composes his in space.

238. (As 235.) 1 ft. 15 frs.
Manager hangs up receiver—hesitates.

239. THREE-QUARTER SHOT. 2 ft. 6 frs.
Jenkins sitting at his desk—staring ahead—indomitable.

240. (As 238.) 1 ft. 12 frs.
Manager rushes back to door in rear.

241. (As 231.) 1 ft. 13 frs.
Runs out door.[7]

The joining together of strips of visual image of greater or shorter length is a device peculiar to the film; but novelists, as we have seen, represent the same effects by verbal description. The musician, the poet and the dramatist likewise have their own means of obtaining variations of tempo. It might seem odd to have the quarrel scene of Shakespeare's *Julius Caesar* quoted as an example of "quick cutting" in the medium of dialogue, but no one who has seen the play performed will easily forget the rapid thrust and parry of Brutus and Cassius hurling their clipped taunts at one another.

CAS:　　　　　Brutus, bait not me;
　　　I'll not endure it: you forget yourself,
　　　To hedge me in; I am a soldier, I,
　　　Older in practice, abler than yourself
　　　To make conditions.
BRU:　　　　　Go to; you are not, Cassius.
CAS: I am.
BRU: I say you are not.
CAS: Urge me no more, I shall forget myself.
　　　Have mind upon your health, tempt me no farther.
BRU: Away, slight man!
CAS: Is't possible?
BRU: Hear me, for I will speak.
　　　Must I give way and room to your rash choler?
　　　Shall I be frighted when a madman stares?

[7] Lewis Jacobs, *The Rise of the American Film* (Harcourt, Brace Co., New York, 1939), p. 195.

CAS: O ye gods, ye gods! must I endure all this?
BRU: All this! ay, more: fret till your proud heart break;
      Go show your slaves how choleric you are,
      And make your bondmen tremble. Must I budge?
      Must I observe you? Must I stand and crouch
      Under your testy humour? ...

The first thing to be observed about the technique of editing is that it affords the film-maker a new field for his powers of selection. The complete action of any given scene will be made up of a large number of detailed movements. Many of them will be going on simultaneously, and obviously we can see only one detail at a time, so that in any case the film-maker who is concerned to concentrate on detail must choose what he will show at any particular stage of the action. Selection, however, can go very much further than this. By means of editing, the film-maker can eliminate all the irrelevances found in the apparent confusion of real life and can concentrate on the significant details in order to articulate the pattern he distinguishes in the chaos.

Even in such a straightforward scene as the gunfight on the wharf in *The Ghost Goes West* selection has been stringently exercised. The whole action is conveyed in thirteen brief shots, the longest of which is on the screen for barely more than four seconds. In the course of it we get seven glimpses of the gangsters, three of the night watchman, and three of Murdoch. The whole of the scene is 51 feet 12 frames in length, which gives a running time of only 35 seconds. Yet when seen on the screen the episode is exciting and complete, and entirely sufficient for its purpose.

A more striking example from D. W. Griffith's film *Intolerance* is referred to by Pudovkin:

Here there is a scene in which a woman hears the death sentence passed on her husband, who is innocent of the crime. The director shows the face of the woman: an anxious, trembling smile through tears. Suddenly the spectator sees for an instant her hands, only her hands, the fingers convulsively gripping the skin. This is one of the most powerful moments in the film. Not for a minute did we see the whole figure, but only the face, and the hands. And it is perhaps by virtue of this fact that the director understood how to choose and to show, from the mass of real material available, only these two characteristic details, that he attained the wonderful power of impression notable in this scene.

Here, once more [continues Pudovkin] we encounter the process, mentioned above, of clear selection, the possibility of the elimination of those insignificances that fulfill only a transition function and are always inseparable from reality, and of the retention only of climactic and dramatic points. Exactly upon this possibility depends the essence of the significance of editing, the basic process of filmic creation.[8]

Where a scene is built up from selected fragments in this way, it is important that they should follow each other smoothly and naturally so that no break or inconsistency is apparent to the spectator; to express it in technical jargon, it is important to establish effective continuity between one shot and the next. We have already seen that one of the most responsible technicians in a film studio is the continuity girl whose job is to prevent any discrepancies (for example, of dress or acting or set arrangement) that would disturb the continuity, and which tend to arise from the fact that shots that are to be joined together may be taken at different times and in different places. Discrepancies of lighting, photography and sound recording arising from the same cause must likewise be avoided.

Again, where a movement in one shot is continued into the next shot, the continuity will be disturbed if there is an unintentional repetition of movement on the one hand, or a noticeable jump in it on the other. For example, the following series of shots might be indicated in the shooting script:

8 *Film Technique*, p. 65.

1. MEDIUM SHOT. An analyst stands by the bench in his laboratory and in one hand holds up to the light a test tube containing a clear liquid. With his other hand he reaches for a bottle on the bench in order to pour a few drops of its contents into the test tube.
2. CLOSE-UP of the test tube. As the drops are poured into it, the liquid in the test tube is seen to grow darker.
3. MEDIUM SHOT. (As in Shot 1.) The analyst replaces the bottle on the bench and walks off-right with the test tube.

In shooting, shots 1 and 3 would be taken as one continuous shot. Then the actor would repeat his action so that the close-up could be taken, and in the process of editing, this close-up would be cut into the middle of the medium shot. If the cutting is done correctly, the three shots when shown on the screen will appear as three consecutive views of one continuous and unbroken piece of action. It would be possible, however, to cut too much from one or both ends of the film to be joined so that there would be an unnatural jump in the action; for example, the end of shot 1 might show us the analyst's hand still in the act of reaching toward the bottle, and then suddenly at the beginning of the close-up he might already be pouring the drops into the test tube. It is equally possible, on the other hand, not to cut one or both ends of the film to be joined short enough, and this will give the unnatural effect of an overlapping of time and a repetition of action; for example, at the end of the close-up we might see the drops poured into the test tube and the bottle begin to move away, and then with the cut to shot 3, we might see once more the drops poured in and the bottle moved away.

It is an important part of continuity to ensure that such unintended inconsistencies do not occur; but all this is continuity considered in a negative sense, the mere *avoidance* of errors in shooting or cutting that would break the smooth transition from shot to shot. There is also a positive aspect of continuity, embracing the means by which the film-maker consciously and deliberately leads the attention of the spectator on from point to point in his narrative; and continuity in this sense is not simply a matter of shooting or editing, but is an integral part of the film's construction and has its foundation in the script.

The establishment of this kind of continuity is not a problem peculiar to the film; it confronts every artist who works in a medium involving sequence and development and the passage of time. The composer, the novelist, the dramatist, the choreographer of ballet, are all concerned with building a structural unity in the dimension of time, just as the painter, the sculptor and the architect are concerned with building a structural unity in space.

Moreover, continuity in this sense is important in every part of the film, from the most general to the most particular. A film derives its unity in the first place, as we have seen, from its plot-theme, and this is made a complete whole by consisting of a beginning, a middle and an end. A cause or series of causes, an act and the consequences, anything that does not contribute to this development is redundant and mars its continuity. When this main action is worked out in terms of a series of minor actions to be represented in scenes and sequences, these likewise must be logically interconnected in terms of cause and effect in order to build up the structure that we know as the plot.

It is indeed in terms of this cause and effect relationship that Mr. E. M. Forster, in his *Aspects of the Novel*, defines the plot. "We have defined the story," he says, "as a narrative of events arranged in their time-sequence. A plot is also a narrative of events, the emphasis falling on causality. 'The king died and then the queen died,' is a story. 'The king died, and then the queen died of grief,' is a plot. The time-sequence is preserved, but the sense of casuality overshadows it—or again: 'The queen died, no one knew why, until it was discovered that it was through grief at the death of the king.' This is a plot with a mystery in it, a form capable of high development. It suspends the time-sequence, it moves as far away from the story as its limitations will allow. Consider the death of the queen. If it is in a story we say 'and then?' If it is in a plot, we ask 'Why?' That is the fundamental difference between these two aspects of the novel." [9]

At both levels then, of action-theme and plot, continuity between the various parts of the action is ensured by establishing one or both of two relationships, the relationship of natural sequence in time, and superimposed on it, the relationship of cause and effect. By seeing A, our minds are prepared to see B, not only because B follows A in time, but also because A is the cause of B, and B the logical consequence of A. "The king died, and then the queen died of grief."

What is true here of action-theme and plot we find to be equally true when we come to consider continuity between the shots of which a single scene is composed. Our attention is carried easily from one shot to the next on the assumption that what we see in shot 1 is immediately followed by what we see in shot 2, and that shot 2 is what we would logically expect to see after shot 1, either because it answers some question raised in shot 1 or because it follows it as effect follows cause, or because there is some natural association of ideas between them.

It is necessary at this point to define more precisely the terms "scene" and "sequence." A scene, as we have already observed, is normally composed of a number of shots. In the jargon of the film studio and in film scripts, these shots themselves are described as "script scenes," or more briefly, "scenes," but in most books of film criticism, and in the present book, ambiguity is avoided by describing any fragment of moving picture that has been taken, either actually or apparently, in one uninterrupted running of the camera as a "shot." [10] Likewise, I always use the term "scene" to

9 *Aspects of the Novel*, p. 116.

10 For certain trick effects (e.g. stop-action photography) the running of the camera may actually have been interrupted during shooting, but if the trick is successfully effected, the interruption will not be noticeable and the shot will still *appear* to have been taken without interruption.

describe a piece of *continuous* action, whether depicted, as in the earliest films, in one shot, or as is much more common today, by a series of shots.

"Sequence" is another word used in film writing somewhat loosely and with several meanings, although the particular meaning in each case is generally apparent from the context. Insofar as it has a particular technical significance, it is used to describe some major part of the action as a whole; usually it is composed of a number of scenes, but it may on occasion comprise one scene only, where the scene is of sufficient length or importance. Quite often, however, "sequence" is used as synonymous with "series" or "succession," as when a writer refers to a certain "sequence of shots," when he may be concerned with no more than a scene, or even only part of a scene. Ambiguity arises in the case of such a phrase as "the mutiny sequence" in *Battleship Potemkin;* without further clarification it is not apparent whether the word "sequence" is being used here in its more precise technical sense to denote the whole group of scenes that, leading up to and including the mutiny, comprise the first main section of the film; or whether reference is being made simply to the fighting on the ship in which that sequence culminates, which would more accurately be described as "the mutiny scene (or scenes)." In order to avoid such ambiguity, in the present book the word "sequence" is normally used to denote a major part of the action of a film, roughly analogous to the movement of a symphony or the act of a play.

In the fiction film conceived in dramatic form, then, shots are joined together to represent pieces of continuous action known as senes, the scenes fall into larger groupings known as sequences and the sequences combined give us the complete film. It is no less important to establish effective continuity between the scenes and sequences than between the shots making up any one scene, and the general principle for establishing continuity are the same. The chief difference lies in the fact that whereas the shots within a scene are essentially continuous in time, there may be a lapse of time between one scene and another, or one sequence and another.

An example taken from literature may help to make this clear. Robert Louis Stevenson's story "The Strange Case of Dr. Jekyll and Mr. Hyde," is told from the viewpoint of a lawyer, Mr. Utterson, who is trying to discover the nature of the relationship between his friend Jekyll and the villainous criminal named Hyde. At one point in the story Hyde murders a well-known public figure and Member of Parliament, Sir Danvers Carew, and immediately upon this follows what Stevenson calls "Incident of the Letter," by which Utterson's curiosity and suspicions are further sharpened, although he still has no inkling that Jekyll and Hyde are the same man. This incident consists of two scenes. The first records a visit paid by Utterson to Dr. Jekyll immediately after the murder. He finds Jekyll in his chair "looking deadly sick." He swears he has finished with Hyde and will never set eyes on him again; but he asks Utterson's advice on a letter he says he has just received:

> The letter was written in an odd upright hand, and signed "Edward Hyde"; and it signified, briefly enough, that the writer's benefactor, Dr. Jekyll, whom he had long so unworthily repaid for a thousand generosities, need labour under no alarm for his safety, as he had means of escape on which he placed a sure dependence. The lawyer liked this letter well enough: it put a better colour on the intimacy than he had looked for; and he blamed himself for some of his past suspicions. . . . "Shall I keep this and sleep upon it?" asked Utterson.

Utterson's suspicions, however, were almost immediately stirred again. Jekyll told him he had burned the envelope in which the letter came, and Jekyll's servant, questioned as Utterson was leaving the house, denied any knowledge of the letter having arrived. And straightway we embark on the second scene:

Presently after, he sat on one side of his own hearth, with Mr. Guest, his head clerk, upon the other, and mid-way between, at a nicely calculated distance from the fire, a bottle of particular old wine.

And while they are sitting thus, Utterson decides to show the letter to Guest, for whose opinion he has a high regard. While Guest is studying it, by a coincidence the servant enters with a dinner invitation written by Dr. Jekyll, and Guest, who is a keen student of handwriting, compares Jekyll's note with Hyde's. He remarks on "a rather singular resemblance; the two hands are in many points identical: only differently sloped." This gives Utterson fresh food for thought, and binding Guest to silence, he locks the note in his safe.

Now each of these two scenes, within itself, is essentially continuous in time; each action or utterance within the scene not only follows immediately on what precedes it, but follows it as effect following cause. Utterson visits Jekyll; as a result he finds him looking unwell (shaken, obviously, by what he knows of the murder that has just been committed); as a result of this, in turn, he expresses the hope that Jekyll is not concealing Hyde, which leads Jekyll to say that he has finished with him; by way of confirmation he shows Utterson the letter; this prompts Utterson to ask to see the envelope, in case its postmark might give some clue to Hyde's whereabouts; Jekyll replies that he has destroyed the envelope, that in any case the letter was delivered by hand; and so on. A similarly continuous chain of cause and effect may also be traced running through the second scene.

Between these two scenes, however, there is a perceptible break: between the point at which Utterson decides to take further advice on the letter and the point at which he is sitting with Guest by the fire, an appreciable passage of time has lapsed, as is made clear in the words "presently after" with which the second scene opens. Certainly, what happens in scene 2 follows as a direct result of what has already passed in scene 1—that is the basis of the continuity between the two scenes—but it does not follow immediately after.

Hence the significance of defining a scene as a series of shots, or fragments of action, that are presented as being essentially continuous in time: it is their continuity in time that is an essential part of their relationship and their meaning. It would be possible for a scene in a hotel room in London to end with one of the characters taking out his watch and saying, "It's exactly ten to nine; John should just be leaving Welwyn," and for the next scene to open with John leaning out of a train as it begins to move out of Welwyn Station. This is an example of a quite common device that scriptwriters use to link one scene with another. Obviously there is no lapse of time here between the end of the first scene and the commencement of the next, but in such a case the continuity in time is not essential: John does not depart from Welwyn Station *because* of what the first character has said, and it would be equally possible for the character to say, "John ought to be leaving Welwyn soon," or "within the hour" without affecting the scene or structure of the two scenes in any way.

In a sense, a scene may be regarded as a unified slice of time; and it is possible for two such slices of time not only to be separated or contiguous, but also to occur simultaneously or to overlap. This happens when a storywriter says "We will leave Paul and Mary talking thus and return to see what befell Mr. Timberley after he had left them at Fountain Grove"; or when a dramatist writes of a scene in a play, "Scene 2 opens ten minutes before the close of scene 1."

The normal method of transition from shot to shot within a scene is by means of the cut, which gives the effect of one shot being instantaneously replaced by the next. The normal method of transition from one scene to another is by means of the mix or dissolve, which is always associated with a sense of the passage of time or of a break in time. A sequence is normally punctuated by a fade-in at the beginning and a fade-out at the end. The fade may be quick or slow according to the emotional mood of the film at the moment it occurs and the degree of emphasis that the director desires to give to the pause at that particular point.

5 · Editing: D. W. Griffith and Eisenstein

*You photograph the natural life, but
you also, by your juxtaposition of detail, create an interpretation of it.*
J O H N   G R I E R S O N

It was by the American director D. W. Griffith that the
principles of film editing outlined in the last chapter were
first developed. No one has had a greater influence on film
technique. As we have already seen, the films made before
1907 consisted of whole scenes taken with a single camera
setup. Occasionally one finds the action broken into two or
three shots, especially in chase scenes, and sometimes even
the close-up was used as a crude inset. Such constructions,
however, were not characteristic, and until the time of Griffith they appear to have been used as exceptional expedients
without any understanding to their potentialities.

David Wark Griffith, born in Kentucky, January 22, 1875,
was a young stage actor who had written one or two unsuc-
cessful plays when he first began to act in one-reel films for
the American Biograph Company in 1908.[1] After he had
played in five films, the company promoted him to film direction and almost at once, fascinated by the new medium in
spite of himself, he began to feel his way forward, in film
after film, toward a radically new technique. From 1908 to
1915 Griffith made on an average two one-reelers a week,
or a total of over 700 reels. Here it is possible to do no more
than note his most significant advances.

In his first film, *The Adventures of Dollie* (released in
July 1908), Griffith used the earliest known flashback. In

---

[1] He had appeared in one film before this date, *Rescued from an Eagle's Nest*,
produced by the Edison Company in 1907 and directed by Edwin S. Porter.

For Love of Gold (August 1908) he had to represent the two chief characters, miners who had struck gold, as growing suspicious of each other's avarice; he solved his problem by moving the camera closer to the actors, getting what is now termed a full shot, in order to show their facial expressions more clearly. A little later, in *After Many Years* (November 1908), a film based on the story of Tennyson's *Enoch Arden,* he moved the camera nearer still into a full close-up of Annie Lee as she sat thinking of Enoch; and he followed this shot by a cutback to Enoch himself on his desert island to begin a new scene. In *The Lonely Villa* (released June 1909) he introduced parallel development for the first time, working up the climax by giving alternately successive fragments of two simultaneous scenes, the one showing a woman and her children at the mercy of burglars, the other her husband hurrying home to their rescue, so that the spectator is held in suspense as his attention is switched from the one to the other; this device was subsequently used in so many of Griffith's films, and with such skill and effect, that it became known as the Griffith last-minute rescue. In *Ramona* (May 1910) Griffith used the earliest known extreme long shot. In *The Lonedale Operator* (March 1911) he used very close shots and further developed the technique of cross-cutting. He also showed in this film a growing command of tempo; both cutting speed and the speed of action within the shot were increased. In *The Massacre* (copyrighted by Biograph in November 1912, but not released until February 1914), in addition to rapid cutting, cross-cutting, parallel development and close-ups of detail, he used for the first time a moving camera in shots of the Indian attack; subsequently, in *Home, Sweet Home* (released by Mutual, July 1914) he used a camera mounted on a moving car to take shots of Jack Pickford galloping on a horse.

Griffith came to the cinema as a man of the theater, but each new experiment led him further away from the methods of the theater and nearer to the true technique of the film. He realized instinctively the possibilities that lay in working through the camera, in using the camera not simply as a recording machine, but as a fashioning tool with which the film-maker's raw material, namely, that which took place in front of the camera, could be molded. His keen eyes saw in the rehearsed scene certain details that he, as storyteller, wanted to accentuate. Instinctively he moved his camera nearer to concentrate on them. Thus he was led to break up the colorless one-shot scene into smaller fragments shown in mid-shot, close-shot and close-up, according to the particular degree of emphasis and concentration he required at each point; thus he established the principles of film editing we have already examined in theory—for, as we have observed, the nearer the camera approaches the scene of action, the more fragmentary does the shot become and the more is the film-maker under the necessity of creating his effects by the particular fragments of the scene he selects to photograph and the sequence in which he joins them. It is sometimes loosely said that Griffith invented the close-up. If this is intended to mean that he first used the close-up, it is demonstrably untrue. The truth is that he was the first to appreciate the significance of the close-up as the keystone of a new technique of film-making.

Griffith, then, broke up the single scene into shots, which enabled him to vary the camera setup from shot to shot and to give a much more intimate and detailed representation of the action. It gave him much greater control over his material by enabling him to select the few essential points of attention out of a mass of irrelevant and distracting detail; in the words of Lewis Jacobs, "he suddenly understood how the art of the movie director differs from that of the stage director; in movie making, guiding the camera, even more than directing the actor, is the trick." [2] It also gave him unprecedented control over movement in what is essentially an art of movement; by playing on shot duration, and on the relationship of actions in successive shots, he was able to

[2] *The Rise of the Amercian Film*, p. 110.

move his audience by skillfully constructed and exciting visual rhythms. He departed, too, from the principle of his predecessors that each scene must be brought to its close before the next was begun. He indulged in a free interplay between the shots of various scenes to emphasize the dramatic relationship between them, as in the cutback, parallel development and other forms of cross-cutting.

This new technique that he had forged Griffith exploited with impressive mastery and power in his two great films, *The Birth of a Nation* (1915) and *Intolerance* (1916). They marked the culmination of his career. He continued to make films for another fifteen years or more, and although some of them still rank as major productions in the history of the film, his work during these years shows a gradual decline. Having reached the limit of his innovations in technique, he stood still, while others quickly learned enough of his methods to appear to equal or even surpass him; moreover, the First World War had given the *coup de grâce* to that Victorianism with which his outlook as both artist and social reformer was so deeply imbued, and he was left with nothing effective to contribute to the entirely new problems of the postwar world.

In his development of the technique of editing Griffith seems to have proceeded largely by intuition, by the inexplicable feeling for his medium that every good craftsman knows. Nowhere, to my knowledge, did he formulate the principles of his method, or even show that he was conscious that such principles existed; he merely solved each problem as it confronted him by means that seemed most appropriate to it. While this safeguarded him from being misled, as many others have been misled, by blind adherence to mere theory, it may also have prevented him from understanding the fundamental character of editing and the full measure of its potentialities. He did not appear to be aware, in particular, that fundamentally the process of presenting a succession of selected visual images, even where its purpose is merely the representation of a dramatic scene as it was actually performed, achieves its effect by building up in the mind of the spectator a particular association of ideas; yet Griffith's own work is full of examples that clearly demonstrate this is so.

For example, in the scenes of *Intolerance* representing the assault on the city of Babylon, Griffith shows men falling from the summit of the high wall to the ground fifty and more feet below. This is done in two shots. The first is a distance shot (vertically masked on both sides, incidentally, to emphasize the sense of height) showing a small figure hurled from the top of the wall and falling into space; this is presumably either a dummy, or a man falling into a net placed below the camera's field of view. The second is a very much nearer shot of the ground at the bottom of a wall and shows a real man falling to the ground and lying there apparently lifeless; in this second case the actor jumped from a wall only a few feet high, but since the top of this wall is not included in the shot, only his drop to the ground is seen.[3] By cutting from the first shot to the second at the right moment, Griffith gives the spectator a most vivid impression of a complete action that in reality did not take place.

A more complex example is to be found in another of Griffith's films, *Way Down East* (1920). The story reaches its climax when the orphan heroine (played by Lillian Gish) is driven from her master's house into a snowstorm. Wandering aimlessly through the blinding snow and growing more and more weary, she makes her way to a nearby frozen river, where she falls down at last in utter exhaustion upon the ice. When the hero (Richard Barthelmess) learns what has happened, he goes out into the storm to find her. Searching everywhere with his lantern and calling her name continually, he too, as dawn breaks, finds himself by the river's edge. During the night the river ice, attacked by

---

[3] This procedure of concealing part of the action necessary to the taking of a shot by excluding it from the camera's field of view is known to studio technicians as "cheating" and the shot as a "cheat shot."

the spring thaw, has been cracking in all directions, until eventually the piece on which the girl is lying breaks away and swings out into the current. It is at this moment that Barthelmess sees her, with her head a few inches from the edge of the ice and her hair straggling in the water. He runs despairingly along the river bank. She is floating nearer and nearer to a huge waterfall over which the massive ice blocks are being hurled into the swirling torrent far below. Barthelmess leaps out onto a piece of floating ice, and thence on to another and another, keeping his balance with the greatest difficulty. Still nearer she moves toward the pounding waterfall, and more quickly as the speed of the current increases. Still he jumps desperately from ice sheet to ice sheet in an endeavor to save her. She is now only a few yards from the waterfall, a few feet, and then, as the ice block prepares to leap over the fall, Barthelmess jumps near to her, seizes her and drags her back to safety.

This sequence is indisputably one of the most vivid, exciting and realistic in the whole history of the cinema, yet the action it presents never in fact took place; it was conceived entirely in the director's imagination and reproduced by skillful editing. Miss Iris Barry, in *D. W. Griffith: American Film Master*,[4] gives the following description of the shooting (p. 29):

In March, when a blizzard conveniently came along, the snowstorm scenes were filmed at Mamaroneck. . . . The ice scenes were then shot at White River Junction, Vermont, under peculiarly uncomfortable circumstances. Albert Bigelow Paine's *Life and Lillian Gish* (New York, Macmillan, 1932) quotes Richard Barthelmess: "Not once, but twenty times a day, for two weeks, Lillian floated down on a cake of ice, and I made my way to her, stepping from one cake to another, to rescue her." The scenes at the brink of the falls, were, however, taken much later in the year at Farmington, Conn., with

4 Published by the Museum of Modern Art Film Library, New York, November, 1940.

wooden ice-cakes. The actual waterfall shown for a brief moment is Niagara. Since scenes of action of this sort are usually produced today by quite different methods, the facts seem remarkable, but might hardly be worth recording save for the effectiveness with which all these scenes taken at remote times and places were finally assembled.

In particular, this account makes it clear that the shots of the ice floe approaching the top of the waterfall, including that in which the heroine appears to miss so narrowly a plunge to death, were cheat shots of the comparatively low falls at Farmington with the lower water level just out of view. Cut into the sequence, however, are other shots of the huge falls of Niagara, and these become inseparably associated in the spectator's mind with the shots of the inert girl on the floe whom he imagines to be moving toward the roaring falls.

In both these cases shots of subjects, which in real life had no immediate relationship with each other, were assembled to create a photographically realistic impression of a purely imaginary event; in both cases the director succeeded in building up in the minds of his audience an association of ideas welded with such persuasive logic and charged with such emotional momentum that its truth was not questioned. It was the directors of the Soviet Union who were the first to understand the full significance of this fact and to exploit it.

The government that came to power in Russia in 1917 was faced with the task of rebuilding the state in one of the most backward countries of the world, whose archaic feudalism, under which the great mass of the people were kept impoverished and illiterate, had suddenly crumpled beneath the stress of a disastrous war into the chaos of revolution. It was for this reason that Lenin declared in 1918 that "for us, the most important of all the arts is the cinema." He was interested in the film primarily as a medium for mass propaganda and education and for the creation of particular social attitudes.[5] In 1919 the Russian film industry was nationalized under the Commissariat of Education, and in the same year the State Institute of Cinematography (the G.I.K.) was established for research and the training of technicians.

The enthusiastic young technicians of the new Russian film industry, inspired by this official encouragement on the one hand, and yet at the same time compelled by the shortage of film stock and production equipment to use every foot of film with the greatest economy and forethought,[6] devoted much attention to the theoretical study of the new medium and especially to the work of D. W. Griffith, whose films were being widely shown.[7]

The Russians argued that a medium that does no more than represent an event as it appears in reality can never serve the purposes of art, however well it may serve those of record. Even though the event be a brilliant actor performing in a most skillfully designed studio setting, if the film simply presents it as it is (i.e., as it would appear to an

[5] "Lenin, as reported in the *Moscow News* for January 24, 1935, speaks of the arts not only as giving pleasure and recreation to the masses, but as indispensable in augmenting social education (i.e. communication) and in welding a vast population into an actual social unity. In Russia the problem of transforming a feudal into a democratic order is most urgent, and this can be done, Lenin realized, more effectively by the arts than by any other agency. Because of the extent of illiteracy, the radio as an avenue of communciation and the motion picture as an art are the primary means by which Russia hopes to democratize its society." (Mortimer J. Adler, *Art and Prudence*, Longman's, New York, 1937, p. 619.)

[6] "Pudovkin now relates with pride the terrible difficulties that had to be overcome in the making of pictures in those early days. There was no coal, no fuel, no light, very little food, hardly room to work in. They studied in thick overcoats and felt boots—when they could get them. They had to gather together material for their scenery from all kinds of flotsam and jetsam. Even the projectors had to be handmade. Every possible thing had to be economized. Every yard of film, every kopeck, had to be fought for." (Herbert Marshall, *Soviet Cinema* [a Russia Today publication], p. 2.)

[7] Miss Iris Barry, in *D. W. Griffith: American Film Master* (p. 24), quotes the following extract from a letter sent by the Soviet director Leonid Trauberg to Griffith in September 1936: "You certainly know what an important effect your pictures have had on Soviet cinema directors and actors. We have seen your pictures in 1923–24—except *Intolerance* [which we saw] in 1919—i.e. in that time when we all—Eisenstein, Pudovkin, Ermler, Vassilieffs, and we two [i.e. Trauberg and Kozintsev]—had just begun our work as directors. Under the influence of your pictures . . . our style has been created." Compare also the references to Griffith and the American cinema in Pudovkin's *Film Technique*.

observer standing where the camera stands), then it merely records, in a quite mechanical fashion, a piece of acting and a piece of studio design; however much art there may be in either of these, the result does not constitute a work of film art. Only if the film itself can be utilized to mold and shape the event, to express an attitude toward it, to express something of the impact it makes on the artist as an experience, has it any claim to be an art form. It is true, as we shall see, that by the choice of a particular viewpoint for the camera, a certain overtone of significance can be implied within the limits of a single shot or even frame, but the potentialities of this device are extremely limited. On the other hand, as soon as we resort to editing, a limitless field of possibilities is opened up; for editing, as the Russians saw, is nothing less than the deliberate guidance of the thoughts and associations of the spectator.

One of the earliest and most influential research workers and teachers at the G.I.K. was a young painter, Lev Kuleshov; it was a chance meeting with Kuleshov that first awakened Pudovkin's interest in the film, and in *Film Technique* there are numerous references to Kuleshov and his experiments:

> From our contemporary point of view Kuleshov's ideas were extremely simple. All he said was this: "In every art there must be first a material, and secondly, a method of composing this material specially adapted to this art." The musician has sounds as material and composes them in time. The painter's materials are colour, and he combines them in space on the surface of the canvas. What, then, is the material which the film director possesses and what are the methods of composition of his material?
>
> Kuleshov maintained that the material in film-work consists of pieces of film, and that the composition method is their joining together in a particular, creatively discovered order. He maintained that film-art does not begin when the artists act and the various scenes are shot

11. *Frames from two successive shots joined to create the illusion of a man falling from the walls of Babylon on D. W. Griffith's* INTOLERANCE *(USA, 1916). Vertical masking of the first shot strengthens the impression of height.*

12. *Two successive shots from the last sequence of Pudovkin's* MOTHER *(*USSR, 1927*), suggesting a simile between the marching workers and the irresistible movement of ice floes on the thawing river.*

—this is only the preparation of the material. Film-art begins from the moment when the director begins to combine and join together the various pieces of film. By joining them in various combinations, in different orders, he obtains differing results.[8]

The Russians, in short, seized on editing as being the vital creative principle in film-making. Dziga-Vertov went so far as to take the extreme view that the director should make no attempt at all to interfere with real life, but should merely go about quietly and unobservedly accumulating material with the camera, his "Kino-eye," relying for his effects solely on the choice of the material and the way in which it was ultimately assembled at the editing table. Eisenstein, on the other hand, staged all his scenes but strove for the greatest realism and rigorously abstained from the use of professional actors, working always in his silent films, with non-actors. Pudovkin, again, used professional actors as well as non-professionals. Whatever their individual differences, however, all these progressive directors of the Russian cinema shared a common conviction in the supreme importance of editing. They clearly perceived, moreover, as Griffith seemed to have been only dimly aware, that editing derived its power not merely from the fact that by breaking up a scene into shots it could be represented more vividly and realistically, but also from the fact that a succession of shots involved a complex set of relationships between them, relationships of idea, of duration, of physical movement and of form, by the skilled manipulation of which an audience could be most powerfully affected.

All the experiments and demonstrations of Kuleshov that Pudovkin records are concerned with this matter of relationship. For example:

L. K. Kuleshov assembled in the year 1920 the following scenes as an experiment:

1. A young man walks from left to right.

8 *Film Technique*, pp. 138-9.

2. A woman walks from right to left.

3. They meet and shake hands. The young man points.

4. A large white building is shown, with a broad flight of steps.

5. The two ascend the steps.   ˙

. . . The spectator was presented with the pieces thus joined as one clear, uninterrupted action: a meeting of two young people, an invitation to a nearby house, and an entry into it. Every single piece, however, had been shot in a different place; for example, the young man near the G.U.M. building, the woman near Gogol's monument, the handshake near the Bolshoi Teatr, the white house came out of an American picture (it was, in fact, *the* White House), and the ascent of the steps was made at St. Saviour's Cathedral. What happened as a result? Though the shooting had been done in varied locations, the spectator perceived the scene as a whole. The parts of real space picked out by the camera appeared concentrated, as it were, on the screen. There resulted what Kuleshov termed "creative geography." [9]

Similarly, "Kuleshov tried to record a woman in movement by photographing the hands, feet, eyes, and head of different women. As consequence of editing resulted the impression of the movements of *one* single person.[10]

On another occasion Kuleshov was assisted by Pudovkin himself in an experiment that he describes as follows:

We took from some film or other several close-ups of the well-known Russian actor Mosjukhin. We chose close-ups which were static and which did not express any feelings at all—quiet close-ups. We joined these close-ups, which were all similar, with other bits of film in three different combinations. In the first combination the close-up of Mosjukhin was immediately followed by a shot of a plate of soup standing on a table. It was obvious

9 *Film Technique,* pp. 60-1.
10 *Ibid.,* p. 117.

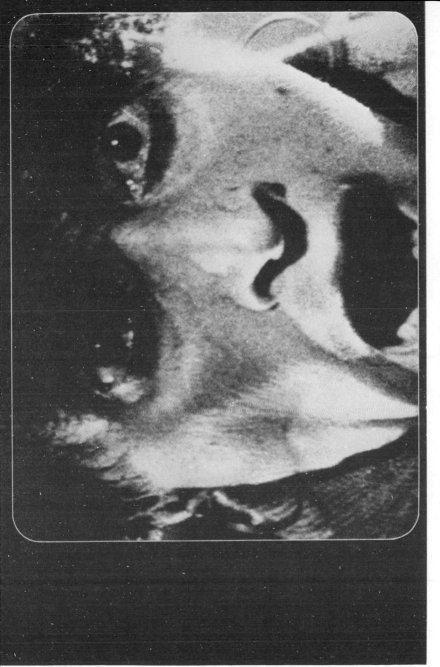

13. *The big close-up. From* BATTLESHIP POTENKIN *(USSR, 1925), directed by S. M. Eisenstein.*

14. *The close-up in a modern film. John Dierkes as the Tall Soldier in John Huston's* THE RED BADGE OF COURAGE *(USA, 1951).*

and certain that Mosjukhin was looking at this soup. In the second combination the face of Mosjukhin was joined to shots showing a coffin in which lay a dead woman. In the third the close-up was followed by a shot of a little girl playing with a funny toy bear. When we showed the three combinations to an audience which had not been let into the secret, the result was terrific. The public raved about the acting of the artist. They pointed out the heavy pensiveness of his mood over the forgotten soup, were touched and moved by the deep sorrow with which he looked on the dead woman, and admired the light, happy smile with which he surveyed the girl at play. But we knew in all three cases the face was exactly the same.[11]

Pudovkin also points out that to alter the order of shots in a scene, without any alteration of the shots themselves, may suffice to change the meaning of the scene. He quotes what he describes as a crude example composed of three close-ups: (1) a man is smiling; (2) a revolver is pointed; (3) the same man is looking frightened. In that order the shots convey the idea of a coward; but if they are reversed they convey the idea of a brave man. Pudovkin indeed was so preoccupied with this question of relationship as to hold that individual shots in themselves had little value:

> To make clear my point and to bring home unmistakably to my readers the meaning of editing and its full potentialities, I shall use the analogy of another art-form, literature. . . . If a writer requires a word—for example, beech—the single word is only the raw skeleton of a meaning, so to speak, a concept without essence or precision. Only in conjunction with other words, set in the frame of a complex form, does art endow it with life and reality. I open at hazard a book that lies before me and read "the tender green of a young beech"—not very remarkable prose certainly, but an example that shows fully and clearly the difference between a single word and a

11 *Ibid.*, p. 140.

word structure, in which the beech is not merely a bare suggestion, but has become part of a definite literary form. The dead word has been waked to life through art.

I claim that every object, taken from a given viewpoint and shown on the screen to spectators, is a *dead object*, even though it has moved before the camera. . . . Only if the object be placed together among a number of separate objects, only if it be presented as part of a synthesis of different separate visual images, is it endowed with filmic life. Transformed like the word "beech" in our analogy, it changes itself in this process from a skeletal photographic copy of nature into a part of the filmic form.[12]

When these Soviet directors came to put theory into practice in their films, they met with astonishing success; the best of their productions, *Battleship Potemkin* (1925), *October* (1928) and *The General Line* (1929) of Eisenstein, *Mother* (1926), *The End of St. Petersburg* (1927) and *Storm over Asia* (1928) of Pudovkin, *Earth* (1930) of Dovjenko, and possibly one or two others, represent the highest level reached by the silent film as an art form. They stirred contemporary audiences to such excitement and enthusiasm that in many countries outside the Soviet Union, including Britain, their public performance was banned on political grounds, and they have withstood the test of time so well that today, when something of their original force as propaganda has been lost, they can still provide sequences more stimulating and aesthetically satisfying than anything that the cinema has produced since, with all its technical development.

Such sequences have to be seen, and indeed seen many times, to be fully appreciated; the effects of the best of them are dependent upon subtleties of shot relationship, especially of timing, movement and gesture, that defy verbal description, that even the reproduction of stills from suc-

12 *Film Technique*, pp. xiii-xv.

cessive shots is inadequate to convey. Here it is not possible to do more than mention one or two of the most obvious realizations of theory in practice by way of illustration.

Eisenstein's long film *October* is for the most part concerned entirely with the presentation of abstract ideas by the combination of visual images. At the beginning, workers are shown swarming over a huge cast-iron statue of the Czar and fastening long ropes to it in order to pull it down. The collapse of the Czar's authority and the beginning of the revolution is symbolized by various parts of the statue falling off in slow motion and the statue itself falling over toward the earth. But with the establishment of the Kerensky Government, the statue floats up into position again and the detached parts move back to their places (an effect obtained by running the previous shots backward). The implication is obvious. The ridicule heaped upon the hapless Kerensky is savage indeed. He is shown in the Czar's palace, in the private library of Nicholas II, where he signs an order for the restoration of the death penalty. He then mounts an ornate wooden stairway, on a landing of which he stands looking down with arms folded. The next shot is of a statuette of Napoleon in a similar attitude. Then comes the news that the royalist General Kornilov is advancing; there is a call for all hands to the defense of Petrograd, "for God and country." The idea of God is presented in a rapid succession of shots and images of gods and primitive tribal deities, the idea of country by shots of medals and other decorations. A shot of General Kornilov on his horse with arm upraised is followed by a shot of a statuette of Napoleon on horseback in a similar position. We return to the figure of Kerensky standing with arms folded, and the statuette of the standing Napoleon, also with arms folded. "Two Bonapartes," says a title. Again Kerensky, and the standing Napoleon; then the Napoleon on the charger with arm upraised; several shots of two statuettes of standing Napoleons confronting each other; a close-up of the heads only, facing each other; a short close-up of a Napoleon head looking to the right; a similar close-up looking to the left; the two opposed statues again, full-length; two primitive wooden figures of tribal gods confronting each other; a series of brief shots of Napoleons and images of gods intercut in rapid sequence; Kornilov raising his arm in a signal to advance; a tank moving forward; Kerensky petulantly flinging himself down into the silken palace cushions in impotent despair, and on that shot the sequence fades out. Such symbolism, which is not characteristic of Eisenstein's work at its best, appears today somewhat naïve, but it indicates the freedom with which these Soviet directors associated individual shots.

A more impressive piece of film-making is the final section of Pudovkin's *Mother*, the story of a woman in pre-Soviet Russia who in trying to shield her son, a political agitator, from the police, is unwittingly led to betray him and is thereby awakened to an understanding of what her son has been fighting against.

When her son is in prison, the mother comes to visit him and surreptitiously slips a piece of paper into his hand. The guard announces that her time is up and she leaves. "And outside," a title tells us, "it is spring." There follow shots of a swollen river, a stream running between the stones, geese waddling through pools, a boy laughing, a baby on the ground as geese come running and splashing through the puddles, a woman picking the baby up, swirling water, the mother walking across the muddy fields and beside a pond on her way from the prison. The scene changes to the son's prison cell again. Furtively he reads the note: "The lamplighter will put a ladder against the wall. At twelve o'clock there will be a cab waiting at the corner." The shots that follow are a large close-up of his eyes, very short (8 frames); a medium shot of him sitting on the edge of the cell bed; a close-up of gushing and foaming water; a close-up of his hand tightly gripping the edge of the bed; a medium close-up of his body on which the shadows of the prison bars form a pattern; swirling water of a stream in

flood (39 frames) ; another (14 frames) ; four brief close-
ups of a child laughing (4 frames, 6 frames, 20 frames and
8 frames) ; two shots of swirling water (14 frames and 13
frames) ; a baby laughing (27 frames) ; a splash subsiding
into turbid water (32 frames) ; a close-up of the son's eyes
(11 frames) ; turbid water (14 frames) ; the son sitting on
the edge of the bed (16 frames) ; a close shot from the rear,
of the son jumping up (13 frames) ; a large close-up from
above, of a mug on a table, and a hand coming forward to
clutch it (9 frames) ; a close shot of the son hurling the
mug onto the floor (21 frames) ; a close shot of the mug
bouncing on the floor; a second shot of the mug bouncing;
it rolls to rest. The son then bangs on his cell door in sheer
exhilaration, until the guard looks in through the observation port and orders him to be quiet.

Now the scene changes to the common cell. Some prisoners sit in a group, others sit alone and silent, lost in their
thoughts. We see what they are thinking; in the case of one,
it is a horse pulling the plough through the rich dark earth;
another sees in his mind's eye a tree in blossom. We learn
that the men are planning a mass prison break "tomorrow
during exercise." The word is passed from man to man.
They lever bricks out of the walls and conceal them under
their jackets in preparation. In another brief scene we are
shown workers in the local factory planning a mass demonstration on the morrow; but they are overheard by an
informer, and the police and military officials also bestir
themselves in preparation. The son in his prison cell is
shown reading a new note: "Everything is ready for your
escape. Tomorrow you will be free again. They are coming
from all parts of the town." The scene ends on a fade-out.

On the next day small groups of workers are seen walking through the town to their assembly point, their figures
reflected in the puddles along the water-filled roads. The ice
on the river is breaking up and large pieces of ice move
slowly downstream. The son looks out of his prison window
at the wall below; a shot of water rippling, another of water

surging; as the son peers through the bars, the prison bell clangs to announce the time for exercise. The top of a ladder is seen moving along the prison wall. A guard orders the son to get down from the window, and when he fails to do so, tells him he will lose his exercise.

The prisoners are marched out into the prison yard in single file; the ice moves down the river; the marching procession of workers is seen from above, moving steadily forward; again we see the river ice; again the procession. The prisoners march sullenly round the yard in a wide circle; one by one they kick a loose stone into position until at last one of them is able to pick it up unobserved. The commander of the military forces in his office receives a note from the chief of police: "Stop the break at once"; he gives an order; soldiers run out of their barracks and horses are brought from their stables, their passing forms being reflected in the puddles; the soldiers mount their horses. We see an end-on view of the town bridge, deserted, followed by close-ups of broken ice rearing and cracking against the pylons of the bridge. A shot from above, of the mass of river ice moving slowly toward the camera, is followed by a similar shot, also from above, of the procession moving away from the camera. A series of nearer views show us the mother marching in the vanguard of the procession, next to the standard-bearer. The river ice is churning; the bridge is still empty.

In the prison yard the prisoners stand in defiant posture. As a guard turns to walk away a brick is hurled and the riot breaks out. Men escaping over the prison gates are fired on, others retreat before a line of firing guards. The son kicks against his cell door, and when a guard comes in to silence him, he overcomes the guard with the help of a fellow prisoner and escapes. In the confusion he manages to get to the outer wall and climb over it into the street. He is pursued down to the river and runs out onto the moving ice, jumping from one floe to another. A guard fires on him from the bank, but misses. A long shot shows him as a minute figure far out on the ice. A nearer view shows him crawling to the edge of the floe and lying there exhausted, his head a few inches from the water. There follow a series of shots showing alternately the workers' procession marching forward with the mother in the van, and the blocks of ice being swept along on the river. The son is seen crouching on a floe as it nears the bank, and then jumping off and clambering up the bank. The mounted cavalry receives an order from the commanding officer to move off and cross the bridge. Clambering over a fence, the son sees the workers' procession advancing across the mud (the marchers are again shown reflected in the pools and puddles). He runs to meet it, is given an enthusiastic welcome, and then turns to meet his mother struggling through the excited crowd toward him. They embrace. At that moment the cavalry officer gives another command; the soldiers, having now come up to the procession, dismount and step into shooting formation. The crowd begins to panic. The soldiers fire. Some of the crowd falls into the mud. The rest scatter. The son sags lifeless in his mother's arms, shot through the head. The mother cries out, wipes the blood from his brow as he sinks inert to the ground. The soldiers remount. The mother, now left alone with the dead and wounded, raises the red flag lying nearby. She gets to her feet and turns to face the soldiers. Their officer gives the order to advance and galloping forward they ride the mother down as she stands facing them defiantly, the flag streaming in the wind. The sequence, and the film, closes with a last shot of the ice blocks rearing and crashing and a brief series of dissolving views of chimneys, turrets and spires culminating in a shot of the flag fluttering against the sun.

Again, it must be emphasized that in a written description it is impossible to convey any real idea of the movement both within each shot and in the transition from one shot to another, which is such an important element of the film itself and which makes this ending of *Mother* so exciting and moving. Nevertheless, this description, imperfect though it is, amply illustrates how Pudovkin could combine shots with a poetic freedom to build up a complex emotional impression. He has himself given an account of the editing of part of this section in the following words: "The son sits in prison. Suddenly, passed in to him surreptitiously, he receives a note that next day he is to be set free. The problem was the expression, filmically, of his joy. The photographing of a face lighting up with joy would have been flat and void of effect. I show, therefore, the nervous play of his hands and a big close-up of the lower half of his face; the corners of the smile. These shots I cut in with other and varied material—shots of a brook, swollen with the rapid flow of spring, of the play of sunlight broken on the water, birds splashing in the village pond, and finally, a laughing child. By the junction of these components our expression of 'prisoner's joy' takes place." [13]

When this account is compared with the film itself, two facts at once become apparent. First, it is not accurate in its details; [14] secondly, and much more importantly, Pudovkin does not do justice to his own craftsmanship. His description gives one the impression that the shots of the brook, the sunlight and the laughing child were introduced quite arbitrarily, as the tribal deities and the statues of Napoleon were introduced into *October*. The filmic tapestry that Pudovkin actually wove, however, was of a much more complex pattern, as an examination of the film shows. All the images that he introduces to depict the prisoner's joy belong to a theme that has already been introduced in a quite natural way, the theme that opens with the words "And outside, it is spring." Certainly they give us a most vivid impression

---

[13] *Film Technique*, p. xvii.

[14] Pudovkin was obviously writing from memory. Anyone who has had an opportunity to see old films again and to check them against his recollection of them knows that the memory can play the most queer tricks with our visual impressions. If Pudovkin could not remember accurately the details of shots to which he must have devoted the most concentrated creative attention three years previously, what are we to expect of the recollections of a mere spectator? Yet most film history and much film criticism has been based entirely (and hitherto perforcedly) on recollected impressions.

of the mingled emotions that surge through the prisoner's brain as he tries to grapple with the sudden news that on the morrow he may be free; but their ability to do this depends mainly on the fact that they are images with which we have already become familiar in the film, and which we have associated with a certain idea, the idea of the winter snows melting, children and animals coming out into the sun again, and the world stirring to life with the coming spring.

The whole of the section that I have described is, in fact, constructed by the interweaving of a number of distinct threads of action or movement. Four of these threads belong to the plot: the son's escape and reunion with his mother, the mass riot in the prison, the demonstration of the factory workers in the town, and the action taken by the army to break up the demonstration. Beyond these, there are two others: first, the general scenes of spring, the running and swirling water of the streams and rivers, the children playing and laughing, and the pools in the muddy ground with their reflections; and secondly, as a more particular element of the spring setting, the blocks of ice moving inexorably down the river, now slowly and placidly, now rearing and grinding against each other. The movement of the section as a whole is built up by the mixture of these subsidiary elements, set off one against the other, and their interrelationships are of a most subtle and varied kind. The shots of spring, as we have already seen, are reintroduced to express the prisoner's joy. The spring theme appears again in the thoughts of the men sitting in the common cell; it is continually recurring in the shots of the procession and the soldiers reflected in the pools in the roadway. The ice on the river is a natural development of the spring theme, which almost at once assumes a special importance of its own. There is a clearly drawn simile between the movements of the ice and the movement of the procession; both begin slowly, both gradually acquire momentum, and in the end, just as the ice blocks rear and crash against the pylons of the bridge, so is the procession confronted with disaster at the bridge and broken up into chaos and confusion. But the ice is also a natural part of the scene and plays a realistic part in the plot development when the son escapes on to a floe and is carried away to temporary safety.

Finally, suffusing the whole section there is a steadily rising undercurrent of hope, which ends on a note of triumph. Materially, everything is lost, the prisoners and the workers are crushed, the son and the mother are killed; but greater than the material disaster is a moral victory. This is the very opposite of that kind of "morbid situation" in which "the suffering finds no vent in action; in which a continuous state of mental distress is prolonged, unrelieved by incident, hope or resistance; in which there is everything to be endured, nothing to be done." [15] Here the mental distress, the hopelessness of the earlier part of the film find release in action of the most violent and tempestuous kind. And once again the constant reiteration of the idea of spring released from the rigid thraldom of winter plays its part as imagery, in this case to point the major theme.

Many writers on the cinema appear to have been under the impression that this selection and combination of shots to suggest ideas of relationship, whether of similarity or contrast, obvious symbolism or subtle imagery, was invented by the Russians, but this is not so; it was implicit in the theory of editing from the very beginning. Pudovkin gave the method a name, "relational editing," but the method itself he took over from Griffith. For example, the savage indictment against modern war, which Pudovkin makes in *The End of St. Petersburg* by intercutting two parallel scenes—one of men fighting and dying in the mud at the front, and the other of hysterically excited financiers bidding on a soaring stock market at home—is justly cele-

[15] Matthew Arnold, *The Choice of Subjects in Poetry* (preface to *Poems*, 1853). Precisely such a "morbid situation" as Matthew Arnold here describes is to be found in von Sternberg's film *The Blue Angel* (Germany, 1931), in which Emil Jannings and Marlene Dietrich played the chief parts.

brated; but in essence this device had already been used by Griffith twelve years earlier, in the modern story of social injustice in *Intolerance*, where he emphasized the condition of working people living at a bare subsistence level by introducing contrasting shots of their wealthy employers walking into a magnificent salon to take part in a rich banquet. The whole of *Intolerance*, indeed, is one massive piece of relational editing, in which four themes are elaborately intercut to make a passionate onslaught against intolerance throughout the ages.

This is not to deny, however, that there are very clear differences between the work of Griffith and the Soviet silent film. In the first place, there is a radical difference in outlook. Whereas Griffith was a romantic and an idealist, an archaic survivor of a vanishing era, the Soviet directors were social realists, imbued with the most advanced political and social ideas of their time. Their approach to life was more dynamic, more analytical, less conventional. They accepted the fundamental principles of technique that Griffith had established, but they worked them out to their logical conclusion. They used them more self-consciously and deliberately, and with greater boldness and freedom. Whereas Griffith appears to have thought predominantly in terms of the scene, and of the relationship of one dramatic scene to another, the Soviet directors tended to think far more in terms of the relationship between single shots, single fragments of action, to express implications, comments, ideas, overtones of significance. They were much preoccupied, as we have already seen, with the potentialities of the fact that by joining one shot to another it is possible to create a *tertium quid*, a third something, which is not present in either of the shots separately, and which is also something more than the mere sum of them.

It is possible that they carried this preoccupation to excess, in their theory if not in their practice; it is obvious that when Pudovkin claims that "every object, taken from a given viewpoint and shown on the screen to spectators, is a

dead object, even though it has moved before the camera,"
and that "only if it be presented as part of a synthesis of
different separate visual images is it endowed with filmic
life," [16] he is overstating his case to the point of absurdity.
"The error," Eisenstein has since conceded, "lay in placing
the main emphasis on the possibilities of juxtaposition,
while less attention seemed to be paid to the problem of
analysing the material that was juxtaposed." [17]

Nevertheless, the work of the Soviet school had a profound influence on the subsequent history of the cinema.
At a time when there was some danger that the real significance of Griffith's discoveries might be lost, partly, perhaps, because they had never been explicitly stated—even
the work for his own films was usually done "in his head"
without a written script—and when editing was already
degenerating in other hands into a merely mechanical joining of lengths of film, the Russians drew attention, in the
most sensational manner, to the fact that primarily editing
was nothing less than a treatment of reality, or rather an
imitation of the process by which we apprehend reality.
Whereas even Griffith appears to have regarded editing as
little more than a most powerful aid for the vivid representation of dramatic fiction, editing for the Russians was the
very essence of creative work in the film, a process of
analysis and synthesis which ideally was already completed
in the script stage before a foot of film had been shot.

This view of editing was very different from that which
obtained in our own commercial studios, where it denoted
merely the process of assembly, the physical cutting and
joining of filmstrips in which the editor engaged after the
shooting was completed, often with the chief object of dis-
guising the mistakes and inefficiencies that had accumulated
during the previous stages of production. In order, therefore, to distinguish the Russian conception of editing, the
Russian term *montage* was introduced into English; for an

16 See above, p. 102.
17 *The Film Sense* (Faber and Faber, London, 1943).

exotic idea, an exotic word. Yet *montage*, as Ivor Montagu pointed out in his translation of Pudovkin's *Film Technique*, is simply the French word for ordinary commercial editing that the Russians themselves had annexed. Unfortunately, seized upon as a catchword by pseudointellectuals, it was used to such excess, and with so little understanding, that both it and the valuable idea it represented fell into disfavor, especially among film technicians, and it is now seldom used.[18]

So far we have considered the relationship of consecutive shots only in terms of content, but they may also be related in terms of visual pattern and movement. The importance of this formal aspect may best be made clear, perhaps, by reference once again to a literary parallel. In his short story "Markheim," Robert Louis Stevenson tells how Markheim murders an old antique dealer in his shop, and how his own conscience subsequently confronts him and forces him to confess his guilt. The skill with which Stevenson builds up the atmosphere on which the success of the story depends is illustrated by the following description of the scene immediately after the dealer has been struck down:

> Time had some score of small voices in that shop, some stately and slow as was becoming to their great age; others garrulous and hurried. All these tolled out the seconds in an intricate chorus of tickings. Then the passage of a lad's feet, heavily running on the pavement, broke in upon these smaller voices, and startled Markheim into the consciousness of his surroundings. He looked about him awfully. The candle stood on the counter, its flame solemnly wagging in a draught; and by that inconsiderable movement the whole room was filled with noiseless bustle and kept heaving like a sea; the tall shadows nodding, the gross blots of darkness swelling and dwindling as with respiration, the faces of the por-

---

18 Note, however, that the word *montage* is used by American film technicians to denote a rapid impressionistic succession of shots, sometimes linked by dissolves, wipes or other optical effects.

traits and the china gods changing and wavering like images in water. The inner door stood ajar, and peered into that leaguer of shadows with a long slit of daylight, like a pointing finger.

Here, one might say, is a perfect fragment of film script, a series of striking visual images, a series of suggestive sounds, crying out to be shot and recorded. Yet if this were done, however faithfully, there is still a *quality* in the literary original that would be entirely lacking in the film version. It is a quality that belongs to the words themselves, to the pattern of sounds and rhythmic stresses, and to the subtle interplay of overtones of association created by their arrangement. In evoking the atmosphere he required, this formal aspect of the word order was no less important to Stevenson than the logical and grammatical aspect.

The function of all representative art, at its highest, is to communicate experience, that is to say, the reaction of the artist, as a complete personality, to a given situation, real or imagined. Because the reaction is that of a complete personality, it is not solely intellectual or solely emotional or sensuous; it is a mixture of all three. When W. B. Yeats, in "The Lake Isle of Innisfree," says:

I hear lake water lapping with low sounds by the shore

he is not concerned merely to present us with a description, a picture, of the poet listening; in addition, by creating certain formal relationships of sound, most noticeably by the alliterative use of the "l," he tries to create for us the sound of the water, reinforcing the intellectual statement of cognition ("I hear lake water") with the sense impression that accompanies it; and by the rhythmic beat of his verse he also evokes an emotional reaction.

Sometimes form and content are spoken of as two separate things, and as though an artist could embellish content by superadding "form," or concentrate on form at the expense of content. This is entirely false. Distinguishable as aspects, they are in essence inseparable. Form is itself a quality of content, and the more highly charged the content of a statement, the more formal in character is it likely to be. To destroy the form of a line of poetry is to rob it of the most vital part of its content.

It is its formal quality—the formal use of sound and rhythm in prose and verse, of composition and color in painting, of movement in dancing, and of rhythm and sound pattern in music—that is the distinctive characteristic of all art and that endows it with permanence. It is in music, of course, that one finds it at its purest, usually devoid of any representational significance whatsoever, and I believe it was Schopenhauer who once observed that "all arts aspire to the condition of music." Mr. Charles Marriott had the same idea in mind when he said of paintings, in a BBC broadcast, that "every picture tells a story, but every picture also plays a tune."

If there is any force in the film's claim to be accepted as an art, then we are entitled to expect that, like all the older arts, it will possess its own characteristic formal potentialities; and many of those who believe the claim to be unwarranted are probably influenced, consciously or unconsciously, more by doubts on this point than any other. It is true that music and verse and the pictorial composition of the painting can all be introduced into a film, but they are not inherent in the film medium. Sir Laurence Olivier's *Henry V* was a very fine filmed version of the play, but the magnificence of Shakespeare's verse alone, although spoken by our greatest actors, is not enough to make a great *film* in the true sense of the word. To adapt a remark made by Jean Cocteau about the theater, what is required is poetry *of* the film, instead of poetry *in* the film.

What has the film-maker to correspond to the color and visual design of the painter, the solid masses of the sculptor, the musical sounds of the composer and the word sounds and stresses of the writer and poet? Undoubtedly the answer to this question is *movement*. The film-maker has pictures, but they are moving pictures, and movement, as we shall see in the chapter on camera work, is the most important element in their composition; he has sound, but again, as we shall see in the chapter on film music, what links the sound and the visuals into a formal unity is the rhythm of the film as an art of movement. Yet the single word "movement" may be misleading unless it is clearly understood to mean *filmic movement,* that is to say, movement controlled and patterned by manipulation of the film medium. The ballet, for example, is an art of movement, but a mere cinematograph record of a ballet will not be a work of film art.

Movement within the shot is, of course, an important part of the movement of the film as a whole, and it need not be limited to movement of the subject only. It may spring from the movement of the camera; or it may be accelerated or reduced to slow motion by alteration of the running speed of the camera; it may be present only potentially, in a composition made dynamic by the use of acute diagonals, or extreme foreshortening or sharp contrast of lighting. Yet movement within the shot, from whatever source, will derive its main formal significance from the extent to which it contributes to a larger and more complex pattern of movement created by the relationship of one shot to another. Even the static shot and the stable composition—even, indeed, the *rigor mortis* of the still picture—may have its place in such a movement pattern.

The film is a kind of ballet, but whereas in the ballet of the theater the spectator sits motionless and watches a pattern of movement unfold before him, in the film it is the spectator's own mind, freed by editing from the body's inertia, that moves. The film-maker who is also a film poet and can discern an underlying rhythm beneath the prosaic and chaotic surface movement of events can induce the spectator to share his experience in precisely the same way as an artist in any medium.

All the great film directors have been aware of this, at

least instinctively, from D. W. Griffith onward, but none has shown himself, in theory and practice, more conscious of its importance than Eisenstein. The mutiny sequence and the Odessa steps sequence in *Battleship Potemkin*, the sequences of the religious procession and the cream separator in *The General Line*, and the raising of the bridge of St. Petersburg in *October* are all brilliant compositions of exactly calculated relationship between the pattern and movement and duration of successive shots, adding vitality and excitement to their representational relationship. They have a richness of design that lends itself to the most extensive analysis.

Unfortunately it is virtually impossible to indicate in the words the precise quality that gives such work its value. The difficulty of describing movement and relationships of movement in exact terms, and the fact that we have no notation for movement similar to that which the musician has for music, is responsible, I feel sure, for the gross neglect that movement has suffered in books on film theory. The only form of film illustration hitherto available to authors—the photographic still—even strengthens this tendency by its entirely static character. I see no remedy beyond urging students not to be content with merely reading books about films, but to take every opportunity to study films on the screen. Many of the old classic films that have an assured place in film history can now be obtained for showing by film societies, clubs and educational organizations, and even by individuals fortunate enough to own a substandard projector.

Although Eisenstein's work, in my view, unmistakably points the way for the development of a true art of the film, his lead has not been followed. Far from having developed its control of movement, the film has, in general, lost much of the sense of movement that it possessed in its silent days. The virtual neglect of movement by film writers and critics, already mentioned, may be partly responsible. In the main, however, it appears to be associated with the development of sound, which brings with it a strong temptation to rely on the use of words in the form of either dialogue or commentary and encourages the adaptation of plays and novels of a literary character; it also tempts producers in some instances to escape the problems of a truly cinematic art while giving a spurious semblance of art to their films by the use of music and verse.

The great complexity of present-day production methods may also be a contributory factor. If, as I believe, a work of art must be essentially the expression of an individual artist, then ideally the film-maker should be able to visualize a succession of images and sounds in an imaginary cinema within his mind and to embody them in a script in the sure knowledge that they will be directly and exactly reproduced as he has imagined them. In the nature of things this is impossible. Between the writing of the script of a film and its final appearance on the screen there must intervene all the other processs of production. The more complicated the production organization, the more difficult does it become for one person to control it, and the less likely is the original conception of the film to find its way to the screen unless it is relatively simple and stereotyped in character; and once again, that which is most likely to get through unaltered is the spoken word.

Even Eisenstein's sound films are far more static than his earlier silent work, although in this case there may be other reasons for the change. His experiments in film aesthetics were apparently checked by the state campaign against formalism in art that was launched in the Soviet Union in the early thirties. It is presumably to this that Eisenstein refers when he says, writing of his early interest in shot-relationships:

> My critics did not fail to represent this as lack of interest in the *content* of the film-shot pieces, confusing *research* in one aspect of a problem with the attitude of the researcher to the representation of reality.[19]

19 *The Film Sense*, p. 19.

In his last years, Eisenstein was preoccupied with the view that "editing" is a process that extends beyond the assembly of images and sounds into every part of film-making, including the composition of the story, the composition of the constituent parts of each frame, the writing of the dialogue and even the interpretation of a character by the actor.

It is quite certain that the film can never return completely to the old silent-film technique, which, even at its best, was forced by the absence of sound to resort to devices we can now recognize as being outmoded and even slightly ridiculous. It is, nevertheless, true that in its silent days, in the hands of D. W. Griffith and Pudovkin and Eisenstein, the film came nearer to being an art form, in its own right, than it has been in most films since. Even with sound, the film remains primarily a visual art, and the major problem of technique with which film-makers should be preoccupied today is that of finding a style that will combine the best elements of the silent film with the peculiar attributes of sound.

The influence of the theories and methods of the Soviet silent cinema is seen most clearly today in the Impressionism of the typical documentary film, in which diverse shots of material taken, either apparently or in fact, from real life, are assembled to build up a generalized survey or statement. The danger of this impressionistic style lies in the fact that since there is no definite content relationship between one shot and another, but only a subject relationship of the most general kind, it is apt to become diffuse and chaotic, even meaningless, unless the shots are linked by strong formal relationships, as they are, for example, in Ruttmann's *Berlin*.

The Russian technique of editing has also left its mark in the use that is sometimes made of filmic imagery, that is to say, the association of shots to suggest visual similes. In Anthony Asquith's early film *Cottage on Dartmoor*, for example, an escaped prisoner, evading pursuit, suddenly de-

cides that life, even with freedom, is not worth living
without the woman he loves, and he turns back in his path
and begins to run toward the cottage where she lives. A
prison officer sees him outlined against the sky, raises his
rifle to his shoulder and fires. Mortally wounded, the prisoner, with a last desperate effort, hurls himself against the
cottage door, and at that moment a shot of a wave crashing
on the rocks is cut in. The result is to give an added
vehemence and intensity to the prisoner's last expiring
movement.

I always feel, however, that imagery and symbolism of
this kind are far more effective if the shots that are juxtaposed are a natural part of the background of the film and
are not introduced arbitrarily, as the wave has been introduced here. A second example from the same film will illustrate the point. The chief character, a barber, tormented
with jealousy because the girl he loves is herself in love
with a customer, finds himself shaving the customer; holding the razor near his throat, he begins to upbraid him, to
frighten him. The girl standing by suddenly moves to intervene, there is a momentary struggle, things are over-
turned, and suddenly everyone stands transfixed with horror. At this moment we are given a close shot of a bottle
lying on the floor and from its narrow neck a dark fluid
slowly pours out into a pool on the floor. We do not need to
be told that the customer had been gashed with the razor. In
this case the bottle is a natural part of the scene, one of the
things knocked down in the struggle, and at the same time
it gives the director precisely the image he wants at that
point. This second kind of imagery (of which the shots expressing the prisoner's joy in Pudovkin's *Mother* are another example) is more effective than the first, I suggest,
not simply because it is more difficult to achieve, but because the film medium, being essentially visual and photographic, demands a higher standard of objective realism
than the other representational arts. This means that where
the film director presents us with a realistic scene in a

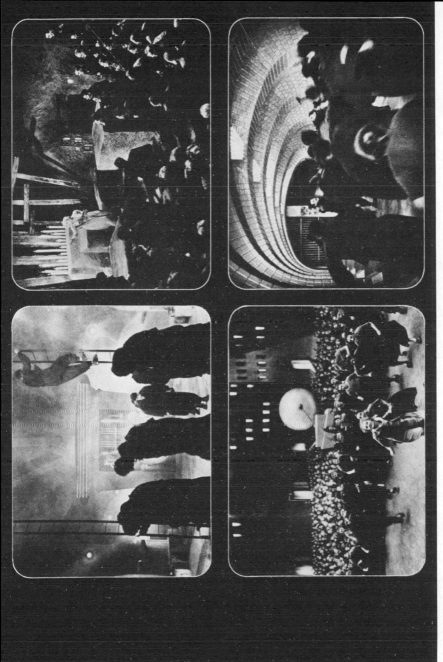

15. Development of movement in Fritz Lang's METROPOLIS (Germany, 1928). (Above left): The static composition emphasizes the subjection of the workers. (Above right): Potentially dynamic composition as they are incited to revolt. (Below, left and right): The revolt breaks into tempestuous movement.

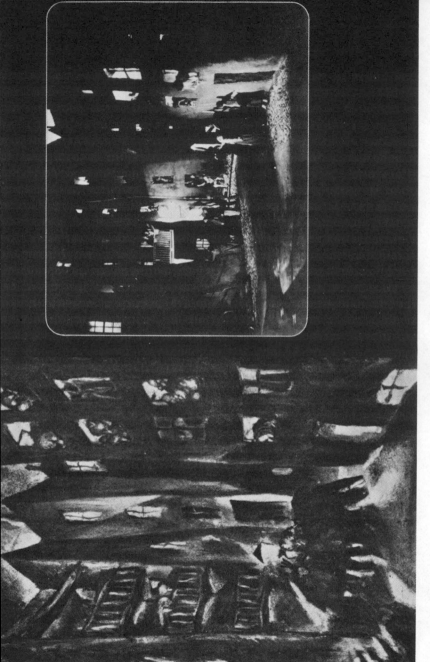

16. (Left): *A set design by Paul Leni for his film* HINTERTREPPEN *(Germany, 1921).* (Right): *The set is constructed. The closed-in effect obtained by vertical composition in the design is largely lost in the horizontal frame of the screen.*

realistic manner, he should as far as possible create the impressions he desires by what might be seen in actuality. This is not calculated to discourage imagination; on the contrary, the image arbitrarily brought in is an easy evasion of the problem. The hallmark of a good film style, as of a good literary style, is its objectivity.

6 · The Use of Sound

The eye, which is called the window of the soul, is the chief means whereby the understanding may most fully and abundantly appreciate the infinite works of nature; and the ear is the second, inasmuch as it acquires its importance from the fact that it hears the things which the eye has seen.
LEONARDO DA VINCI

For those who remember the great days of the silent film, and still look back to them as a golden age of cinema, it is a healthy shock to be reminded that few people today under the age of fifty can have any clear recollection of watching silent films. For most of them the film has always been something to be heard as well as seen. While, therefore, the historical accident that gave the visual side priority of development has justified our giving it priority of consideration, it is now high time to redress the balance.

Although the sound film as we know it dates from 1926, the desire to make the film talk is as old as the film itself. Indeed, it is older; for Edison first discovered, in 1877, how to record and reproduce sound by means of his Phonograph, and it was the success of the Phonograph that suggested to him the possibility of adding to it a moving photograph. In 1891 he invented the Kinetoscope, a peepshow machine by means of which moving photographs could be displayed to one person at a time, and the Kinetoscope was subsequently combined with the Phonograph to make the Kinetophone.

In 1896 Charles Pathé in Paris and Messter in Germany made attempts to combine the newly invented cinematograph with the Berliner gramophone. This idea received a new lease on life in 1908, when the Warwick Company in England introduced their Cinephone apparatus, to be followed rapidly by the Hepworth Vivaphone and the Gaumont

17. *D. W. Griffith was at one time popularly credited with the discovery (or rediscovery) of the close-up, but it was no less essential to his practice of editing to be able to draw the camera back for a long shot, as here in* THE BIRTH OF A NATION (USA, 1915).

18. The extreme long shot. From SHE WORE A YELLOW RIBBON (USA, 1950), directed by John Ford.

Chronophone, all depending on the playing of gramophone records with films and incorporating some mechanical device to ensure synchronization between the two. Two limitations prevented these systems from becoming anything more than a fashionable novelty; the volume of sound produced by the ordinary gramophone was insufficient, and the methods of synchronization were imperfect.

A more fruitful line of research was pursued by Eugène Lauste, who in 1906 took out in Britain the first patent for a system of recording sound vibrations photographically on the film itself, by which perfect synchronization could be automatically ensured. It was the development of this idea, coupled with the parallel development of devices for the electrical amplification of sound, that made the modern sound film possible. What ultimately brought it to birth was the decision of Warner Brothers, faced with a slump in their fortunes, to gamble on the novelty of sound. Their first sound feature, *The Jazz Singer*, made in 1927, was such an astonishing success that within a few months the film industries of the world began a stampede to wire studios and cinemas for sound, and by 1929 the era of the silent film was virtually at an end.

Sound added a new dimension to the film, a new extension of realism. One could not only see a man speaking or singing, one could also hear at the same time what he said, or what he sang, matched perfectly to the movements of his lips. If he slammed a door, one heard the bang at precisely the right moment. If a dog barked, one could hear the bark perfectly timed to the movement of his jaws. If an actor knocked over a vase, one heard the smash and tinkle of broken glass as it struck the floor. It was marvelous; it was unbelievable. Just as audiences in 1896 had been thrilled chiefly by the idea that pictures actually moved and had been content to sit and watch such simple things as a train entering a station or workers coming out of a factory, so in the earliest days of the sound film they were chiefly excited by the fact that the sound was realistic and perfectly timed to match the action. Naturally, the producers exploited this curiosity to the full. Sound was used without discrimination, and wherever possible in obvious synchronization with the picture; and since it was in speech that synchronization could be displayed to the greatest advantage, it was the "hundred-per-cent talkie" that became the most popular film of the day.

Films made in this way, however, had little artistic merit and fell far below the standards of even the moderately good silent film. In the first place, much of the freedom with which the visual image had been used in the silent film was suddenly lost. The film script was written in terms not of pictures, but of long passages of dialogue, like a stage play, and this imposed severe limitations on the distance within which the camera could be moved; for if speech is to be heard clearly, the listener must not be too far away, and in a film the "listener" is the imaginary observer represented by the camera. Variation of camera angle and freedom of cutting were also seriously reduced since they would have tended to distract attention from the dialogue, which was of principal significance, and would have been incompatible with the emphasis on synchronization. The "hundred-per-cent talkie," in short, represented a throwback to the stilted, monotonous style of the cinematographic reproductions of stage plays that had been common from 1908 to 1914, when the film was still groping to discover itself.

Moreover, the compensating gain from synchronization was negligible. A silent film can show a dog barking; to add the sound of his bark is certainly a gain in realism, but it tells us nothing more than we knew before, it adds nothing to the expressive qualities of the image; it is still merely a dog barking. Even dialogue was often used to say in words what the silent film was able to express as well by images alone. The picture of the angry father pointing his wretched erring son to the door is made no more significant if we add the words: "Get out of here and never darken these doors again." The silent image, in such a case, may well be more, rather than less, impressive.

The more intelligent critics were quick to attack these faults, and some were even goaded into a reactionary attack on sound itself as being a step backward. An art, they argued, thrives on the limitations of its particular medium, and every gain in realism (as, for example, the painting of sculpture in lifelike colors) must be accompanied by an aesthetic loss. They grimly prophesied the ultimate invention of a film capable of representing life and its sensations so perfectly as to be entirely useless for the purposes of art. An echo of these misgivings was heard when the color film was introduced and will doubtless be heard once more when the stereoscopic film appears. Such attacks, however, are both impotent and ill-founded; if they had any validity, the addition of movement to photography, which led to the birth of the film itself, would stand condemned by the same token, and cinematography would be a far less expressive and resourceful medium than still photography, which is apparent nonsense. A gain in realism must, of course, mean a loss of certain limitations that previously may have been used with great effect (compare the remarks on *Ladies in Retirement*, p. 56), but it also brings with it, by way of compensation, new scope for selection and, indeed, new limitations of its own.

The microphone, like the camera, is unselective. As we have already seen, the camera records everything within its field of view without discrimination; but by means of editing we can join together a number of shots taken by the camera in different positions and reproduce the impressions of an observer looking now in one direction, now in another. The microphone likewise picks up all sounds within its range without discrimination. Can we, in this case also, reproduce the impressions of a selective observer by mechanically cutting and joining various pieces of sound track together? Pudovkin experimented with this method in his sound film *Deserter* [1] and secured some striking results, but it is not capable of general application; for the simple fact

1 See p. 38, footnote.

is that the way in which we hear is different from the way in which we see.

When we were considering the way in which we see, we were helped by one or two quotations from the descriptions of novelists. Let us, therefore, discover what help they can give us now in this matter of hearing. At one point in Tolstoy's *War and Peace* one of the chief characters, Pierre, is compelled to watch the military execution of five men. The death of the fifth, a young factory worker, is described as follows:

> The word of command must have sounded, and after it the shots of the eight muskets. But Pierre, however earnestly he tried to recollect it afterwards, had not heard the slightest sound from the shots. He only saw the factory lad suddenly fall back on the cords, saw blood oozing in two places, and saw the cords work themselves loose from the weight of the hanging body, and the factory lad sit down, his head falling unnaturally, and one leg bent under him.

The striking part of this description from our present point of view lies in the words: "But Pierre . . . had not heard the slightest sound." The word of command must have sounded, and after it the shot of the eight muskets," and these sounds must have fallen on Pierre's ears; but transfixed with horror at what he saw, he *heard* nothing.

A moment's reflection will persuade us that this is so far from being an uncommon thing as to be part of our everyday experience—part, in fact, of the normal mechanism of hearing. At any particular moment a considerable number of sounds may be impinging on my ear drum, as I can confirm if I consciously pause in what I am doing to listen to them; but I am seldom conscious of more than one or two of these sounds, which have caught my attention or to which my attention is deliberately directed, and I may on occasion hear nothing at all. The distant note of the cuckoo to a countryman, the tumultuous roar of street traffic to the city dweller, although clearly audible, may be entirely unheard if their minds are held by some other sound or sight or thought. I well remember how, as a boy, I would become deeply engrossed in an exciting book and how my mother would call me again and again without any effect, until at last she had to come and shake me forcibly by the shoulder; it was not that I was inattentive or indifferent—I had not heard, so entirely was my attention turned in one direction. On the other hand, if one's attention is in a mood to wander, all kinds of incidental noises may force themselves on the mind and prove a distraction to reading or whatever else one may be doing; the rustle of paper or the ticking of a clock in an otherwise silent library can be, on occasions, more disturbing than the deafening roar of a factory working at full pressure.

In the case of the eye, we turn our attention from one thing to another by looking now near, now far away, now in one direction, now in another. The very fact of looking at one point excludes the possibility of looking at any other, not merely mentally, but physiologically; if I am looking before me, it is a physical impossibility to see what is behind me, and vice versa. But in the case of the ear, all the sounds within audible range are striking our ears all the time and are able to be heard; which of them we in fact hear depends on a purely mental process of selection that allows some sounds through and stops others, that may even on occasion stop all sounds, according to the preoccupations that hold our attention at that moment. It is as though between the ear and the conscious mind there were an automatic sound-control device, by means of which incoming sounds were separated, some being allowed to come through clearly and loudly, others more faintly, and the rest not at all, the balance between them being changed all the time as the control responds with the greatest sensitiveness to the fluctuations of attention in the mind.

Now let us turn for a second quotation to Dickens's *Bleak House*. The chief character, Esther Summerson, accompanied by her two young friends Richard and Ada, visits the house of a certain Mrs. Jellyby, who is so taken up with public duties that she neglects her home and her large family. Here is a fragment from Esther's own description of the visit:

> We passed several children on the way up, whom it was difficult to avoid treading on in the dark; and as we came into Mrs. Jellyby's presence, one of the poor little things fell downstairs—down a whole flight (as it sounded to me) with a great noise.

> Mrs. Jellyby, whose face reflected none of the uneasiness which we could not help showing in our faces, as the dear child's head recorded its passage with a bump on every stair—Richard afterwards said he counted seven, besides one for the landing—received us with perfect equanimity. . . .

> The room, which was strewn with papers and nearly filled by a great writing table covered with similar litter, was, I must say, not only very untidy, but very dirty. We were obliged to take notice of that with our sense of sight, even while with our sense of hearing we followed the poor child who had tumbled downstairs: I think into the back kitchen, where somebody seemed to stifle him.

Here Esther describes certain things she sees and certain things she hears; and yet, as she herself indicates, the one set of sense impressions is quite independent of the other. She observes the undisturbed face of Mrs. Jellyby, the consternation on the faces of Richard and Ada, the room strewn with papers, but what she hears is something else: "We were obliged to take notice of that with our sense of sight, even while, with our sense of hearing, we followed the poor child who had tumbled downstairs."

This again, is a far from uncommon experience. Very frequently we find ourselves looking at one thing and listening to sounds coming from some other source altogether; and because this is so, a continuous insistence on synchronism throughout a film, far from being realistic, will produce an unnatural effect. The free association of sound and image, the bringing together in certain instances of the sound of one thing with the image of another, is not only truer to life, it also enables sound and image to complement each other instead of merely duplicating each other. Arnheim instances a moment in the film *Men Behind Bars* of Paul Fejos; the picture on the screen shows convicts in the prison chapel passing weapons from one to another in the shadow of the pews, but the sound that accompanies it is the voice of the priest intoning "Thou shalt not kill." [2]

Thus, in opposition to those critics who attacked the introduction of sound as retrogressive, we arrive at the conclusion that the hundred-per-cent talkie was crude and artless, not through an excess of realism, but on the contrary, through an excess of artificiality. It ignored the fact that in hearing we are exercising all the time an unconscious selection from the indiscriminate mass of sound that is playing upon the drums of our ears; and, secondly, while very often a sound will cause us to turn our eyes toward the place from which it is coming, so that we apprehend the sound and its source together, it as often happens that while we listen to one thing we may be looking at another.

The skillful and imaginative use of sound in the film lies in taking advantage of these facts, and as we saw in an earlier chapter, "The Film-Maker's Tools," the methods of recording sound offer no obstacle to its free and selective use; on the contrary, they are especially suited to it. By means of the re-recording panel and post-synchronization, that is to say by the recording of separate sound tracks and the subsequent re-recording of these onto a final track, the film-maker can compose any assembly of sound that his imagination can conceive. And in the second place, because the picture and the sound are recorded on different lengths of film and can be manipulated independently of each other, the

2 Rudolf Arnheim, *Film* (Faber and Faber, London, 1933), p. 257.

film-maker can obtain whatever relationship between them at any point he desires. The sound engineer in fact, sitting at the volume controls of his re-recording apparatus, fading each track in and out and constantly maintaining the required balance between simultaneous sounds as they are registered on the final composite track, is fully analogous to that automatic sound control that we have imagined to exist between the ear and the conscious mind; the intelligence he obeys and to whose preoccupations of attention he responds is that of the film director through whose eyes, we the audience, are to see, and through whose ears we are to hear.

In our analysis of the editing of the visual image, we found that the one fundamental principle on which all else hinged was that of the camera as an observer, watching through the director's eyes. With the addition of sound, the scope of that observer's power of apprehension and the range and complexity of what the imaginative director can reveal to him is greatly increased, for he now becomes a listener as well. What he hears should enrich and add to what he sees, not merely duplicate it.

A most effective use of sound that comes to my mind occurred in Jean Renoir's film *La Bête Humaine*, adapted from Emile Zola's story of that sexual mania that expresses itself in the lust to kill. An engine driver, Jacques Lantier (played by Jean Gabin), has fallen in love with a young married woman, Séverine Robaud (played by Simone Simon). So that they can go away together, he conspires with her to kill her husband, but at the crucial moment he cannot bring himself to carry out the deed. Séverine, disappointed at his lack of courage, runs from him, and there follows a period of estrangement between them. One evening, Jacques, frustrated and gloomy, goes to a dance concert arranged for the railway workers, where he sees Séverine dancing with a younger man. Jacques approaches her and leads her outside to the veranda so that they can talk; when he learns that she still loves him, he tries to persuade her to go away with him, but she replies that it will be useless, since her husband will find her wherever she goes. She then leaves the dance hall to return to her flat across the railway yard.

Jacques follows her there and declares that he now has sufficient resolve to kill her husband. She tries to dissuade him, but he is adamant and takes Robaud's revolver out of a drawer and loads it. Hearing a noise that they believe to be Robaud returning, they run to the door. While they embrace each other to give themselves courage, the footsteps pass upstairs to the floor above; it is not Robaud. As Jacques continues to caress Séverine, the mania for sadistic murder, which he believes he has inherited from his ancestors, rises to uncontrollable intensity within him, and his fingers fasten round her throat. She breaks away and runs into the bedroom, but he pursues her and finally kills her; one hears only her stifled screams through the open doorway and catches a glimpse of his savagely bending form. The whole of this scene in the flat is played in silence, save for the few words of dialogue, the footsteps on the stairs and the woman's screams.

The scene changes for a moment to the dance hall, where a tenor is singing a light cabaret ballad of a young girl and how she suffered for love. Then we return to the flat, where Jacques walks slowly away from the body of Séverine to the parlor sideboard, against which he stands in weary self-disgust, all his passion spent. With this return to the apartment, however, the tenor's song does not cease to be heard, as we might expect, but on the contrary is carried over into it without any drop in volume. This device is both dramatically effective and psychologically sound: dramatically effective because the introduction of the song helps to relieve the intense emotional excitement that has been built up during the murder scene, and because the words of the ballad itself form an ironic commentary on the horrible fate of Séverine; and psychologically correct because (we may suppose) the music of the dance band and the singing was all the time audible within the apartment, but the characters (and likewise the spectator), absorbed first in the anxious waiting, and then in the struggle and murder, were unconscious of it, as Tolstoy's Pierre was unconscious of the shots of the eight muskets. The murder over, however, the murderer would inevitably become conscious of the awful stillness in the room, and it is then that his mind, no longer rigidly directed to some purpose, but relaxed, would become aware of the singing. It is for this reason that the audience can accept, and welcome as relief, a musical accompaniment that in the earlier part of the scene in the flat would have been only an irritating distraction.

The proper relationship of picture and sound in a film has been compared to that of the parts in a musical duet; neither part of the duet is complete in itself, but played together they combine to produce a complete composition. It should be noted, however, that in the case of the film the two parts are generally not of equal importance. Normally, the visual part of a sound film is the more important in the sense that it carries more of the total significance. This is hardly surprising; sight, after all, is the most important of our senses, and we know and learn far more of the world around us through our eyes than through our ears. This fact has a bearing particularly on the use of dialogue in the sound film.

In the stage play dialogue is everything; it is itself the medium in which the playwright works. And since it is found profitable and easy to make film adaptations of stage plays and since unskilled scriptwriters find it easier to write in literary than in visual form, many films also are conceived primarily in terms of dialogue; the ghost of the hundred-per-cent talkie still haunts the production studios. Even with sound added to it, however, the film remains primarily a visual medium, and there is generally no justification for allowing speech to play more than a subordinate part; even on the sound track it does not rule unchallenged, but must frequently give way to other natural sounds and noises, and to music. Whereas dialogue in the stage play is a highly conventionalized medium through which everything must be expressed, almost everything done, in the sound film dialogue can be used quite naturally; in some parts a certain amount of dialogue will be appropriate, in others it can be quite sparse, even monosyllabic, and in still others it may be dispensed with altogether, the significance being carried entirely by the action. It follows that the dialogue script of a film, which has no indication of the action, will as a whole be incomprehensible.

So far we have considered only a naturalistic use of sound; that is to say, we have considered only sounds that were presented as a natural part of the scene and that might be heard by anyone who could be imagined as standing in the same place as the camera. Sometimes, however, sound is used to give an impression of a character's state of mind; this is usually done either by the introduction of sounds that could not conceivably be a natural part of the scene represented, or else by the obvious distortion of naturalistic sounds. An example will make this clear.

In *Scarlet Street* (produced in America in 1944 and directed by Fritz Lang) Edward G. Robinson plays the part of an elderly bookkeeper, Chris, who ruins himself over an infatuation for a worthless girl. When he learns that she has been interested only in his money, he kills her and allows her boy friend Johnny to be tried and condemned for the murder. Chris travels to a distant town and takes a room in a cheap boardinghouse, but he cannot escape from his conscience. As an electric sign outside flashes continually on and off, he begins to hear the voice of the girl echoing from different corners of the room and calling the name of Johnny. Chris tries to shout it to silence, to shut his ears against it, but the half-muffled, echoing voice goes on, until he is finally driven to an attempt at hanging himself.

Although such a non-naturalistic use of sound can on occasion be effective, it requires management of the greatest care if it is not to appear clumsy and forced. In the French film *Beethoven*, for example, the director, Abel Gance, represents the onset of Beethoven's deafness by a loud clanging sound, which is presumably to be understood as the noise ringing in his head; with a cut to a shot of a shepherd boy watching him, the sound vanishes, but it returns as soon as we see Beethoven again. Elsewhere in the film a beggar is seen and heard playing his violin in the street; the deaf Beethoven comes into the shot, and as he approaches the beggar, the sound dies away completely, although the beggar can be seen still playing; as Beehoven moves out of the shot, the sound comes back again. The effect in both cases is forced and unconvincing.

Where occasional non-naturalistic effects are introduced into a sound track conceived generally in naturalistic terms, the spectator is involved in a change of viewpoint in passing from one to the other. In the naturalistic sections his viewpoint is objective, whereas in the non-naturalistic sections he finds himself suddenly invited to look at the action through the mind of one of the characters. Such a change should be clearly established and properly motivated, so that the spectator realizes what is happening and has been led to expect it. Arnheim describes [3] an example from which this point may be illustrated. In the sketch for what was to have been his first sound film, *Life Is Grand*, Pudovkin planned the following scene: A woman is shown saying goodbye to her husband at a railway station. Suddenly she remembers that she has something to tell him, but she cannot remember what it is. Agitatedly trying to collect her thoughts, she imagines that the train is already starting. The engine whistle and the puffing of steam are heard, growing in speed and loudness and scattering her thoughts entirely. Yet although these sounds are reproduced on the sound track, the picture on the screen shows that, in fact, the train is still standing motionless; they are entirely the product of her panic-stricken imagination. Ultimately, the film was made silent, under the title *The Story of a Simple Case*, so that there is no possibility of judging the effectiveness of this scene. The description suggests, however, that

[3] In *Film*, p. 266.

anyone not aware of Pudovkin's intention might well have regarded the sound of the starting train as a naturalistic background sound coming from some other part of the station, and so might have entirely lost its significance.

Alfred Hitchcock's first sound film, *Blackmail*, has a classic example of non-naturalistic sound used successfully. In self-defense a girl has murdered an artist in his studio with a bread knife. All night she walks through the streets in a daze, creeping home to bed in the early morning just before her mother comes to call her. At breakfast she is nervous, distraught; her experiences of the previous night and the lack of sleep have left her in a state bordering on hysteria. A gossiping woman neighbor comes in to talk to the girl's parents. She is full of the details of the murder spread across the morning newspapers. In her harsh, metallic voice she speaks of the knife that has been found. Again she mentions the word "knife." The girl is asked by her father to cut some bread; a close shot shows the look of terror staring from her eyes. The woman's gossip has become a continuous mumble in which only one word is heard clearly at intervals: "knife . . . knife . . . knife." The girl stretches out her hand for the bread knife, and as she touches it, the word "knife" is suddenly shouted out, and she drops it with a clatter; in the silence that follows, everyone stares at her in amazement.

There is perhaps something to be said for the view that this is a clever and unusual use of the selection of sound rather than mere distortion; the word "knife" is certainly a natural element of the scene, and it is conceivable that it might seize the attention of the distracted girl to such an extent as to drive all understanding of the rest of the talk from her mind, reaching its maximum intensity when her hand actually touches a knife. The reason for its success, however, is the fact that the whole of the immediately preceding action, her struggle with the artist, the murder, her wanderings through the night, and finally (and most importantly), her pathetically desperate attempt to appear normal in a world whose every movement and sound has suddenly become the stirring of an avenging justice, has built up in the spectator a sense of dramatic tension in which his sympathies are so completely with the girl that he is already, in effect, looking at everything from her point of view, and so accepts the subjective approach quite naturally and readily.

Despite this example from *Blackmail*, however (and many others equally effective might be quoted), I personally cannot help feeling that where the film-maker can secure the result he wants by the relating of images and sounds singled out by selection from the natural circumstances of the scene, the result is likely to be more forceful and convincing than if he introduces sound effects adventitiously. In *La Bête Humaine*, for example, the introduction of the tenor's song adds greatly to the effectiveness of the scene and is all the more striking because it is not arbitrarily brought in for that purpose, but is also part of the actual background of the scene and is introduced at (quite literally) the psychological moment.

If I were pressed to justify this prejudice against non-naturalistic sound, I should perhaps find myself in some difficulty. We do not cavil when Virginia Woolf in *Night and Day* writes: "To Cassandra's ears the buzz of voices inside the drawing-room was like the tuning up of the instruments of the orchestra"; or when Kenneth Grahame in *The Wind in the Willows* describes how the Sea Rat beguiles the Water Rat with his travels, saying: "And the talk, the wonderful talk flowed on—or was it speech entirely, or did it pass at times into song—chanty of the sailors weighing the dripping anchor, sonorous hum of the shrouds in a tearing North-Easter, ballad of the fisherman hauling his nets at sundown against an apricot sky, chords of guitar and mandoline from gondola and caique?" To deny altogether to the film-maker a similar freedom of expression would be absurd, and I should certainly not go so far; the most one can say is that non-naturalistic sound, in a narrative film conceived generally in naturalistic terms, should be used with great caution. The reason lies in the fact that the film medium is a naturalistic medium, not a conventionalized one; it is direct, not indirect; it represents not by description, but by the reproduction of actual sights and sounds. Now there is normally a considerable difference of intensity between our subjective and objective impressions; they exist, as it were, on different planes, and we do not confuse a mental image of a chair or of a sound with an actual chair or an actual sound (unless, of course, the mind is in an abnormal state). In an indirect medium such as that of the storywriter, this difference between the objective and subjective can be indicated, or else the reader himself automatically makes the necessary adjustment. In the film this is infinitely more difficult to achieve, since everything seen or heard is on the same plane of realism.

In other kinds of film the same objections do not hold. In documentary films sound has frequently been used with considerable freedom and success. *Cable Ship*, for example, made by Stuart Legg for the G.P.O. Film Unit, falls into three sections. The introductory sequence shows the international exchange in London, its operators making connection with the furthermost parts of the world. Then follows the main part of the film showing the work of the men on the cable ship examining the submarine cables for defects and making repairs. Finally, in the concluding sequence we again see the operators at the switchboard, but what we hear is not their voices, as before, but sounds from the cable-ship sequences, the creaking of the winch, the shrill blast of the whistle, the voices of the men. The whole film, in fact, is a piece of screen rhetoric. First comes statement one, then statement two, and finally, in a kind of filmic peroration, the two statements are brought together to imply a general conclusion, namely, that the bedrock, as it were, of this vast system of international telephonic communication is the constant watchfulness and labor of the men in the cable ships.

There are two forms of non-naturalistic sound that merit special attention; the film commentary and film music. Both are accepted conventions and are recognized as being on an entirely different plane from the representational elements of the film. Film music is a subject of such importance that it will have to be given separate consideration, and for the moment we shall consider commentary only.

The commentary is used almost entirely as an explanatory device, either descriptive, didactic, humorous or rhetorical. Its use is therefore mainly confined to that group of informational films that includes the newsreel, the educational film, the travelogue, the interest film, the documentary and the propaganda film. The great temptation to which such films too often succumb is to say nearly everything through the commentary and to leave the minimum to the picture. The *March of Time* films, for all their excellence, erred conspicuously in this way, and the same fault could be laid at the door of many documentaries. Such films are sometimes basically little more than illustrated lectures, the visual illustrations being at some points highly effective, at others merely stopgaps. There are several reasons for this, and on occasion they may be insuperable. In the first place, we are accustomed by education and habit to express ourselves in literary terms, in writing and in speech, and it is therefore easier for the unskilled scriptwriter, whether he be a professional film technician or (as may happen in these cases) a subject specialist who is an expert in his own field but a tyro in the film, to set his ideas down in literary terms; to express them in the visual terms of the cinema requires a special training and a high degree of visual imagination. Secondly, a film that sets out to present an argument or to trace a series of factual developments may for the sake of completeness be compelled to cover ground for which satisfactory visual material cannot be obtained. Thirdly, where a film is being sponsored by a government department or a public organization or commercial undertaking, and the script has to be approved before production,

it may often be easier to secure approval for a literary
script in which the content is fully set out in the commentary than for a highly technical script that the sponsors
find difficult to understand.

Granting all this, however, the fact remains that it is the
visual part of the film that leaves the deepest and most
lasting impression on the great majority of people, and
those films are most effective that appeal primarily to the
eye and only secondarily to the ear.

In a number of documentary films some interesting experiments in the use of commentary have been carried out.
Paul Rotha, in *The World Is Rich* and *Land of Promise*, has
developed a free and lively method in which numerous
voices carry on the argument in the form of a dialogue, the
commentator, subject experts and representative members
of the community interrupting each other, asking questions,
contradicting and speaking in their turn. In *Nightmail, Our
Country* and the American documentaries of Pare Lorentz,
attempts have been made to use verse, but it will be more
suitable to consider these when we come to deal with film
music.

From time to time there have been experiments in the use
of commentary as one of the elements of the story film.
Gold Is Where You Find It, a Technicolor film directed by
Michael Curtiz, telling a story of rivalry between pioneer-
ing oil prospectors and the farmers whose land they are
ruining, opens in the manner of an interest film with scenic
shots of American oil areas, accompanied by a commentary
on the conditions under which oil mining began. Other
films, such as *Our Town* (directed by Sam Wood), employ a
method known as *narratage*, in which one of the characters,
usually a minor character in the film, is depicted as telling
the story: at the beginning, and perhaps occasionally
throughout the film, we see the narrator talking; at other
times the film becomes entirely naturalistic; and there may
be still other portions, intermediate between these two, in
which we see the action of the story, but hear the words of

the narrator, which thus become, in effect, a form of commentary.

While it would be foolish to discourage such experiments, or to seek to limit in any way what Charles Morgan, writing of the art of the storyteller, has called "freedom of attack," [4] it must be said that these attempts to use commentary in the fiction film have not been strikingly successful. It is difficult to see what is gained by commentary to balance the loss involved; for there is a loss, the nature of which Charles Morgan himself indicates:

... There are a hundred methods in which a subject or a scene may be treated.

To shift from one to another is necessarily to sacrifice something in consistency of illusion; the reader, if he is violently and frequently dragged from one point of view to another, may cease to be spell-bound; this is the risk inherent in the ... exercise of ... "freedom of attack."

A variation of the commentary, which has been used comparatively little despite its possibilities, is the internal monologue, in which the thoughts of one of the characters of the film are heard as though spoken aloud. Eisenstein was at one time so enthusiastic about it as to declare (in capital letters) the "THE TRUE MATERIAL FOR THE SOUND FILM IS, OF COURSE, THE MONOLOGUE." [5] Assuming that this was neither a mistranslation nor a leg-pull, we must accept it as the momentary excess of a great film and theorist. Although he intended to experiment with the monologue in a film version of Theodore Dreiser's *An American Tragedy* to be produced in Hollywood by Paramount, his treatment was rejected and the film was never made.[6] To judge from his later films, *Alexander Nevsky*

---

[4] "The Central Tradition," an essay published in *The Sunday Times* (London) of April 21 and April 28, 1946.

[5] *Close-up*, June, 1933, pp. 120-3.

[6] See *The Film Sense*, by S. M. Eisenstein, p. 171, for an extract from the treatment.

and *Ivan the Terrible*, his enthusiasm for the monologue vanished.

One of the few films in which the internal monolouge has been used to any extent is a short, *Low Water*, made by Arnot Robertson and H. E. Turner in 1937. An unemployed seaman, who has lost almost all hope of finding work again, looks aimlessly down into the water at the dockside. The skipper of a small vessel calls him over and offers to give him a trial as mate. Since there are no other members of the crew it means, in effect, that he must sail the boat himself. As he moves about the vessel grappling with each task, his heart sinks steadily within him. He has had no decent food for months; he is weak and out of practice; he is sure he cannot make good. When the boat returns to shore he prepares to leave and go on the search for work again, but suddenly, to his joy, the skipper offers him a permanent berth, and it is on that note of hope that the film ends. The main element throughout the sound track is the voice of the seaman himself giving utterance to his thoughts, first of despair, then of chagrin and humiliation at his weakness and clumsiness, and finally of elation. The contrast between the sound of the voice on the one hand, low, intimate and casually extempore, and on the other hand the shots themselves, detached and objective, gave the film an unusual quality.

It is also of interest to recall that two well-known and successful British films of their day, *The Seventh Veil* and *Brief Encounter*, were cast mainly in the form of a monologue, although in each case a great part of the action within the monologue was represented, of course, in the normal way.

Glancing back over the path we have so far traced, we find that the nature of the film medium has in its main elements already revealed itself. It is a medium of fragments of recorded moving visual image and fragments of recorded sound, which can be assembled in any order that has significance for the mind. They can be assembled in narrative order (the mind watching and listening), or to point some relationship (the mind judging and commenting), or to create a general impression of a subject (the mind reflecting) or even to represent the free association of ideas that takes place in our subconscious mind (the mind dreaming). Any association of visual or sound impressions, in short, that is possible to the mind in any condition can be represented in the film. This composition of moving images and sounds can be so arranged as to give the spectator the continuous impression of moving in and out of a sequence of events, approaching to examine this, receding to regard that, following a figure moving down a corridor, sweeping his gaze up a stairway; out of a concourse of possible sounds, real or imagined, now this is heard, now that. Anything in a film that is clumsy or abrupt or meaningless is so because the spectator's mind has been jarred or checked or led astray.

Of all who are engaged in production, those most directly and immediately concerned with the manipulation of this medium are the scriptwriter, the director and the editor. It is perhaps misleading to describe them thus, as three persons, because, as we have already seen, the three functions may be carried out by one person; even where three are involved, their contributions cannot be equal; if the film is to have unity of purpose and of effect, one mind must dominate the creative work. Usually it is the mind of the director.

Since the introduction of sound the film director has no longer been able to work with the same *physical* freedom as in silent days, when whole films were shot "off the cuff" and could be radically altered by cutting after shooting had been completed. That is to say, he can no longer juggle with the actual celluloid pieces in the way that was then possible. The complexities of sound-film production demand the most careful and detailed planning. Much more work goes into the script, and after the script has been completed and shooting begins, there is much less scope for alteration and improvisation than there used to be.

19. *Models floating in a studio tank* (above) *are photographed in close-up to appear as full-size warships in the finished film* (below). *From* FIRE OVER ENGLAND *(Great Britain, 1937).*

20. Shooting a scene for CHRONIQUE D'UN ÉTÉ (France, 1961), directed by the French anthropologist, Jean Rouch. The use of the hand camera gives the film director free and direct contact with the real world.

This does not mean that the film itself has undergone any fundamental change. It means only that the burden of creative effort has now shifted from the shooting and cutting stages toward the scripting stage. The director who is conscientious for the success of his film and who regards himself as its ultimate coordinator and creator is compelled to conceive it in more exact terms in the earliest stages of production, and this inevitably draws him into the scripting process. He must carry out in his imagination a process that is at once analysis and synthesis; breaking each scene up into fragments of observation, as it were, in order to select those particular fragments that, when assembled, will convey precisely the image he wishes to present. The shooting and editing of the film, one may say, should have already occurred in the mind of the director before a foot of actual film is shot.

Where, on the other hand, the director is content to be merely an interpreter, the scriptwriter will have a correspondingly greater importance. In all cases, however, the editor's contribution is today less than it once was, since there is little he can do to influence the main concepts that have guided the script and the shooting, whatever improvements he may be able to make in matters of details. Of the numerous subordinate artists, technicians and craftsmen who assist the director in realizing the conception of the film, the three chief are the cameraman, the actor and the composer, and it is their work we must now proceed to consider.

7 · The Art of the Cameraman

Painting is concerned with all the ten attributes of sight, namely, darkness and brightness, substance and colour, form and place, remoteness and nearness, movement and rest; and it is with these attributes that this, my small book, will be interwoven . . .
LEONARDO DA VINCI

Of the assistant technicians in film production none is more important than the cameraman. The creative work of scriptwriters, set designers, costumers, actors and director is all designed to one end, to the securing of a transparent photographic image that can be projected onto the screen. Without the cameraman their labor can lead nowhere; whereas the cameraman, on the other hand, if he wishes can constitute himself producer, director, photographer and editor all in one, and make his own film entirely unaided, as Flaherty in 1920 made *Nanook of the North* in the Hudson Bay territory of Canada, with the Eskimos as his only companions. Nevertheless, such an event is rare, and the cameraman must ordinarily be content to photograph, under the instructions of the director, the shots that have been planned in the shooting script.

The director will usually discuss each shot with his cameraman, either in the preparatory stages or during shooting, and he will listen to any advice the cameraman may have to offer. The final decision, however, and the ultimate responsibility for the shot as it appears, rests with the director. One may imagine a director sitting, perhaps, in the quiet of his own home, working through the script and trying to visualize how he wants certain shots to appear; it may be his first detailed study of the script prior to shooting, or shooting may already have begun and he may be concentrating particularly on the shots that are to be taken on the following day. In his mind's eye he sees the screen, a plain white rectangle. How shall he arrange his picture within this space? What factors govern his choice and what resources of the camera can he call upon?

He seems to be in a position very similar to that of an artist planning a picture to be painted on canvas, but in fact the problems that confront him are fundamentally different. First, and most importantly, the shot he is planning is not meant to be self-sufficient, like an artist's picture, and to be studied at length as a complete whole. It will be on the screen for only a brief space of time, a fleeting period that the spectator is powerless to prolong, and it will be preceded and followed by other shots: that is to say, it will be merely a single element in a continuous flow of images, and its character, indeed, the justification of its very existence, are dependent on the contribution it can make to that visual flow. The ruling consideration in the director's mind will be the part that he wants the shot to play in the edited scene, the way in which the shot is to be related dramatically, logically and pictorially to those preceding and those following, so that with them it forms a unity.

A second vital difference between painter and director is that the director's picture is a moving one. This virtually nullifies the ordinary laws of pictorial composition. Movement becomes the vital factor in composition and overshadows everything else. A still taken from a certain shot may look pleasing to the eye because a mass of trees in the distance on the right is balanced by a building in the left foreground and a white winding road links the two in a unified pattern; but when the same shot is shown on the screen, the figure of a man, so small as to escape notice and have no importance in the still, may be moving, and immediately that movement is the most compelling focal point in the whole picture. Or again, a still may show a rider on a rearing horse, their figures making a perfectly proportioned arrangement within the rectangle of the still; but the frame from which that still is printed may be one of a hundred or more in the shot, and the only one among them all that gives such a pleasing picture. When the shot is projected we follow the movement as a whole: we do not linger over the one flashing moment that the still reproduces.

That is why stills are so misleading when used as illustrations of films. To select, out of the 150,000 frames of which a film may be composed, the few that make pleasing pictures is itself a minor art that, like poker work and the jigsaw puzzle, requires a certain niceness of judgment, and the pictures so selected may revive memories for those who have seen the film; but of the things that really matter in a film they can tell us almost nothing.

There is one further difference between director and painter that merits attention: whereas the painter is normally free to compose his picture in a space of any size and shape he may choose, the film director is forced to work, at least in standard film, with a standardized horizontal rectangle in the fixed proportions of four to three. These proportions do not, unfortunately, lend themselves equally to every type of composition. They do not allow the director to set off most effectively extended panoramic shots (such as that of the Teutonic knights in Eisenstein's *Alexander Nevsky* advancing out of the horizon across the ice of Lake Peipus), which require a frame horizontally elongated; they are not altogether suitable to single portraits or group compositions requiring a single compositional center; and they are entirely inimical to a narrow upright composition.[1]

In an attempt to break away from the fixed proportions of the screen, D. W. Griffith occasionally masked either the top and bottom of the picture (for a horizontal composition) or the sides (to emphasize the vertical quality of an upright composition). He and other silent film directors also

[1] The wide-screen systems introduced since 1950 are even more restrictive. They favor and impose one type of composition (the wide-sweeping panorama) at the expense of all the others.

frequently used some form of circular masking to concentrate attention on the center of the screen. The French director Abel Gance designed his film *Napoleon* for showing on three screens side by side (the triptych screen) and was thus able to dispose panoramic massed battle scenes extending across the three screens. In 1930, in an address he gave to the Academy of Motion Picture Arts and Sciences in Hollywood, Eisenstein proposed the introduction of a circular frame into which rectangles of different proportions could be introduced to meet the needs of different types of composition. Nothing came of this proposal, however, and the proportions of the screen still stand in the ratio of four to three. Today not even masking is ordinarily used. Director and cameraman accept the limitations that the rectangle of the screen imposes on them and they endeavor to adapt their compositions as far as possible to its shape.

One way in which the rectangle is sometimes used as a positive element in composition is in setting the vertical axis of the frame at an angle to the vertical axis of the subject. This is done by taking the shot with the camera tilted to one side, so that the lower and upper limits of the film frame are not horizontal but on an incline; when this shot is projected onto the screen, the frame will, of course, be horizontal in the projector gate, and it is the subject that will appear to be tilted sideways. One of the sequences of Julien Duvivier's *Carnet de Bal*, showing the broken life of an epileptic doctor chained to a harridan of a wife, living out his hopeless existence in a disordered flat to the noise of a clattering crane outside, was shot in this manner, and the lack of equilibrium in the composition, prolonged throughout the whole episode, adds considerably to its nervous tension.

A similar device was used in *Brief Encounter*. Just after Alec (Trevor Howard) has left Laura (Celia Johnson) for the last time, she is shown sitting benumbed with grief at the railway refreshment-room table. Slowly the image tilts to one side. At the sound of an approaching express she rushes out to the platform (shown in two shots, with the same tilt). Then as we see her face in close-up, the lights from the train rushing across her face and her hair streaming in the wind, the image slowly returns to the horizontal. The crisis, the impulse to throw herself beneath the train, has passed. Again, in showing the feverish preparations for the defense of Petrograd in *October*, Eisenstein obtained a strikingly dynamic composition by shooting workers marching up a ramp with the camera tilted at the same incline as the ramp; with the frame restored to the horizontal in projection, the workers appeared to lean forward at an unnatural angle.

This lateral tilting of the camera, however, is not a device capable of wide application. For the most part the director must accept the fact that he looks on life always, as it were, through the same window. It is a window that has the greatest freedom of movement: it can stand nearer to a scene or farther away, it can be placed at an angle, and with each change of position the content and the pattern of the picture isolated within its margins will be different, but the rectangle itself remains unchangeable.

There are numerous factors that govern the composition of a shot, but they can be grouped under three main heads: first, the form or movement of the subject itself; secondly, the position or movement of the camera in relation to the subject; and thirdly, the way in which the subject is lit.

In the earliest films it was the first of these, of course, that was all-important. The story was told entirely by the settings and the action, the camera remaining stationary throughout the whole of a scene and simply recording what took place in front of it. The set was lit by ordinary sunlight, either in the open air or beneath the glass roof of a studio. The development of film technique brought a much greater flexibility in both camera viewpoint and lighting. The first was associated with the development of editing, which brought the camera, as it were, into the midst of the action, and caused it to look now at this detail, now at that, now in one direction, now in another; the second was associated with progress in studio lighting and in the sensitivity of photographic emulsions.

First among the factors that determine the character of the picture in the frames is the distance between the camera and the subject. If the distance is very great, the result will be an extreme long shot, or distance shot. If it is very short, the result is a big close-up. Somewhere in between lie the long shot, the medium long shot, the medium shot, the medium close shot and the close-up. These distinctions are necessarily relative and it is impossible to fix precisely the dividing lines between them. The normal standard of measurement is the human figure. A shot taken at such a distance from a man as to make him appear quite small in the rectangle is a long shot. If the camera is brought nearer, until the figure of the man, standing upright, is just within the rectangle, we begin to enter the region of the medium shot; a position nearer still gives a medium close shot, with the man shown from the waist up. A close-up is a shot taken from such a distance that in relation to the human figure, only the face would be shown; and a big close-up would show no more than a portion of the face.

The general character of the shot having been fixed in terms of distance from camera to subject, the next thing to consider is the viewpoint. Should the shot be taken at normal eye level, or above it, or below it? Should the subject be shot from the front or the back or one side? It is clear that the shorter the distance between camera and subject, the more marked is the change that can be produced by a given change of viewpoint; to put it in another way, the close shot, for the purposes of composition, is much more under the cameraman's control, more plastic, than the long shot. In the case of a near subject, there are dozens of different viewpoints from which the shot may be taken; the director's task is to choose precisely the one that will be most effective for his purpose.

One or two examples will give some indication of the

possibilities involved. If the camera is raised above eye level so that it looks down on the subject it will produce a picture in which the subject appears dwarfed and of diminished importance; contrariwise, if placed below eye level and directed upward, the size and importance of the subject will appear exaggerated. The German film of 1925, *The Last Laugh*, directed by F. W. Murnau, depicts the bitter humiliation of the doorman of a large hotel who has become too old for his job and is made the lavatory attendant. All the shots of the doorman as he struts about in his magnificent gold-braided uniform in the early part of the film are taken from a point a little below eye level to enhance his grandeur; after he has had his uniform stripped from him all shots in which he appears are taken from a point a little above eye level, looking down on him to emphasize his dejection. The difference between the two points of view is very slight, but it is, nevertheless, deliberate and effective.

One finds much more exaggerated effects of a similar kind in the Soviet silent films. In *The End of St. Petersburg* the capitalist, Lebedev, sits at his desk brooding over the stock market prices. He decides that the time has come to act. Rapping out the order, "Buy everything!" he suddenly rises from his chair and towers upward above the camera. His movement has knocked over the table and its contents, and his clerk drops to his knees with servile haste to recover them; he looks up at his employer, and there follows another shot, likewise taken from a low angle, of Lebedev towering imperiously, and suddenly this cuts to a simple shot of a statue of Peter the Great viewed from a similar angle.

Sometimes a shot is taken from a particular viewpoint to create a suggestive relationship between separate figures or objects in the shot. A classic example is to be found in that scene in Eisenstein's film *The General Line*, where the peasant Martha Lapkina comes to beg the loan of a horse from a wealthy kulak sunning himself on his raised veranda. A shot taken from a point immediately behind him and looking downward puts the huge bulk of his barrel-like back and fat creased neck in the foreground, while away below in the background stands the pathetically minute and timid figure of Martha.

One could multiply such examples almost endlessly. In each shot in a well-made film in which the director has had the choice of several viewpoints, the one finally chosen, whether it appears quite ordinary or strikingly unusual, will have been chosen deliberately and for definite reasons; and once again, the overriding consideration must always be the part the shot is to play in relation to the other shots with which it is associated.

Most shots are taken from a single viewpoint with a stationary camera, but a director is not obliged so to limit himself; he can, if he wishes, take his shot with a moving camera. All kinds of movement are possible. A camera can be turned horizontally on its stand or tripod through a part or the whole of a complete circle of 360 degrees to produce what is known as a "pan." It can be tilted vertically up and down through an angle of 90 degrees. If it is placed on a vehicle known as a truck or dolly, it can be carried forwards or backwards or sideways to produce what is variously known as a tracking, trucking, dolly or perambulator shot. Camera and operators can also be placed on a crane that will swing them through the air. And finally, of course, the camera can be carried in a car or strapped to the front of a railway engine or taken up in an airplane. There is virtually no limit to the effects of camera movement that can be produced.

The possibilities of the moving camera appear at first glance to be considerable, and it is notorious that the novice in amateur cinematography can seldom resist the temptation to swing his camera about in every direction. The experienced film-maker, on the other hand, uses camera movement with great restraint. This restraint is imposed partly, it is true, by the fact that in professional film-making a moving-camera shot usually presents special problems of lighting, planning of the action and timing that all add to the cost and difficulty of shooting. Fundamentally, however, the case against an excessive use of camera movement lies in the fact that it represents a visual impression that we experience in real life only in special circumstances. If, while I am looking out of the window, the sound of a knock calls my attention to the door, I do not swing my eyes steadily and slowly round the walls of the room from the window to the door; my glance turns instantly from the one to the other. This abrupt change of glance is properly reproduced in the film by means of the cut, the instantaneous replacement of a shot by its successor; and since this is the normal method by which the mind turns from one point of visual attention to another when it is alert and not wandering aimlessly, the normal method of carrying forward the attention of the film spectator is by cutting from one shot to another.

Some directors have gone so far as to avoid camera movement almost entirely. There are very few moving-camera shots to be found in the silent films of Eisenstein and Pudovkin, for example: "Tracking (and panning)," wrote Ivor Montagu in 1928, "are in disfavour with the left-wing Russian school, for, naturalists, they hold such methods easily tend to remind the spectator of the presence of the camera." [2] Others also condemned camera movement on the ground that it made it impossible to reduce the length of a shot, since one could not cut into the middle of the movement and the possibility of quick cutting was therefore lost. Whatever force this argument may have in the case of the actuality film, where the circumstances of shooting are sometimes difficult to foresee and where the material is not fully under the director's control, it has no force in any other kind of film; the length of the shot should already have been determined, at least approximately, in the script.

While our gaze, as we have already observed, normally turns from one point of attention to another instantaneously, there are occasions when it moves more slowly and

2 *Film Technique*, p. 186.

21. (Above): *In Julien Duvivier's* CARNET DE BAL *(France, 1937) the tilted camera is used to convey nervous tension.* (Below): *In Eisenstein's* OCTOBER *(USSR, 1929) it expresses the tension of physical effort (see p. 154).*

22. Camera angle, lighting and setting combine to accentuate the peril of a man about to fall to his death to escape his Nazi pursuers. Tadeusz Janczar in a shot from A GENERATION (Poland, 1954) directed by Andrzej Wajda.

23. *Masterly landscape photography, including strongly filtered cloud effects, were a feature of the superb hunting scenes in* Jean Renoir's LA RÈGLE DU JEU *(France, 1939).*

24. *Montgomery Clift and Susan Kohner in John Huston's* FREUD *(USA, 1962). Although in an exterior shot, the figures are molded by supplementary lighting.*

deliberately. When we are searching for something, whether it is a book on a bookshelf, a concealed door in a wall, a figure in a landscape, or a ship at sea, we carefully scan the given area with our eyes. If we are confronted with an expanse we cannot take in at a single glance and we wish to study the interrelationship of its various parts, or if we wish to appraise the mutual relationship of several objects within our field of view, we instinctively look back and forth from one part to another or from one object to another in order to observe how they are placed with respect to each other. If we wish to take in the contents of a room or study the members of an audience, we view them in turn carefully and systematically. And when, of course, we are ourselves moving, in car or train, the moving view is inescapable. To attempt to deny the film the use of the visual impression one gets in such circumstances as these would be ridiculous. Movement of the camera for its own sake is obviously to be avoided, but there may be numerous occasions when a director feels that the role he wishes a shot to play, psychologically, dramatically and visually, in the flow of images of which it is a part, demands a certain movement of the camera, and in such a case he will be justified in using it.

Camera movement is often used to emphasize the spatial relationship between objects. For example, in *Gold Is Where You Find It* (not a film of especial distinction) there is a lavish banquet scene in which the camera tracks slowly forward from one end of a long table to the other, looking down on the colorful and appetizing array of foods and drinks and plate with which it is laden. If the director had tried to convey the same idea in a series of static close shots or a single static long shot, he would have produced a different and less successful impression. There is a scene in Carol Reed's *Bank Holiday* in which a girl (played by Margaret Lockwood), spending the night with her boy friend on the crowded beach at Brighton, finds herself unable to sleep; she is a hospital nurse and she cannot forget the tragic figure of the bereaved man (played by John

Loder) whom she has left earlier in the day just after the death of his wife. Quietly she gets up and goes down to the water's edge. As she stands there staring into space, the camera tilts slowly down to the sea washing the pebbles at her feet, the shot mixes through to another shot of water of a different kind, and the camera tilts up again, this time to reveal the figure of John Loder leaning over the Thames Embankment. The tilting shots establish clearly the spatial relationship between the girl and the sea, the man and the river; but the dissolve from sea to river establishes a relationship of another kind altogether, a smiliarity of idea, by which our thoughts are easily and unambiguously turned from Brighton to London.

Where camera movement is not used simply to emphasize relationships in space, it very often carries with it a certain subjective impression. The movement of the camera draws attention to the imaginary observer whose movement it reproduces. The content of the shot is seen, not directly, but through the eyes, as it were, of someone who is reacting to that content in a certain way. Sometimes this effect is used very obviously. Giddiness, intoxication, the action of falling, may be indicated by shots showing the scenery moving round (shot with a camera turned rapidly on its vertical axis) or swaying uncertainly (shot with a rocking camera) or showing the floor suddenly coming up toward the spectator. In his film *Metropolis* Fritz Lang wanted to convey the wild fear of hundreds of children struggling through rising floods in their underground city toward a small iron door that is their only means of escape. In order to take certain shots for this scene, he had the camera mounted on a swing so that it could be swayed backward and forward in the direction of the iron door. A publicity brochure issued by the original distributors of the film makes its purpose clear: "The distorted lights of the swaying surroundings create in the mind of the spectator the feeling of fear. It conveys to one the impression that the world will collapse in the next instant. . . . The spectator feels that he is actually there, and is taking part in the scene. He is moving about amongst the others, and at the same time his eyes are travelling from one part to another, and not merely standing by, looking on as a spectator would. If the camera were placed on his head, so that it moved from place to place with him, turned when he turned his head, and altered its focus as that of the eyes altered, then such an effect might be obtained, but to carry the camera in such a manner was out of the question. So the impression was gained by the swings and turns of the 'flying camera.' "

On other occasions the subjective impression conveyed by camera movement is much more subtle, sometimes to such a degree as to make it difficult to analyze precisely its quality. In Thorold Dickinson's *Next of Kin* a young soldier and his girl, who have met to spend the afternoon together, are shown sitting on a lonely part of a clifftop by the sea. As they talk their minds are not entirely at ease. The soldier has acted and spoken in a way he knows in his heart to be contrary to security orders; the girl cannot forget the black-mailing threats of her employer, who is a German spy. But suddenly their love for each other wells up and obliterates their cares and they turn to embrace each other; at that moment the camera turns slowly away to the white clouds and the blue sky. One is conscious of the ideal observer, through whose eyes we watch, deliberately averting his gaze from intimacies into which it is not his business to pry.

Again, in the film *They Knew What They Wanted,* Charles Laughton played the part of a well-to-do farmer who marries a young waitress from a café in the city. At the wedding feast he drinks more than is good for him, and to display what youth and strength are still left in him, he insists on climbing onto the roof of his house. While he is balancing his way along the ridge, he slips and falls to the ground. He is so seriously injured that he has to be carried into the house, and the wedding guests crowd around door and windows trying to peer into the room. At this point the camera circles round the house at the back of the crowd, moving up to a gap here or a space there, precisely in the manner of a spectator hovering on the fringe of the crowd and trying vainly to find an opening where he can see what is going on. The figure of the injured man is not shown; everything is suggested by implication in that unsuccessfully inquisitive movement of the camera.

It should be added that pictorially the movement of the camera in a tracking shot can increase the illusion of depth; objects in different planes will appear to move at different speeds according to their distance from the camera lens (just as near objects seen from a moving train appear to travel past the window at a greater speed than more distant objects) and the relationship between these various movements can, on occasion, suggest almost a three-dimensional effect; this is the principle behind the multiplane technique employed in the making of cartoon films. Movement of the camera may also compensate to some slight extent for the limitations imposed by the fixed proportions of the frame: for an extended horizontal subject it can pan or track, for a tall, narrow subject it can tilt up and down—movement of the camera in both cases replacing the movement that the eye would make in following the composition of a static picture. Finally, camera movement may also serve, on occasion, to give a certain sense of movement to a static subject. In *Acciaio*, for example, Walter Ruttmann's documentary film of a steel works, one scene showed sheets of molten steel being passed to and fro between a series of rollers. At one point a shot of stationary finished steel sheet was introduced, with the forms of the workers reflected in its polished surface; because the shot was taken with a moving camera it dovetailed smoothly with the movement of the other shots and caused no interruption in the tempo of the scene. There is no justification, however, for attempting to realize any of these pictorial effects purely for their own sake; let it be said once again that camera movement, as any other photographic effect, is permissible only where it can be justified psychologically and dramatically, as well as pictorially.

Camera movement can also be used to follow a moving subject, as in Basil Wright's *Song of Ceylon*, where in a series of panning shots the camera follows the flight of a bird; or in the Swedish film *En Natt*, where the camera faces the head of a column of marching soldiers from a low angle, and moves backward in time with their advance; or in Pabst's *Westfront 1918*, where the camera follows a line of men from behind as they march toward the front-line trenches; or in the opening of *The Thin Man*, where the camera tracks from right to left to keep William Powell in view as he walks along pursued by a horde of importunate press reporters, and stops at regular intervals as he is jerked to a standstill together with the reporters, the cause of each stop (as we discover when the view opens out to a medium shot) being the fact that the dog Asta, whom he has on a lead, has come to another tree. Of this use of camera movement little need be said, except to observe that where a camera moves in order to keep a moving subject continually in view, as, for example, where two characters are walking along a street talking and the camera recedes before them to keep them continually in a close shot, its movement is designed to preserve a static relationship to the moving subject.

When the camera setup has been decided, the lighting of the subject can be arranged. It is here that the camerman comes preeminently into his own. Whether the shot is to be a medium shot or a close-up, whether it is to be taken from this viewpoint or that, whether the camera is to be static or moving, all these things will have been decided by the director and may be set down, more or less explicitly, in the script; but when it comes to lighting, it is upon the cameraman that the detailed work must fall. Nowadays the first cameraman in a production unit has comparatively little to do with the camera itself; he leaves its manipulation to his assistants and concentrates on the supervision of the lengthy, difficult and important business of arranging the lighting. The function of the lighting, at its lowest level, is, of course, to illuminate the subject, but the degree of control that the cameraman now exercises over his lighting effects enables him to do a great deal more than this. Pouring in light first from one side, and then from another, throwing a shadow here, picking out a point of brilliance there, he gradually builds up his picture, as it were, out of the darkness, using his lights to delineate and mold the contours and planes of his subject, to create the impression of spatial depth, to convey emotional mood and atmosphere, and even upon occasion to reproduce certain dramatic effects.

Inside the studio, where he relies entirely on artificial illumination, the cameraman's control of his lighting effects is complete. The two principal types of light he uses are, first, the "broad," a floodlight with a spread of some 60 degrees, which will illuminate a large area; and secondly, the spotlight, with a beam spread that can be varied from approximately 8 to 45 degrees, and which is used for concentrating light upon a limited area or spot. In addition to these, there are various kinds of special lamps in use. To shield light from the camera or from some part of the subject, the cameraman has at his disposal screens of various shapes and sizes (*nigger* and *gobo* being studio slang terms for two popular types of screen). The quality of the light can also be controlled by the use of diffusing screens. These are of two principal kinds. The first, which are made of some such substance as gelatine, frosted glass or silk, are placed over the lamps, either to modify their hard direct light into a softer, more diffused illumination or to alter the color of the light for certain effects (as when an actress with light-blue eyes which, owing to their high actinic value, would appear in a photograph abnormally "washed-out" and expressionless, is lit with a magenta-colored spotlight to give them depth and sparkle). The second class of diffusing screens are those placed directly over the camera lens to soften the definition of the picture; they are usually made of fine gauze, finely frosted gelatine or glass covered with a network of fine lines, and they can produce effects varying from a barely perceptible softening of the picture to a strong haze.

In outdoor work the cameraman naturally has less control over his lighting, but it is nonetheless more considerable than one might suppose. From quite an early period in film history, reflectors have been used to illuminate the shaded parts of a subject; these are either of polished metal, which give a hard, direct reflection, or of white-painted board, which give a softer, more diffused reflection. Artificial lights are often used as a substitute for such reflectors. Canopies of muslin or similar material known as "scrims" are sometimes erected over the players to soften the natural light of the sun. Another device that has been in use for many years now is the filter, a piece of colored glass that is placed in front of the lens to alter the tone relationships of the picture. If the cameraman wishes to lighten the tone of a color, he uses a filter of the same color; if he wishes to darken it, he uses a filter of a complementary color. Sensitive though modern super-panchromatic film is, it does not give an entirely true reproduction of the relative tone values of a scene; by using the right filter, the cameraman can correct for this deficiency. By the same token, he can "overcorrect," that is to say, make a color much darker or lighter than it appears in real life. If he wishes to darken the blue of a sky, for example, in order to emphasize by contrast the whiteness of the clouds, he will use a filter of a color complementary to blue, the particular filter selected depending on the degree of darkness he wishes to obtain; he can make his sky as black as ink if he desires. Tisse, in shooting for Eisenstein the material for his never-completed film of Mexico, *Que Viva Mexico*, photographed the skies in certain of his shots in a very heavy tone, which produced not only strong contrasts, but the sense of a most oppressive atmosphere.

There are three principal ways in which the cameraman can control his lighting: in direction, in intensity and in degree of diffusion.

The main source of illumination in a picture is known as the key light, and the first problem is to decide the direction from which the key light should fall. In outdoor work the key light will naturally be the light of the sun, coming from high overhead at midday and falling more obliquely in the early morning and late afternoon. In exterior sets construted in the studio, the key lighting will be designed correspondingly to simulate the sun. In interiors also, where no special effects are required, the key lighting will come from above. There will be many occasions, however, when the key lighting must fall on the subject from some other direction; as, for example, when we are to suppose the main light in the scene to come through a single window, or from a table lamp or the glow of a fire. The direction of the main light source can sometimes affect considerably the impression a picture makes on us; it is common knowledge that a face, when lit predominantly from below, can be made to appear more sinister than when it is lit in the normal way. It is also possible, by placing the main light source in a certain position, to obtain shadows that may be dramatically effective. In Clarence Brown's *Marie Walewska* Marie (played by Greta Garbo) comes to Napoleon (Charles Boyer) at nighttime and is conducted to a room where he is engaged in issuing instructions to his staff officers. The room is lit by many candles standing in low candelabra that half light the faces of the occupants and cast shadows of their figures onto the surrounding walls. On one wall hangs a large map of Europe. Napoleon, completely absorbed in his military affairs, fails to notice Marie Walewska. Striding up and down the room amid his officers, talking, gesticulating, ordering, he presents a personification of restless, purposeful energy. At one point he stands still and throws up his hand to emphasize his words. At that instant we are given a shot of the huge map of Europe and, stretching right across it, the sinister symbol of his grasping shadow.

When the direction of the key lighting has been settled, consideration must be given to its intensity, for upon this will depend the lighting tone of the picture as a whole. The importance of the general tone has been well indicated by the American cameraman, Mr. John Arnold, in the following paragraph:

Consider a very simple scene; a bedroom in which a sick child lies while its mother keeps constant vigil. If this scene be presented in sombre tones with long menacing shadows on the screen, you feel at once that the child is gavely ill and may never recover. If, on the other hand, the room is in lighter tones, with the sunlight streaming through the windows and a cheerful sparkle evident everywhere, instinct tells you the crisis has passed, and that the child is on the road to recovery.[3]

Dark tones, in short, tend to depress our spirits and a great abundance of light helps to raise them; but, of course, while it lies with the cameraman to decide what power of lighting to use and how the film should be exposed and processed to obtain a given effect, he cannot depart from the script. If the script and the director insist that the saddest scene in the film is to take place in a brilliantly lit ballroom and the happiest one in a cellar lit by one candle, there is little the cameraman can do about it in terms of lighting tone; he can only protest that in his view the script should have been written differently.

Finally, the cameraman must decide the degree of diffusion he should introduce into his lighting. Where the subject is illuminated by a single light source of great intensity, the lighting is described as direct or "hard"; the areas of light and shade are sharply defined and harshly contrasted, and there are very few intermediate tones between the two extremes of light and dark; the picture is said to have a narrow tonal scale. Direct, harsh light of this kind reveals sharply the main contours of a subject and emphasizes linear perspective; on the other hand, it gives a picture that is simple and flat and tending to monotony. If one imagines a stylization of the subject in areas blocked in with ivory black and chinese white, one gains an idea, somewhat exaggerated, of its defects. Normally, therefore, a cameraman will seek to give warmth and interest to his picture by bringing in other subsidiary lights. In lighting a

3 *We Make the Movies*, p. 145.

human figure, for example, if the key light is falling on the figure from above and in front, he may introduce a back light of lower intensity to throw the figure into relief by outlining its shape and bringing it forward, as it were, from the background. He may also throw a subsidiary front light onto the side of the figure that the key light leaves in shadow. He may direct a bright spotlight onto one or both sides of the figure to heighten the effect of the backlight, or on a portion of the figure to heighten some particular feature (the tonal spot or light accent). In this way, by securing the registration of a different intensity of light from as many planes of the subject as possible, the cameraman adds to his picture liveliness, interest and depth. The more subsidiary lights he adds to his single-direction key lighting, however, the more soft and diffused will his whole lighting become; for diffused lighting is the effect obtained when the subject is illuminated from many sources, each source having a relatively low intensity. It is as though the key lighting, instead of being closely concentrated at one point, were spread in dilution all around the subject; the contrast is reduced, deep, black shadows and bright, clear highlights are almost completely eliminated and the tonal scale is broadened with a multiplicity of halftones. The purpose of diffusing screens and soft reflectors is likewise to spread light so that it falls on the subject from a large number of points of relatively low intensity instead of in a concentrated glare.

It is obviously impossible to establish any principles for the use of given lighting effects. Each scene and each shot in a film has its own characteristics and its own problems, the solution of which calls for the widest skill and experience. Even the texture of materials may have to be taken into account: a rough surface, for example, reveals its texture best under a direct, intense light, while a polished metal surface shows best in a soft diffused radiance. The most that can be said here is that in view of the close association between lighting and mood, we may expect the

25. Low-key lighting in a scene from George Cukor's A STAR IS BORN (USA, 1954), with Judy Garland.

lighting of a film to correspond in its general character with
the mood or key in which the film as a whole is conceived,
and in its variations with the changes of mood that are
bound up with the film's rhythmic structure. Tragic films
are frequently lit in a predominantly low key with soft
contrasts: D. W. Griffith's *Broken Blossoms,* John Ford's
The Informer and Marcel Carné's *Quai des Brumes* are
cases in point. For melodrama likewise, low key lighting is
commonly used, but with sharp contrast. Romances one may
expect to find in a brighter tone with soft contrast, and
comedies in a much lighter tone still. These are merely indications of general tendencies, however, and must not be
taken as hard and fast rules. Although *Quai des Brumes*
opens in a dense fog on the Havre road at night and closes
with a stray dog being swallowed up again in the fog and
darkness, there are scenes in the middle of the film, showing
the hero and heroine at the peak of their brief happiness,
that are bathed in radiance. It should perhaps be added that
a still cannot be accepted as an infallible guide to the lighting of a scene, since the tone and contrast of the still can
be altered appreciably by exposure and development in the
course of printing.

The lens of the camera, through which all the light from
the subject has to pass in order to register on the sensitive
negative film, is another most important means of modify-
ing the photographic image. It was implied earlier in this
chapter that in order to make the change from a medium
shot to a close shot, or from a medium shot to a long shot,
it was necessary to alter the distance between the camera
and the subject. In fact, however, a similar result can be
obtained merely by changing the lens in the camera. By replacing his lens with one of shorter focal length, the cameraman can obtain the equivalent of a more distant view; by
replacing it with one of greater focal length he can obtain
the equivalent of a nearer view. With a telephoto lens it is
possible to obtain a close-up of some detail of a subject that
is at a considerable distance from the camera. Lenses of

variable focal length have now been devised that make even the replacement of one lens by another unnecessary; as the focal length is increased or decreased, so the camera appears to swoop toward or away from the subject.

This interchanging of lenses is a great convenience in actuality work of all kinds—to the newsreel cameraman, for example, who from his site in the grandstand at a cricket match wants to take a close shot of the batsman; to the naturalist who wants to record close-ups of a shy bird or animal; or to the documentary film-maker who wants to shoot a close-up of a factory worker without bringing the camera so near as to make him self-conscious and nervous. Nevertheless, there is only one type of lens that at any given camera distance will produce an accurate picture, and lenses of longer or shorter focal length cannot be used at that distance without producing some distortion of the image. No one who has seen a close shot of a cricket pitch taken with a telephoto lens will forget the curiously vehement and ineffective up-and-down movements of the batsmen taking what seems to be an age to cover the distance between two wickets apparently standing almost on top of each other. A long-focus lens produces an effect of flattened perspective; a short-focus lens deepens the perspective and exaggerates the size of foreground objects.

In studio work, therefore, a lens of abnormally small or great focal length will be used not simply as a matter of convenience, but in order to obtain certain optical effects. Where the cameraman, for example, wishes to enlarge the relative size of objects in the foreground, or to exaggerate foreshortening or to give emphasis and impetus to movements to and from the camera, he will use a short-focus lens. Again, the greater the focal length of a lens, the less depth of focus does it possess, so that if in a close-up taken with a given lens the background can be dimly discerned, the cameraman can either take his close-up with a lens of greater focal length, from a greater distance, and reduce the background to a hazy flatness by putting it out of focus;

26. Peter Ustinov and Martine Carole in a scene making effective use of mirror reflections, from Max Ophüls' LOLA MONTES (France, 1955).

or he can use a lens of shorter focal length, and bring the background into sharper focus so that it plays a more important part in the shot.

There have been numerous occasions on which directors have sought to obtain certain subjective effects by putting the whole of the image slightly out of focus or by altering the focus during shooting. A mother, for example, looks up from her sewing to see her long-absent sailor son standing unexpectedly in the doorway; the shot of the son quickly grows hazy and confused, and when we see the mother again her eyes are filled with tears. In the cream-separator sequence of *The General Line,* Eisenstein reverses the device. Peasants are being introduced to the first cream separator they have ever seen; when the dustcover is snatched from it, the separator is shown out of focus; gradually it comes into focus until it stands with its polished metal parts sharply defined and brightly gleaming; the peasants gasp with amazement. Here the purpose was presumably to suggest that perceptible interval during which the peasants gradually took in the unaccustomed object. In the film *Der Träumende Mund,* there is a scene in which Elisabeth Bergner sits in a concert hall listening to a violinist; one shot is taken from a point immediately behind the violinist and looking down over his shoulder toward the audience. At first, the violinist in the foreground is sharply defined and the audience beyond is indistinguishable; then the violinist goes out of focus and the face of Elisabeth Bergner looking up among the audience is brought sharply into focus. The purpose was clearly to shift the attention of the spectator from foreground to background and back again without any change of camera setup, although why it should have been preferred to a simple cut is a little difficult to understand.

By the use of special lenses and mirrors the cameraman can obtain optical distortions of every conceivable kind. There are multiplying lenses that produce a number of images of the same object side by side; there are lenses that give a thin elongated image or a fat distended image. There have even been occasions when the cameraman has obtained a desired effect by smearing his lens with Vaseline. By multiple exposure, either in the camera or in the course of printing, it is possible to obtain a superimposition of several images on one length of film. The bewildering effect of street traffic in a large city, for example, may be represented by taking a shot of one stream of traffic approaching the camera, a second shot of another stream moving obliquely from right to left, and a third of another moving obliquely from left to right, and then superimposing the three so that on the screen vehicles appear to be crossing and cross-crossing confusedly in all directions at once. All these optical distortions were used frequently in silent films to convey states of mind, such as intoxication, bewilderment, dizziness and the like. They have been used less frequently in sound films, partly perhaps because sound has imposed a greater naturalism, and partly because sound itself can be used for expressing ideas that before could only be expressed visually.

There are various kinds of optical trick work, such as back projection, the Dunning process, the Schufftan process, the model shot, the glass shot and the traveling matt, by means of which the cameraman can combine either action and backgrounds shot in two different places, or miniature models and full-size sets, or two different roles played by the same actor so successfully as to be entirely deceptive. While these are of great technical interest they need not detain us here, since they perform no expressive function and therefore have no critical importance, unless indeed when they are so badly and obviously done as to destroy the spectator's credibility. By this I mean that it does not matter whether an express train shown tearing through the countryside is a real train or a model, so long as we accept it as real; nor does it matter when an actor plays a dual role, as Robert Donat does in *The Ghost Goes West,* whether we know how the obvious trick is done. What is important is whether the train is shot from effective viewpoints that are combined to make an exciting editing construction, or whether the characterization of the two roles is convincingly portrayed; for the rest there is even, perhaps, something to be said for the view widely held in the film industry that the less the public knows of these technical tricks the better.

There remains one resource of the camera, commonly regarded as a trick and often used as such, that may, nevertheless, play an important part in expressive representation, namely, the variation of camera speed that produces the effects of slow motion and accelerated motion. If the camera is run at double the normal speed, forty-eight frames will be exposed in a second, and when these are subsequently shown at the normal projection speed of twenty-four a second, the action of the shot will appear in slow motion; conversely, if action is shot with a camera running at half speed, the result on the screen will be an accelerated movement. Accelerated motion is frequently used in comedy scenes, as, for example, where the hero is driving at breakneck speed along a busy street and veers and turns recklessly between cars and buses that dart crazily about in every direction. Slow motion was used effectively in two British documentary films: one was Evelyn Spice's *Spring on the Farm,* in which a young boy was shown in slow motion riding a horse bareback through a field of waist-high billowy grass; the second was Marion Grierson's *Beside the Seaside,* in which holidaymakers, dancing to the seaside band on a sultry afternoon after lunch, move in a slow, dreamlike rhythm. When the heroine of *The Seventh Veil* attempts to commit suicide by throwing herself from a bridge into the river below, her fall is shown in slow motion.

It was the Soviet directors, however, who made the most effective use of slow and accelerated motion as elements in the tempo of their editing constructions. Pudovkin describes [4] how on one occasion he watched a man scything grass just after a heavy summer rain-shower:

4 *Film Technique,* pp. 145 *et seq.*

He was bared to the waist. The muscles of his back contracted and expanded with the even sweep of the scythe. Its damp blade, flying upwards, caught the sunlight and burst for a moment into a sharp blinding flame. I stepped near. The scythe buried itself in the wet, rank grass, which, as it was cut away beneath, slowly gave down on to the ground in a supple movement impossible to describe. Gleaming in the slanting sunrays, the raindrops trembled on the tips of the pointed drooping grass-blades, trembled, and fell. . . . And once more I found myself gripped by an unaccustomed feeling of excitement at the grandeur of the spectacle. Never had I seen wet grass like this. . . . The question was how to capture, how to reproduce to others this full and profound sensation. . . .

He then describes how he arrived at a solution. When a director wishes to show some detail of an action he moves the camera nearer to take a close-up; then why not, argued Pudovkin, momentarily slow down the speed of a movement to show some detail that could not be seen at normal speed, and thus secure, as he describes it, a "close-up in time"? In his own words:

Why should not a given detail be momentarily emphasized by retarding it on the screen, and rendering it by this means particularly outstanding and unprecedentedly clear? Was not . . . the grass falling to the ground retarded, in relation to me, by my sharpened attention? Was it not thanks to this sharpened attention that I perceived ever so much more than I had ever seen before?

He continues:

I tried in my mind's eye to shoot and construct the mowing of the grass approximately as follows:
1. A man stands bared to the waist. In his hands is a scythe. Pause. He swings the scythe. (The whole movement goes in normal speed. . . .)
2. The sweep of the scythe continues. The man's back and

shoulders. Slowly the muscles play and grow tense. (Recorded very fast with a "slow-motion" apparatus, so that the movement on the screen comes out unusually slow.)

3. The blade of the scythe slowly turning at the culmination of its sweep. A gleam of the sun flares up and dies out. (Shot in "slow motion.")
4. The blade flies downward. (Normal speed.)
5. The whole figure of the man brings back the scythe over the grass at normal speed. A sweep-back, A sweep-back. A sweep . . . And at the moment when the blade of the scythe touches the grass—
6. —slowly (in "slow motion") the cut grass sways, topples, bending and scattering glittering drops.

Pudovkin explains that this is a very approximate sketch and that after the actual shooting he edited it differently— "more complexly, using shots taken at very various speeds." When he saw the result on the screen he realized that the idea was sound: "chance spectators, who were ignorant of the nature of the method employed, confessed to having experienced an almost physical sense of moisture, weight and force." He is careful to make clear that he is not concerned here with the single slow-motion shot standing in isolation. He alludes to previous directors who have made use of slow motion:

Suppose they have been using "slow motion" to shoot a horse jumping, then they have shot it as a whole, and as a whole inserted it in the picture, almost as a separate "dragged-in" sequence. I have heard that Jean Epstein shot a whole film in "slow motion" (I think it was *The Fall of the House of Usher,* from E. A. Poe's story), using the effect of retarded motion to give a mystical tinge to every scene.

That is not at all what I mean. I refer to the incorporation of various degrees of retarded speed of movement

integrally in the construction of a given editing phrase.
. . . The full processes shown upon the screen by the
editing together of shots recorded at various speeds seem
endowed with a rhythm peculiar to themselves, a sort of
breath of life of their own. They are alive, for they have
received the vital spark of an appraising, selecting, an
all comprehending concept. They do not slip like landscape past the window of a railway carriage beneath the
indifferent glance of a passenger familiar with the route.
They unfold and grow, like the narrative of a gifted observer, who has perceived the thing or process more
clearly than anyone else has ever done before.

8 · Film Music

*Taking place in the open air, on the sunny slope of a hill,
. . . the moving pageant, thus from the first set in tune
with nature, brought to a focus of splendour the rays of
every separate art. More akin to an opera than to a play,
it had, as its basis, music. For the drama had developed
out of the lyric ode, and retained throughout what was at
first its only element, the dance and song of a mimetic
chorus. By this centre of rhythmic motion and pregnant
melody the burden of the tale was caught up and echoed
and echoed again, as the living globe divided into spheres
of answering song, the clear and precise significance of the
play, never obscure to the head, being thus brought home
in music to the passion of the heart, the idea embodied in
lyric verse, the verse transfigured by song, and song and
verse reflected as in a mirror to the eye by the swing and
beat of the limbs they stirred to consonance of motion.*
LOWES DICKINSON, describing the Greek drama in
The Greek View of Life

Accustomed though we are to speak of the films made before
1927 as "silent," the film has never been, in the full sense
of the word, silent. From the very beginning, music was
regarded as an indispensable accompaniment; it is recorded
that when the Lumière films were shown at the first public
film exhibition in this country in February 1896, they were
accompanied by piano improvisations on popular tunes. At
first, the music played bore no special relationship to the
films; an accompaniment of any kind was sufficient. Within
a very short time, however, the incongruity of playing lively
music to a solemn film became apparent, and film pianists
began to take some care in matching their pieces to the
mood of the film.

As cinemas grew in number and importance, a violinist,
and perhaps a cellist, would be added to the pianist in certain cases, and in the larger cinemas small orchestras were

formed. For a number of years the selection of music for each film program rested entirely in the hands of the conductor or leader of the orchestra, and very often the principal qualification for holding such a position was not skill or taste so much as the ownership of a large personal library of musical pieces. Since the conductor seldom saw the films until the night before they were to be shown (if, indeed, he was lucky enough to see them then), the musical arrangement was normally improvised in the greatest hurry.

It was to help to meet this difficulty that film distributing companies started the practice of publishing suggestions for musical accompaniments. In 1909, for example, the Edison Company began issuing with their films such indications of mood as "pleasant," "sad," "lively." The example was followed by others, the suggestions became more explicit, and so emerged the musical cue sheet, containing indications of mood, the titles of suitable pieces of music and precise directions to show where one piece led into the next.

Certain films, some of them outstanding, some merely pretentious, had music especially composed for them. In 1908 Saint-Saëns wrote music for the Paris performance of the first *film d'art, The Assassination of the Duke of Guise*; this was his Opus 128, for strings, piano and harmonium, consisting of an introduction and five tableaux, with each part carefully cued to the film. In 1911 in America Walter Cleveland Simon composed an original score for *Arrah-Na-Pough,* and in Germany in 1913 Guiseppe Becce composed the music for a film called *Richard Wagner.* The most famous of these early special scores, however, was that composed and arranged by Joseph Carl Breil for D. W. Griffith's film *The Birth of a Nation,* which Seymour Stern describes as follows:

> The orchestral score as a whole was not original, consisting as it did of folk-tunes and symphonic selections. Some notable examples of the latter were *In the Hall of the Mountain King,* from the *Peer Gynt Suite* (played

during the evacuation of Atlanta scenes) ; strains from the *Ride of the Valkyries,* mingled with *Dixie* and also with other Wagnerian and other dramatic music (for the ride of the Clansmen) ; and innumerable fragments or mixed strains from Beethoven, Lizst, Rossini, Verdi, Tschaikovsky and other composers. However, the score did contain a number of original themes and tunes, specially composed by Griffith and Breil for the film, and of these, several have long since become famous: namely, a theme expressing barbarism, insolence and menace, played during the film-prologue, in the scenes depicting the introduction of Negro slavery into colonial America, and more especially, during Part II, in virtually all scenes depicting the rise to power of the Negroes after the Civil War; a somewhat related theme, expressing insolence, sadism and villainy, played during the scenes featuring the Hon. Rustin Stoneman or his protégé, Silas Lynch; the love-theme music for the romantic "business" between the Little Colonel and Elsie Stoneman . . . ; and, most famous of all, that weird blend of reed-whistles and horn-blasts, the clan call, composed by Joseph Carl Breil, and played during the scenes showing the birth of the Ku Klux Klan, the summoning of the Clans and the ride of the Clansmen. However, regarding the last, the conviction persists in my mind that Breil may have based the Clan-call motif on a motif of two similar notes, which occur in the latter part of Dukas's *The Sorcerer's Apprentice.*[1]

Other notable original scores were Edmund Meisel's music for *Battleship Potemkin* (so effective that in some European countries the film itself was passed for exhibition, but the music banned)and for Ruttmann's *Berlin,* and Arthur Honegger's music for the Abel Gance films, *La Roue* and *Napoleon.* The number of films provided with original

1 *The Griffith Index: An Index to the Creative Work of David Wark Griffith;* Part II: *The Art Triumphant;* (a) Monograph on *The Birth of a Nation,* July 1945. Published by *Sight and Sound,* British Film Institute, London.

scores were, however, very few, for reasons Dr. Kurt London has summarized:

> The "general release" theatres did not possess completely equipped orchestras. It could not be expected of music publishers that they should print this kind of music, save for a few self-contained numbers which they brought out for concert and light entertainment purposes. It would have been much too costly and unprofitable to publish, as it would have involved the printing of several arrangements for different orchestral combinations. The film companies would not entertain the idea of taking shares in, or themselves taking charge of, the publishing; for them, original music was, if not a mere luxury, at best a good means of propaganda, intended to heighten the general impression among press and other interested parties at the first performance of the film. They did not think of the general public, which would see the same film with inadequate music and go away with an inadequate impression. This music, too, was often boycotted by ambitious conductors in the local houses, because they wished to compile their own, and because a quick and good rehearsal was for technical reasons impossible.[2]

For the most part, therefore, the arrangement of film music throughout the whole of the silent-film period remained in the hands of the pianist, leader or conductor attached to each cinema, making use of such resources as were available to him and of music with which he was already familiar. Inevitably, he came to look on his music entirely from a utilitarian point of view, regarding certain pieces as suitable for comedy scenes, others for romantic scenes, others for sad scenes and so on, and in course of time, composers and music publishers found it profitable to issue small fragments of original music under these labels. In this way there came into existence a large library of mood music consisting of many thousands of short pieces express-

[2] *Film Music* (Faber and Faber, London, 1936), p. 62.

ing every conceivable degree of mood, feeling and sound impression: *Galloping Horses, Pursuit, Despair, Impending Doom, Uncanny Agitato, Dramatic Agitato, Lament, Triumphal March, Tender Love*—these are only a few titles from a list that could be extended almost indefinitely.

Owing to the shortness of film scenes and the rapidity with which one scene might give way to another, there was no place in the silent film for any leisurely development of musical form. The pieces of mood music rarely lasted longer than two or three minutes, and their structure was of the very simplest kind, so that they could either be extended by repetition on the one hand, or condensed or suddenly interrupted on the other, without a noticeable jar or without loss of their original characteristics.

Obviously, as the titles of these fragments of mood music remind us, one of the chief functions of music in the silent film was to illustrate the narrative, to give musical expression to each mood of the action, and so intensify it by arousing through the ear the same feelings as were being stirred through the eye.

This function alone, however, is not sufficient to explain the clearly deep-seated and instinctive demand for music with the silent film that film audiences have always felt, or the curiously shadowy and flat effect of seeing a silent film without music—seeing it "in the cold," as it used to be called. This desire springs from the fact that the film is, above all, an art of movement. There has always been a close relationship between music and movement. Instinctively a child sways and dances to the rhythm of an orchestra, and an elderly gentleman sunning himself on a seaside promenade taps his foot or his hand to the strains of the military band; a musical accompaniment would add nothing to our enjoyment of a painting—would, in fact, be incongruous—but a dance without music is hardly conceivable.

Primarily, then, it is the actual physical movement one sees upon the screen that creates an instinctive need for the accompaniment of sound, a need met in the case of the silent film by music. Yet because the music, as we have seen, had to bear some relation in rhythm and mood to the visual scene it accompanied, it was able to perform a further ser-vice—to accentuate the rhythm of the film as a whole. That is to say, the narrative and dramatic structure, which was already implicit in the first treatment, and had been still further developed as the film passed through all the proc-esses of production, could be even more clearly articulated by a well-chosen musical accompaniment, which, reflecting and intensifying the mood of the film at each moment, be-came, in its changes of mood and tempo, a reflection of the shape of the film as a whole.

In the sound film music continues to be used, and here too the fundamental justification is the rhythm of the film as an art of movement; in all other respects, however, the role of music in the sound film is essentially different from that of music in the silent film.

To begin with, music is no longer the only form of sound possible. Human speech and every kind of audible sound and noise can be reproduced, and throughout considerable por-tions of a film these may predominate; in such places music will be both unnecessary and inappropriate. This means that music now requires to be used with far greater dis-crimination.

It should perhaps be said here that not all producers ex-ercise this discrimination. There are still far too many cases where music is used continuously, or almost continu-ously, throughout a film in the descriptive style of the silent-film accompaniment—as a background to dialogue and sound effects or to commentary. *Escape to Happiness,* in which Leslie Howard and Ingrid Bergman played the chief parts, is only one of many films that have been spoilt by an excess of sentimental music played as a background to much of the dialogue; and the short interest films in which com-mentator and music compete persistently for attention all the way through are a constant affliction for those of us who go to the cinema with any regularity. This use of background music cannot be too strongly condemned. It is a gross offense against reason and good taste and causes such widespread irritation, even among the least critical of filmgoers, that it is difficult to see why the habit continues.

Another respect in which music in the sound film differs from silent-film music is that with perfect and automatic synchronization a much more exact relationship between music and picture is possible. Instead of being something apart from the film, superadded during the whole of its length, it now appears, it is true, only occasionally (at least in the naturalistic narrative film), but is a carefully calculated element *within* the film, forming an integral part of its structure.

In the sound film there is no longer any need for mere descriptive illustration. Instead the music, where it is used, has to advance the action, to link one dialogue section to another, to establish associations of idea and carry on developments of thought, to intensify the lyrical and emotional climaxes of the film, occasionally to provide emotional relief. This is true even of music introduced as a naturalistic element, as in the case of the tenor's song in *La Bête Humaine* already described.[3]

Finally, whereas the quick changes of scene in the silent film caused difficulty to the musical arranger and compelled him to work with short fragments of music that had no pretensions to musical form, within the sections of a sound film that have been especially designed for a musical accompaniment there is often room for some degree of formal finish, and the shape of the music may even on occasion have some influence on the visual form of that part of the film.

Whereas under the conditions of performance of silent-film music an original score was a rarity, the new conditions of the sound film were highly stimulating to original composition, and such men as William Alwyn, Arthur Benjamin, Arthur Bliss, William Walton, Walter Leigh, Vaughan Wil-

3 See p. 184.

liams and Benjamin Britten in Great Britain, Arthur Honegger, Maurice Jaubert, Darius Milhaud and Georges Auric in France, and Dmitri Shostakovitch and Sergei Prokofiev in the Soviet Union—to name only a few—were attracted to the new medium. The result of their work has been to raise the standards of film music to a far higher level than was possible in silent days; film audiences hear better music and they hear it played by the finest orchestral combinations, which more than compensate for the imperfections of reproduction.

It should be noted, however, that it is not the intrinsic quality of the music in a film that is so important as its dramatic appropriateness and a proper synchronization between its rhythm and the visual rhythm of the film. Music so good that it calls attention to itself at the expense of the film is out of place, hence the common observation that the best film music is that which is not heard. This is as much as to say, of course, that music in the film is a servant art, but this is nothing new; music has been a servant art throughout the greater part of its history. In many cases exceptionally fine film music has been written by composers who in the realm of pure music were not in the first class; Edmund Meisel, who wrote the score for *Battleship Potemkin*, and Hans Eisler, who composed the music for Joris Ivens's film *Zuyderzee*, are two cases in point.

Music in a film may call undue attention to itself not only where it is too good, but also where it has a strong and clearly defined melodic line. The spectator's attention is drawn to the melody and he half-consciously listens to hear it played to its conclusion. The composer who wishes to keep his music in the background will work rather on changes of harmony and rhythm. The use of well-known music is even more distracting and has the additional disadvantage that it often has certain associations the producer wishes to establish in his film. The most painful case of this kind in my experience was Disney's treatment of Beethoven's Pastoral Symphony in *Fantasia*, which was so destructive of my feelings about this music that for a long time I feared I should never be able to efface Disney's images from my mind and my enjoyment of it would be permanently marred. The use of classical music for sound films is entirely to be deplored; fortunately, this is generally recognized and nowadays even the most modest type of documentary usually has music composed especially for it. *Brief Encounter* and *The Seventh Veil*, two successful films in which well-known pieces of classical music were heard, might appear to be exceptions, but in both the music is used realistically as a part of the action and not merely as accompaniment. In the first, Celia Johnson, turning on the radio, happens to hear the Rachmaninoff Concerto No. 2 and its music afterward runs through her mind. The pieces heard in *The Seventh Veil* were played by Ann Todd as a concert pianist. It is doubtful whether even in such cases the use of classical music is fully justified, but probably only a purist would insist on the point.

The extent to which music is used in a film and the importance of the role it plays will depend very much, of course, on the type of the film. It is, in general, true that if one takes the well-established categories of film and sets them down in an order ranging from the virtually untreated actuality of the record film at one end of the scale to the abstract diagram film depending exclusively on the appeal of visual form at the other—as, for example, record film, newsreel, lecture film, teaching film, interest film, documentary, story film, puppet film, cartoon, abstract diagram —one finds that whereas non-naturalistic music has no place in the record film, it gradually acquires more and more importance as one moves toward the other end of the scale. In the Disney cartoon it is an integral element, and in abstract films of the kind made by Norman MacLaren in Canada it is the fundamental element providing both the form and the justification of the film. The whole value of the record film lies in its content, in the use of the camera as a recording instrument with an absolute minimum of human interference, of formal treatment. But as the film-maker's purpose lies further away from mere record, as he is more concerned to persuade, to express an idea or a point of view, so form becomes more important to him; and since music, after all, is nothing other than a highly elaborate formalization of sound, it is hardly surprising that it should be most important in those types of film in which the formal element is most pronounced.

It has already been observed that one of the chief differences between the use of music in the silent film and its use in the sound film is that in the naturalistic story film (which comes at some middle point in our scale) non-naturalistic music will be used for certain portions only. This raises new problems. First, when should music be used? In view of what has been said of background music, we shall not expect it to be used in naturalistic dialogue scenes. But that is a negative direction; can anything more positive be said? Obviously, in any particular film, the decision as to when music shall be used and of what kind it shall be must rest with the good taste and judgment of the producer or director concerned, but some clue to a general principle is afforded by what has already been said about the relationship between visual form and music. Form becomes more important to an artist the more he is concerned to express the emotional and the lyrical, and it is in the parts of a film that reach these levels that the use of music will be most appropriate. The French composer Maurice Jaubert, after condemning background music to dialogue—music, as he describes it, "called upon to annotate the action"—goes on to say:

> If I reject entirely all musical annotation or synchronization, it is because I believe, as I said above, in the essentially realistic character of the screen. Into the raw materials of cinema—which acquire artistic meaning only from their relations to one another—music brings an *unreal* element which is bound to break the rules of objective realism. Is there no place for it in the film?
>
> Certainly there is. For just as the novelist sometimes

interrupts the telling of a story with an expression of his feelings, argumentative or lyrical, or with the subjective reactions of his characters, so does the director sometimes move away from the strict representation of reality in order to add to his work those touches of comment or of poetry which give a film its individual quality, descriptions, movements from one point to another in space or time, recalling of earlier scenes, dreams, imaging of the thoughts of some character, etc. Here the music has something to say: its presence will warn the spectator that the style of the film is changing temporarily for dramatic reasons. All its power of suggestion will serve to intensify and prolong that impression of strangeness, of departure from photographic truth, which the director is seeking.[4]

When it has been decided where in a film music should be used, there follow the secondary problems of deciding precisely at what point it should begin and end, and how the transitions from and to the adjacent parts of the film, particularly the adjacent parts of the sound track, are to be effected. As far as the first point is concerned, the problem is largely one of motivation: the audience must be prepared and ready for the change, and the director must sense where it should properly come. The second point is largely a technical one. "One may, in a moment of extreme dramatic tension, make use of the shock of a brutal attack (an orchestral fortissimo linked to a cry, for instance). One may also subtly mingle a musical with a non-musical sound (the noise of a train developing a rhythm which merges gradually into actual music; the shrilling of violins replacing imperceptibly the whistling of the wind, etc.). There are a thousand and one possible solutions to a problem which never twice presents itself in the same way. But it is precisely the function of the film musician to feel the exact moment when the image escapes from strict realism and calls for the poetic extension of music."[5]

4 *Footnotes to the Film*, p. 109.
5 *Footnotes to the Film*, p. 109.

I have been concerned here only with the use of non-naturalistic music in the dramatic film and have said nothing of musical films as such; these have their own conventions that are commonly understood and accepted. Those, however, who are especially interested in them are recommended to turn to Dr. Kurt London's *Film Music*, where various types of musical film are described and discussed.

Closely related to the use of music in films are the experiments that have been made in the use of poetic commentary or commentary cast in a rhythmic form. All these experiments, as far as I am aware, have been made in documentary films, and although they have not always been successful, one must acknowledge the courage of the producers who made them.

In Basil Wright's *Song of Ceylon* (1935) the commentary was taken from the description of the island written in 1680 by Robert Knox, and although not in verse, was recited in a slow, soft, rhythmical monotone that formed a complete whole with the musical portions and the lyrical conception of the entire film. Pure verse was used in Harry Watt's *Nightmail* (1936). Toward the end of the film, after the work on the nightly postal special from Euston to Glasgow has been shown in considerable detail and with a very considerable feeling of dramatic excitement, the spectator is moved away from the detailed view into a series of long shots of the express speeding toward its destination in the slowly breaking dawn. This is precisely one of those lyrical moments mentioned by Maurice Jaubert, one of those moments "of departure from photographic truth," what we hear at this point, however, is not music chiefly, but the following verse of W. H. Auden, spoken in a rapid, rhythmical tone imitative of the pulsation of the wheels over the rails:

> This is the night mail crossing the border,
>   Bringing the cheque and the postal order,
> Letters for the rich, letters for the poor,
>   The shop at the corner and the girl next door,

Pulling up Beattock, a steady climb—
  The gradient's against her but she's on time.
Past cotton grass and moorland boulder,
  Shovelling white steam over her shoulder,
Snorting noisily as she passes
  Silent miles of wind-bent grasses;
Birds turn their heads as she approaches,
  Stare from the bushes at her blank-faced coaches;
Sheepdogs cannot turn her course
  They slumber on with paws across,
In the farm she passes no one wakes,
  But a jug in a bedroom gently shakes.

Dawn freshens, the climb is done.
  Down towards Glasgow she descends
Towards the steam tugs, yelping down the glade of cranes
  Towards the fields of apparatus, the furnaces
Set on the dark plain like gigantic chessmen.
  All Scotland waits for her;
In the dark glens, beside the pale-green sea lochs
  Men long for news.

Letters of thanks, letters from banks,
  Letters of joy from the girl and boy,
Receipted bills and invitations
  To inspect new stock or visit relations,
And applications for situations,
  And timid lovers' declarations,
And gossip, gossip from all the nations,
  News circumstantial, news financial,
Letters with holiday snaps to enlarge in,
  Letters with faces scrawled on the margin,
Letters from uncles, cousins and aunts,
  Letters to Scotland from the South of France,
Letters of condolence to Highlands and Lowlands,
  Notes from overseas to the Hebrides;
Written on paper of every hue,

The pink, the violet, the white and the blue,
The chatty, the catty, the boring, adoring,
The cold and official and the heart's outpouring,
Clever, stupid, short and long,
The typed and the printed and the spelt all wrong.

Thousands are still asleep
Dreaming of terrifying monsters
Or a friendly tea beside the band at Cranston's or
Crawford's;
Asleep in working Glasgow, asleep in well-set
Edinburgh,
Asleep in granite Aberdeen.
They continue their dreams
But shall wake soon and long for letters.
And none will hear the postman's knock
Without a quickening of the heart,
For who can bear to feel himself forgotten?

This verse sequence, however, is the least successful part of *Nightmail*, which is in all other respects one of the finest of the prewar documentaries; the reason lies, probably, in the fact that Auden's verse is complex enough to stand on its own as a self-sufficient poem. Where commentary aspires to a poetic style, the connection between words and images necessarily becomes very much closer than in the case of the merely informative commentary that remains detached and aloof, describing something outside itself. The poetic commentary, like good film music, should be conceived as an integral part of the film, as part of an unbreakable artistic unity. It is useless to conceive the visual side of the film on the one hand, and the commentary on the other, and then seek to give the film some special quality by casting the commentary in verse. If picture and verse commentary are not conceived on the same level from the outset—if they are not designed, in short, to express a unified idea at a single emotional level—the result is almost bound to be a failure.

27. *The dramatic use of shadow in Eisenstein's* STRIKE *(USSR, 1924).*

28. Shadow used suggestively to create a prison cell in THE TRIALS OF OSCAR WILDE (Great Britain, 1960), directed by Ken Hughes, with Peter Finch as Wilde.

Nowhere was this division between picture and commentary more clearly discernible than in the Ministry of Information film *Our Country* (produced in 1945) for which Dylan Thomas wrote the verse.

In the two American documentaries made by Pare Lorentz, *The Plow That Broke the Plains* (1936) and *The River* (1938), a form of free verse commentary was used with greater success, due, perhaps, to the fact that Lorentz made himself responsible for the conception of the whole film, commentary as well as picture. As the following example shows, Lorentz's verse is not subtle or complicated; it is a measure of its fitness as an accompaniment to the visual images that, when these are taken away, it stands a little threadbare:

We built a hundred cities and a thousand towns:
    St. Paul and Minneapolis,
Davenport and Keokuk,
    Moline and Quincy,
Cincinnati and St. Louis,
    Omaha and Kansas City. . . .
Across to the Rockies and down from Minnesota,
    Twenty-five hundred miles to New Orleans.
We built a new continent.
    Black spruce and Norway pine,
Douglas fir and red cedar,
    Scarlet oak and Shagbark hickory.
We built a hundred cities and a thousand towns—
    But at what a cost!
We cut the top off the Alleghenies and sent it down
        the river.
    We cut the top off Minnesota and sent it down the river.
We cut the top off Wisconsin and sent it down the river.
    We left the mountains and the hills slashed and burned,
And moved on.

Or again:

> Down the Judith, the Grand, the Osage and the Platte;
> The Rock, the Salt, the Black and the Minnesota;
> Down the Monongahela, the Allegheny, Kanawha and
>   Muskingum;
> The Miami, the Wabash, the Liking and the Green;
> The White, the Wolf, the Cache, and the Black;
> Down the Kaw and Kaskaskia, the Red and Yazoo.
> Down the Cumberland, Kentucky and the Tennessee. . . .

The distinguishing characteristic of this commentary is its rhythmic repetition of phrases and sentences and place names that, without importuning the attention with too great complexity of meaning, provide an effective lyrical accompaniment to the images.

9 · Film Acting

*Those dreadful pictures of real people in their real sur-
roundings, who by their obvious self-consciousness make
the spectator squirm, are not interpreters of truth merely
because they are real. Between being natural and appearing natural there may have to be a bridge of art.*
GEORGE PEARSON

Toward the beginning of this section the fiction film was
defined as one representing men in action, things happening
in terms of human behavior, and now we come at last, very
near the end of this section, to those who impersonate the
men in action—the actors. There are many, perhaps, who
think that the place of the actor in the film is so important
that it ought to have been considered very much earlier, but
it would be unwarrantable to assume that last means least;
in fact, it would have been impossible to examine the place
and distinctive character of acting in the film and the ways
in which it differs from acting on the stage without first
establishing a clear understanding of the nature of the film
medium.

In a stage play the actor is all-important. His performance, in fact, is itself the dramatic medium; it is the stuff
out of which a play is made. When the curtain rises on an
empty stage we do not look on the play's beginning, but only
its setting; the play does not begin until the actor walks on,
and it cannot proceed very far until he begins to speak. The
medium of the drama is dialogue, written to be spoken by
actors. To the actors, moreover, belongs the sole responsibility of carrying the performance forward. While in rehearsal it is the producer who shapes the general character
of the performance, he has no active part in the performance itself; the actors are not even subject to the same

sort of guidance as an orchestra following its conductor, but are in the fullest sense "out on their own." Again, each actor plays his part through as a single whole, interrupted only by the periods when he is offstage. Imaginatively and emotionally, therefore, he is able to cast himself into a frame of mind for the performance in which, in a sense, he "lives" the part he has to play. Finally, he plays, as it were, on the living sounding board of the audience, which responds and resonates to his performances and reinforces it.

None of this is true of film acting. In a film that is not simply a cinematographic record of theater acting, the actor is not all-important; he is no more than one of several technicians who combine their talents to produce a number of film shots, and it is these shots, not the actor's performance, that constitute the filmic medium. Not only does the film actor perform under the immediate guidance and control of the director, but the effect of his performance may be modified by his other collaborators, by the camera angle or lighting used by the cameraman, or by the way in which the separate fragments of his performance are cut and arranged by the editor.

In the theater the spectator is stationary as he watches and listens to the spectacle moving before him. If an actor has to give emphasis to a particular gesture or expression, he must draw the attention of the audience to himself by taking up a conspicuous position or by striking a pose or making a movement or pause that will lead the other actors to look at him; and whatever he does must be performed so obviously that it cannot fail to be observed by the most distant members of his audience. His makeup, even his stage whispers, must be exaggerated for the same purpose.

In a film none of this is necessary; the director simply cuts to a close-up of the detail he wants to emphasize. In Alfred Hitchcock's *Blackmail*, for example, two detectives come to arrest a wanted man in bed at his lodgings. They quietly push the door ajar and see him sitting up reading a newspaper held fully open in front of him. In a close shot of the wanted man's face we see his eyes move slightly to the left to look beyond the paper. There follows a shot of the washstand mirror, with the detectives reflected in it sideface; we know that he has seen them. Back again to the wanted man. Without betraying himself to the detectives by the slightest movement he turns his eyes down toward the right; there follows a close-up of a revolver lying on the table by his bedside, and at once we know what he is thinking. The spectator of a film, considered as a spectator, is no longer stationary, as in the theater; he is made by the art of editing an active observer, moving about in the midst of the action wherever the director chooses to lead him.

This fundamental difference between the methods of the theater and the film involves considerable differences between the technique of stage acting and that of film acting. In the first place, the exaggeration and overstatement the stage actor has to employ become quite unnecessary in the film. On the contrary, because the camera can approach so close and give such an enlarged view of the least detail, it is restraint and understatement that are required. "I had always believed," George Arliss tells us, "that for the movies acting must be exaggerated, but I saw in this one flash that *restraint* was the chief thing that the actor had to learn in transferring his art from the stage to the screen." [1] All that is essential and effective on the stage, the wide sweep of gesture, the makeup, the declamatory style of speech, becomes false and ridiculous on the screen simply because it is out of place. "When we speak of the 'unnecessary staginess' of a film actor's performance, we so term it not because staginess necessarily involves anything of itself wrong or unpleasant. We simply register an unpleasant sensation of incongruity, and therefore falseness, as though at the sight of a man striving to negotiate a non-existent obstacle." [2]

[1] George Arliss, *Up the Years from Bloomsbury* (Little, Brown and Co., Boston, 1927), p. 289.

[2] Pudovkin, *Film Acting* (Newnes, London, 1937), p. 106.

A second difference is that whereas on the stage an actor's chief instrument of expression is his voice and his movements are almost entirely an accompaniment to, and an extension of, what is said, in the film he acts with the whole of himself. A glance, a movement of the hand, a slight shrug of the shoulders, may be far more significant than anything said. This means that the film actor must exercise a far higher degree of self-control. Falseness and insincerity are much more apparent in a screen performance than on the stage where, as Robert Donat has testified, it is easier for the actor to disguise an imperfectly assimilated characterization. "In the theatre," he says, "it is the audience which receives; in the studio it is the camera, with this surprising difference—that whereas one can get away with flippancy, sloppiness and insincerity in the theatre, infinite care must be exercised in front of the camera. In the theatre the broad methods necessary to reach topmost galleryite and lowermost pittite sometimes cover a multitude of sins." [3]

To make the same point in a slightly different way, whereas stage acting is to a considerable extent conventionalized and stylized, film acting is in the highest degree naturalistic. Nothing is so effective on the screen as complete sincerity, provided always that it is tempered with restraint; and those who have a naturally easy and genuine personality and who always give the appearance of being simply themselves, unmarred by any self-consciousness or sense of strain, are most consistently successful—Fred Astaire, Bing Crosby and the late Gary Cooper, for example. It is the knowledge of this fact that encourages the film industry to continue in that exploitation of personality known as the star system. The word "star" is sometimes loosely applied to any actor who takes a principal part in a film, but its correct meaning is more limited than this: it denotes an actor whose appearance in a film is the main guarantee of its commercial success, and who is paid ac-

[3] *Footnotes to the Film*, p. 29.

cordingly. Many producers with a wealth of experience behind them believe that the mass of the film-going public is
more interested in personalities than in stories or film
craftsmanship, and they take the greatest pains to build up
and to publicize interest. If a film star has genuine acting
ability, he is seldom given the opportunity to demonstrate
it, because it is of the essence of his status as a star that
he should display the same personality in picture after
picture.

Given all that has been said about the exacting nature of
film acting, it might be doubted whether it is possible for
anyone to play widely differing roles with conviction and
success. It might seem that to expect an actor to behave
naturally and easily before the searching lens of the camera,
with every gesture, every word, every twitch of a muscle
perfectly coordinated in a sincere portrayal, and in so doing
to be anything other than what he really is, is to expect
more than human nature can achieve. It is certainly true
that film acting is in many ways a more difficult and exacting art than acting on the stage. It is also true that the
range of roles a film actor can play successfully is usually
very much narrower than that of a stage actor. As Miss
Dilys Powell has put it: "On the stage the great actor is
often unrecognizable from part to part: there is no finding
the Laurence Olivier of Oedipus in the Laurence Olivier of
Justice Shallow; and this kind of metamorphosis is not confined to the great actor either. On the screen the complete
transformation of personality is rare; in the American
cinema so rare as to be almost non-existent.[4] Nevertheless,
such players as Paul Muni and Bette Davis, and the Russian
actor Cherkasov (*Deputy of the Baltic, Alexander Nevsky,
Ivan the Terrible,* etc.), have demonstrated that it is possible for an actor to express his personality in different
ways in entirely different situations, and to give in each of
them a convincing interpretation. Paul Muni tells us: "Personally, I prefer parts that are unlike myself, and not those

4 *The Sunday Times* (London), March 31, 1946.

exhibitionistic parts that are given to many Hollywood stars, who act as themselves on the screen." [5] And Bette Davis, in a parallel essay, says: "I should like to add, here, that I have never played a part which I did not feel was a person very different from myself. The character I am playing stays behind in my dressing room at the end of the day, and is waiting for me there the following morning." [6]

One factor which greatly increases the difficulty of acting for the film is the conditions under which the actor has to work. The needs of editing require that the action be broken up into small fragments, and these will not even be shot in the order in which they are finally to be shown. This means that during the period of shooting, which may be anything from a month upward, the actor will concentrate the whole of a day's efforts on one small action, the next day he will work at another, four days later at a third, and so on. If he is working on location, bad weather may stop shooting for days on end, and after kicking his heels he must be ready to take up his performance again with the same zest as before as soon as the sun shines. Robert Donat has amusingly and feelingly described the taking of one such shot:

On the screen, suppose we see a modern young man dangling a leg over a modern office desk with modern New York receding in the background. Suddenly we come closer to him. In other words, the camera moves into close-up. His eyes flash a look of doubt and that is all. I have purposely chosen something elementary. That flicker of doubt is created in a blaze of light in a dreadful fug under the very nose of that terrifying taskmaster, the camera lens, with a "mike" on a boom hovering overhead, surrounded by a gang of electricians and props boys and faced by the unit staff headed by the director—who is expecting results. Behind him are the plaster walls and an unglazed window with an enlarged black-and-white

5 *We Make the Movies.*
6 *Ibid.*

picture postcard of New York propped up behind it; above him and everywhere else, lights.

In actual fact, the young man's behind is probably propped up on a couple of cushions or books, and the desk raised up on wood blocks to improve matters for the camera, so that his leg dangles at a very unnatural height from the ground, and he must gauge his movements so that at the moment of the close-up his head will be momentarily still and his eyes—almost imperceptibly—will flash their story; not into the lens itself (for the lens, though our most inquisitive neighbour, must be ignored completely if we would win it over completely), not precisely into the lens, then, but at a spot dangerously close. And an exact spot; remember, he is to convey a flicker of doubt—not a flicker of doubt as to where he should look, and so insidiously faithful is the lens that it will blurt out the whole story if given half a chance: "Damn! I'm looking into the lens." "Hell! I looked too low." [7]

The essential discontinuity of the film actor's work makes it extremely difficult for him to conceive and feel his part as a complete whole. As Paul Muni says, "On the stage you have a strong sense of security. You are sure of your four weeks' rehearsals, with the entire cast, from the beginning to the end of the play. You can work gradually into the part, knowing the timing and the rhythm, letting the process become subconscious, and later you may color and change and add to the characterization. But in acting for the screen you do not have the same sense of security." [8] Yet it is clear that if the actor is to fulfill his proper function, and if his abilities and training are not to be wastefully neglected, he must have the opportunity to imagine himself into his part as a whole and make it an expression of his personality. Only in this way can he endow it with sincerity and with unity and consistency of development in the changing circumstances of the story of the film.

7 *Footnotes to the Film*, p. 31.
8 *We Make the Movies*, p. 138.

In many cases directors who lean considerably on the work of their actors and who realize their need to feel their acting in its entirety seek to help them by avoiding frequent breaks in the action and by shooting whole scenes with very few cuts. This is simply to throw away the characteristic virtues of the film medium and to revive all the demerits of the photographed play. Pudovkin, on the other hand, has proposed in his book *Film Acting* that the dangers of discontinuity might be met by special rehearsal methods involving the use of actors' scripts that might even contain supplementary action having no place in the film. Effective though this might well be, it is most unlikely that such an innovation would be generally acceptable in current production practice. The problem remains one that each director must solve in his own way, and the solution of which will become part of his personal approach to the actors who come to work under him.

If the danger of sacrificing the benefits of editing to assist the actor leads to the theatrical film, the danger of exploiting editing to the extent of ignoring the needs of the actor altogether leads to his becoming a mere automaton in the director's hands. This danger was particularly strong in the days of the silent film. When D. W. Griffith wished to portray the extreme anguish of a woman hearing her husband condemned to death, he showed a close-up of Mae Marsh's face and followed it with another close-up of her clenched hands. The face, as we can see, is passive enough, and the hands may not even be hers. Inevitably the question arises: Why use a Mae Marsh at all? Would not any girl have done as well?

The more extreme directors of the Soviet silent cinema followed precisely this line of thought. They argued that the fundamental creative process in film-making was editing, which not only enabled the director to escape entirely from the limitations of the theater, but in fact compelled him to seek his material in the natural world and to rely for his results, as far as possible, on the way in which it was

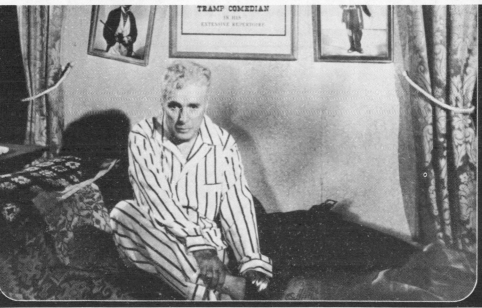

29. *Charlie Chaplin in* (above) CITY LIGHTS *(*USA, *1931) and* (below) LIMELIGHT *(*USA, *1952). The greatest artist in mime in the history of the cinema, he is now virtually the only director whose creative control extends over every part of the films he makes.*

30. *The versatility of the great actor, changing his personality from role to role.
(Left): Sir Laurence Olivier in his own production of* RICHARD III *(Great Britain,
1955) and (right) in* THE ENTERTAINER *(Great Britain, 1960), directed by Tony
Richardson.*

selected and assembled. In order to secure the fullest control over his material and to obtain with economy precisely what he wanted, it might be necessary for the director to stage the content of each shot, but the essentially realistic character of the film medium demanded that any such staging should be as natural as possible. If one of the characters in his film is a workman, the director should employ a real workman to play the part; he will, of course, have to carry out certain actions under the director's instructions, but it will not be necessary for him to act in the theatrical sense, since his performance, as a whole, will be created primarily by the director through editing. Such a nonactor, it was argued, could not fail to be more realistic and convincing than the stage-trained professional, dressed up and made up and performing actions to which in real life he was unaccustomed.

In all his silent films Eisenstein consistently used nonactors, and Pudovkin used them to a considerable extent for his minor roles, although not generally for his chief parts. In the sound film nonactors are used more rarely, although often with great success, as in De Sica's *Bicycle Thief*, Satyajit Ray's *Pather Panchali* or Flaherty's *Louisiana Story;* outstanding children's performances (Bobby Henrey in Carol Reed's *Fallen Idol* or Hayley Mills in Lee Thompson's *Tiger Bay,* for example) fall into the same category. Pudovkin has described the taking of a shot with a nonactor in his film *The Story of a Simple Case*:

> There was a scene as follows: a father and his small son . . . who have not seen each other for a long time, meet. It is early morning. The boy is just out of bed. He is stretching and flexing his muscles after sleep. At his father's question, "How's life, Johnny?" he turns towards him, and instead of an answer gives him a sweet, rather shy, smile.
>
> . . . I decided, first and foremost, to make the boy experience a real pleasure from the process of stretching,

more even, feel a need for it. To achieve this, I bade him bend forward, grip his feet with his hands, and hold them in this position until I gave him permission to straighten up.

The boy was really interested, I felt it. Now I further reckoned thus: when I give him permission to straighten out, and he stretches with genuine pleasure, I shall interrupt his movement with a question: "Well, Johnny, isn't it grand to stretch?"

Talking during the shot was not allowed; the boy knew he had to keep silent. I knew his nature well, and I was convinced that he would answer me with precisely the smile I needed, acquiescent, and a little confused and shy at the unusualness of the situation.

The scene began. The boy stood bent downwards. I allowed him to straighten out, he stretched; I saw on his face a satisfaction both of physical pleasure and from his feeling that the game I had suggested to him was going without a hitch. I put my question and received in reply the beautiful and sincere smile I wanted.[9]

In such a case as this, "the raw material is nature itself, unmodified by any conscious process except that of editing, when it is not modified itself but is involved in a series of juxtapositions with other raw material to form a general concept. This concept is the *director's* modification of reality, not the performer's and it must be borne in mind that the performance of a nonactor remains unmodified to the end.[10] Carried to its extreme this directing of nonactors is not dissimilar from the process of directing animals in which shots of isolated fragments of behavior and reaction are taken and subsequently joined in an order that gives the animal concerned the appearance of displaying an uncannily human intelligence.

The addition of sound to the film enabled personality to

9 *Film Acting*, pp. 122-3.
10 Bernard Miles, "Are Actors Necessary?", published in *Documentary News Letter* for April, 1941.

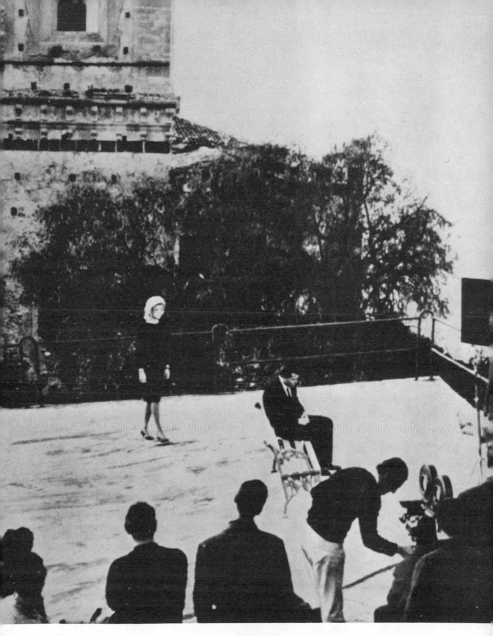

31. *In the gray dawn the lonely penitent weeps. The woman he has wronged approaches to touch his head in compassion, but the actors (Monica Vitti and Gabriele Ferzeti) have to live this single moment of tenderness that ends Michelangelo Antonioni's* L'AVVENTURA *under the glare of camera and lights and calculating technicians.*

32. *The art of the film can be used for documentary and historical record: it can also appear (though with loss of scale and detail) on the television screen. This picture of the composer Igor Stravinsky at work, by Gjon Mili, comes from the Robert Snyder "Time"* production SKETCHBOOK NO. 1—THREE AMERICANS, *shown in Britain by* BBC *Television (Monitor program).*

be portrayed, as it were, in a new dimension. It enabled characterization to be drawn with greater depth and greater individuality. In the silent film it was the portrayal of emotions that had received the main emphasis; speech, with all the fine shades of meaning and feeling it could express, added a new element, primarily an intellectual element, which the film had till then been unable to compass. Into this new world of characterization in depth the nonactor found it more difficult to enter, for the moment he spoke he revealed his limitations; he became awkward and self-conscious. It is true that even in sound films gifted and patient directors have occasionally obtained remarkable results with nonactors (Vittorio de Sica's *Bicycle Thief* is a conspicuous case in point), but these are now isolated exceptions. The use of the nonactor, which had never been general in the entertainment film industries of the West, was abandoned even by the Soviet directors. Eisenstein, for example, used well-known professional actors (notably Cherkasov) in all his sound films after the abortive *Que Viva Mexico*, and today the Soviet film industry honors its professional actors and actresses no less than its directors and cameramen.

There was, however, one school of film-makers, working outside the commerical entertainment film, that continued to rely almost exclusively on nonactors long after the silent film had disappeared, namely, the British documentary school founded and led by John Grierson. In a manifesto of "first principles" published in the Winter 1932 issue of *Cinema Quarterly*, Grierson declared:

We believe that the original (or native) actor, and the original (or native) scene, are better guides to a screen interpretation of the modern world. They give cinema a greater fund of material. They give it power over a million and one images. They give it power of interpretation over more complex and astonishing happenings in the real world than the studio mind can conjure up or the studio mechanician re-create. We believe that the materials and the stories thus taken from the raw can be finer (more real in the philosophic sense) than the acted article. Spontaneous gesture has a special value on the screen. . . . Documentary can achieve an intimacy of knowledge and effect impossible to the shim-sham mechanics of the studio, and the lily-fingered interpretations of the metropolitan actor.

Grierson's attitude, stated here with his characteristically uncompromising vigor, was formed partly under the influence of the Soviet cinema and of Robert Flaherty, who had likewise relied on nonactors in his dramatized records of primitive life; partly, perhaps, it was the result of an independent reaction against the influence of the theater, which has always been strong in England owing to the economic fact that the film industry here was not until recently sufficiently large or well organized to give security of employment to specialist film actors and had therefore to draw its actors from the stage; but what committed him more heavily to the theory of the nonactor than anything else was that belittlement of the individual as such that became an integral part of his documentary theory and that he has expressed on numerous occasions. The following is a characteristic statement of Grierson's anti-individualism:

You may think that the individual life is no longer capable of cross-sectioning reality. You may believe that its particular bellyaches are of no consequence in a world which complex and impersonal forces command, and conclude that the individual as a self-sufficient dramatic figure is outmoded. When Flaherty tells you that it is a devilish noble thing to fight for food in a wilderness, you may, with some justice, observe that you are more concerned with the problem of people fighting for food in the midst of plenty. When he draws your attention to the fact that Nanook's spear is grave in its upheld angle, and finely rigid in its down-pointing bravery, you may, with some justice, observe that no spear, held however bravely by the individual, will master the crazy walrus of international finance. Indeed, you may feel that in individualism is a yahoo tradition largely responsible for our present anarchy, and deny at once both the hero of decent heroics (Flaherty) and the hero of indecent ones (studio). In this case, you will feel that you want your drama in terms of some cross-section of reality which will reveal the essentially cooperative or mass nature of society; leaving the individual to find his honours in the swoop of creative social forces. In other words, you are liable to abandon the story form, and seek, like the modern exponent of poetry and painting and prose, a matter and method more satisfactory to the mind and spirit of time.[11]

It is not part of our present purpose, of course, to embark on a discussion of the very important social and political questions that this statement raises, and which would lead us far away from film acting. What is important to our subject is to observe that this contempt for the individual and for the experience of the individual, and the deliberate reliance on the nonactor in which it found expression, imposed a definite character on the documentary approach to reality. It is, of course, true that at a certain level, the level of public behavior, the non-actor may give an impression of greater authenticity; if a conductor has to be shown on his bus calling "Any more fares?" or an auctioneer on his stand repeating the bids, it may be more effective to employ a real bus conductor or a real auctioneer. But as soon as one wants to go below the surface of public behavior, the non-actor fails; even at its best his performance is bound to be both limited and static, and it only ceases to be either inasmuch as he abandons his function of non-actor and begins to act, that is to modify his behavior by the light of his own creative imagination.

The nature of the limitation to which the British documentary movement thus subjected itself was so ably anlyzed

11 *Grierson and Documentary*, ed. Forsyth Hardy (Collins, London, 1946), p. 82.

by Bernard Miles in an article in *Documentary News Letter* of April, 1941, that I make no apology for quoting from it at some length:

> In all the documentary films that I have seen, and I have seen some dozens in the past three or four weeks apart from isolated examples in the course of ten years' steady cinema going, I think that non-actors achieve all, or at any rate most, that the very best professional actors could achieve in the same circumstances. But this is only because most of these pictures avoid the implications of human action, or where they do present it, present it in such a fragmentary way as never to put to the test the training and natural qualities which differentiate an actor from a non-actor. It seems to me that in this lies the whole crux of the matter, because when I say that documentary has never faced up to the problem of sustained characterization and development on the human side of its material, I am simply implying that the leaders of documentary are guilty of a kind of escapism, a deliberate side-stepping of the very central problem in that interpretation of reality which is their avowed aim, I mean Man and his efforts to find his bearings in the universal set-up.
>
> . . . in documentary film, man is nearly always implicit but rarely explicit. It seems that documentary insists upon placing the major emphasis upon circumstances and environment and only by inference upon the human being as an individual. I contend that this is a limitation and a cul-de-sac which documentary directors will sooner or later find themselves forced to revolt against. Man's hopes, his doubts, his fears, his yearnings, his aspirations . . . from all these documentary seems to turn away— only the economic and natural forces which condition his behaviour and set the scene of the struggle, but never the struggle itself. Always the circumference, never the centre.

It seems to me that documentary displays with the greatest clarity the material world and the environment in which all our problems have to be solved, that it shows with equal clarity most of the problems themselves, but that it makes little or no attempt to grapple with the most important thing of all, *the act of solution.* To this extent documentary is a passive rather than an active medium. But I suggest that true social analysis can have only one object—action towards the solution of the problems analysed. And I further suggest that these inescapable social and propagandist aims can best be served, from the screen point of view, by a marriage of documentary as we know it, with a more and ever more human story value and by an ever-increasing concentration upon people. And that this can best be achieved by the isolation of the particular typical people, and that for this purpose actors trained to portray the development of human character and the intensification of thought and feeling that go with it, will have to be used more and more.

I will leave these quotations to stand beside Grierson's as a statement of two opposed points of view, and will only add, as a matter of some interest, that in a number of documentaries made during the war, actors were used with considerable success, and Bernard Miles himself has given several notable performances that fully bear out his contention that "it is possible for a sensitive actor to achieve the whole range of understatement so effective and so attractive in non-actors, together with a passion and a concentration and a power of development quite outside the range of his untrained rival." The war also gave an impetus to that marriage of documentary and story film that he suggested. The first completely balanced and successful fusion of the two forms is probably to be found in Harry Watt's *Nine Men,* which told a fictional story of nine soldiers cut off by the enemy in a deserted fort in the North African desert with documentary naturalism. Watt had gained his film experience under John Grierson, but *Nine Men* was made for Ealing Studios. Apart from this, however, there were many story films that were imbued with a documentary quality. The war broadened the scope of the documentary film and at the same time compelled the studio film to take more account of the realities of life; the net result was to bring the two closer together.

PART THREE
CRITICISM

10 · Film Criticism

As soon as a man becomes aware . . . that he likes this thing better than that, criticism begins; which is as much as to say that criticism begins when literature begins. But criticism as a noticeable activity in literature begins when vague instinctive preference passes into consciously defined choice which can be rationally justified; when, that is to say, there is an appeal to intellectual principles.
LASCELLES ABERCOMBIE

No one is likely to have started to read this book, and certainly to have continued with it so far, unless he had been interested in films and wished to know more about them. For the great majority this can have amounted to no more than simply a desire to get greater enjoyment from the films they see and to develop an ability to discriminate between them. Nowadays anyone pursuing such an end is said to be concerned to develop a sense of film appreciation; previously, he would have been described as developing his powers of criticism. The value of words, like the value of money, tends to depreciate as time passes, and the word *criticism* has suffered more than some others. For many people it now has the meaning, or at least the association, of fault-finding. This is a pity, because the alternative word, *appreciation,* tends to lean overmuch in the opposite direction toward an indiscriminate (that is to say, uncritical) admiration, and the ill effects of this are seen in a watering-down of standards such that almost every film can be found praiseworthy for some reason or other. I therefore propose to eschew *film appreciation* and to retain the more vigorous term *criticism;* and by *criticism* I mean enjoyment enriched in two ways: first, by the pleasure of being as fully conscious of it as possible; and secondly, by the pleasure of being able, as a result, to discuss it with others.

Now one cannot begin to enjoy an art, or even to comprehend it, until one understands its language. Therefore we have been mainly concerned up to this moment to break down the technique of the film into its elements, to dissect it in order to understand its nature and its grammar. Some people, in their approach to criticism, never pass beyond this stage and continue to analyze the films they see in terms of their editing, their acting, their camera work and their use of sound and music, appraising each of them as separate elements. Their interest, in short, develops into an interest primarily in technical aspects, and like all who are preoccupied with the technical approach to art, they fail to see the woods for the trees. "They murder to dissect," and their dissection, instead of being an aid to enjoyment, may positively hinder it; with them enjoyment and criticism, instead of being one integrated function, are two separate functions, enjoyment remaining the same unreflecting satisfaction that it always was, and criticism being an arid intellectual anatomizing they have learned to exercise as the occasion requires.

In order that criticism and enjoyment can become one, all that has been learned about the elements of film technique must be allowed to sink into the background of the mind, to be called on as needed, and then not for its own sake, but only to clarify one's thought about the film-maker's purpose and his success in achieving it. For all that we have considered so far are means to an end, and it is to that end, the finished film and its content, that we now have to turn.

Some people believe that no such thing as objective criticism is possible. Assessment of a film or any work of art, they would contend, is solely a matter of personal opinion, in which one man's meat is another man's poison, and neither is more right than the other. In the final analysis this is true. If a painter bases the composition of a picture, as Van Gogh does in his still-life study of fruit and table utensils grouped around a black coffeepot, on the juxtaposition of two principal colors—a certain shade of blue and a certain shade of yellow—one either finds this conjunction pleasing and satisfying or one does not. This is a simple act of personal judgment, and if two people differ as to the result, I know of no way whereby one can convince the other than he is right.

An instance of the same kind of judgment applied to the film is to be found in the analysis Eisenstein made of a sequence of shots immediately preceding the famous massacre on the steps of Odessa in his own film *Battleship Potemkin*.[1] A medium shot of two figures standing on the steps waving to the battleship is followed by a similar shot of two figures, and then by a close-up of the face of one man only who is also waving. Eisenstein subsequently found this sequence of groupings (two, two, one) displeasing. Of the second shot he says: "Generally speaking, an unfortunate combination with the preceding shot. It would have been better to have introduced between them a shot of three faces. . . . A correct alternation of faces (if we make the suggested correction . . .) two, three, two, one." This criticism is a question of judgment, beyond the reach of rational proof. All that Eisenstein can argue in support of his conviction is that it is "a common compositional variation: an even number of people is replaced by an uneven number"; and that "this 'golden rule' of change of the *mise-en-scène* has behind it a tradition which can be traced back to the Italian *Commedia dell' Arte*." [2]

Criticism of any work of art resolves itself ultimately into such problems of judgment, and they cannot be evaded. This is not the same thing, however, as to say that one's reaction to a complete work is a simple matter of personal like or dislike. A work of art is a complex structure, and a consider-

1 *The Cinema as a Graphic Art* by Vladimir Nilsen (Newnes, London, 1940), p. 118. Nilsen explains that his analysis is "in the exact form given by Eisenstein" (p. 116).

2 *The Cinema as a Graphic Art*, p. 117.

able degree of analysis and understanding is possible, and indeed essential, before one arrives at those elements of simple judgment of which its total effect is composed. A not dissimilar situation is found in mathematics in the distinction between the axiom and the theorem. A schoolboy asked to prove the theorem of Pythagoras is expected to subject it to the required analysis, and would get short shrift if he answered that it was true simply because he had always found it to be so; nevertheless, the whole structure of mathematics rests ultimately on such simple assumptions (axioms) as that two and two make four, which are incapable of further analysis or proof and are perforce accepted on the grounds that we have always found them within our personal experience to be so.

Critical ability is the ability to ask and answer rational questions about a work of art. The purpose of these questions is to resolve a highly organized and complex structure into its basic elements so that the judgments that have to be made are clearly identified; not to settle by logical analysis to discover what these issues are. The further this process can be carried, the more assured is one's judgment, and the richer one's pleasure where the work is capable of giving pleasure.

Many people, in their appreciation of life and the pleasures that life can give, including the pleasures of man's own creative imagination, exist in a mental and emotional fog. The object of criticism is to dissolve that fog so that things stand out, sharply and clearly defined. Of course, one result will be that much that was before tolerated, and thought to be enjoyable, can no longer be accepted; the rest, however, will yield pleasure of a richness and intensity never previously suspected.

The critical attitude is an attitude to art and to living and he who adopts it embarks on an endless voyage of exploration and discovery. Since the evidence for this is essentially personal, perhaps I may be allowed to illustrate the point by a personal experience. I had long been familiar with Beethoven's piano Rondo in C Major, Opus 51, and gained a certain pleasure from listening to it and attempting to play it, although it is one of the least ambitious of his pieces; then I read Sir Donald Tovey's little book on Beethoven,[3] the first part of which deals with key relationships and with Beethoven's modulations from key to key in one work or movement. The music of the Rondo, being accessible, simple and familiar, was an obvious piece in which to study the working out of these ideas in practice. As a result, I found, first, that this little work, unpretentious though it is, runs through a fascinating range of key changes, precisely according to the principles Tovey had described, and secondly, that it was this pattern of moods, with its accompanying rhythms, that had been the source of my enjoyment from the very beginning.

To any musician all this would seem most elementary, and I was indeed in a position similar to that of Molière's Monsieur Jourdain, in *Le Bourgeois Gentilhomme*, who suddenly learned that the mysterious thing the grammarians called prose was nothing more than what he had spoken every day for forty years. Yet both of us had made an important critical discovery, and I could echo Monsieur Jourdain's "Sirs, I am infinitely obliged to you for having taught me that," for what I found exemplified in the Rondo has since enriched for me my appreciation of all Beethoven's work and of all music. Something of which I had been only dimly aware suddenly came sharply into focus.

To say that one's appreciation of a work of art is simply a matter of personal opinion, and that one person's opinion is as good as another's, is simply the lazy man's excuse for a disinclination to use his mind. The surprising thing is that when the complex structure of an imaginative creation has been broken down by analysis until analysis can go no further and we are faced with simple problems of judgment, our judgments are far more likely to agree with each other than to disagree. One of the features of composition in paint-

3 *Beethoven* by Donald Francis Tovey (Oxford University Press, London, 1944).

ing is the pattern of propositions created where the lines of the composition meet or intersect, and this pattern may be complex so that only those who study it carefully are fully aware of it. Yet the elements of which it is compounded are so much a part of common human experience that if a number of people are asked, for example, to divide a straight line at the point that gives them the greatest satisfaction, most will make their mark not in the middle of the line (which produces a monotonous pair of equals) or very near one end (which gives a sense of unbalance) but at some point between these two positions. Again, if they are asked to divide a rectangle by drawing a horizontal line across it, they will not draw it so as to divide the rectangle into two equal rectangles or into two grossly unequal rectangles, but somewhere between these two extremes. In fact, so constant are the proportions into which people will thus instinctively choose to divide a line or rectangle that it has long been supposed that they approximate to a "golden section" or "golden mean" in the ratio of approximately 1:1.6. Sir Donald Tovey, in the book on Beethoven I have already mentioned, refers to the familiar experience that the playing of a scale up to the leading note ("te" on the tonic sol-fa) creates an instinctive sense of incompleteness unless the tonic (doh) is added. "There is a legend," he says, "that when the infant Mozart insisted on lying slug-abed he could always be got out of bed if you played a scale which stopped on the leading note." And he uses this illustration to reinforce what he has to say about another such instinctive expectation, the expectation of the tonic after a prolonged harping on the dominant. So consistent is this expectation among all listeners that it can be used as a systematic method ("dominant preparation") of moving from one key to another. In short, the fundamental esthetic reactions that are beyond the reach of rational justification require no justification to be understood and discussed, for like the acceptance of the mathematical axiom they are common to us all; it is the fact that they are common that makes communication in any field of art possible.

This does not mean that judgment cannot develop. An uneducated and unsophisticated person who was asked to divide a line in two might perhaps put his dividing mark in the middle of the line simply because he lacked confidence in his own judgment and might prefer to cling to a naïve balance of equals, either not daring to trust himself to experiment with any alternative or finding it impossible consciously to justify any alternative to himself or to others. As we test our reactions, however, against works of art whose creators have been more adventurous than we dared to be, and above all as we become conscious and articulate about these reactions, so we are likely to find that our judgments themselves develop and acquire greater self-confidence.

Thus we see that the critical process, the process of enriching our enjoyment by a keener awareness, involves two activities, an activity of feeling and apprehension, and an activity of rational analysis designed to clarify for us what our feelings and apprehensions really are (in fact the questions and answers that are the fabric of the rational activity are really put to ourselves rather than to the work of art); the two react to one another, the analysis being made possible by the existence of the feelings, and the feelings themselves developing and acquiring greater definition as the result of the analysis.

The important consideration that emerges from this definition is that before one can analyze, one must feel and apprehend. The intellect should never be allowed to prejudge an aesthetic response. The first requirement of all sound criticism is that the critic should lend himself with all his faculties, sensuous, emotional and intellectual, to the work of art in a state of rapt and receptive attention. To put it more simply, he should do his utmost to listen to what the artist has to say. This may seem too obvious to need emphasizing, but it is so often disregarded as to be, perhaps, the most common cause of bad and misguided criticism. For example, a visitor to an art exhibition may turn away in bewilderment or disgust from a painting by Chagall because the fiddler, which is the central figure in it, appears to be crudely drawn, with a green face, and a violin and bow held in sausage-shaped fingers in a way no true violinist would hold it. He misjudges the painting because instead of savoring it and allowing it to have its effect on him (on the not unreasonable assumption that since the artist has made no attempt to be realistic he must have some other purpose), he stifles all possibility of apprehension by the purely intellectual presumption that Chagall wanted to draw a realistic violinist but lacked the skill or the patience to do so, and must therefore be a bad artist. Yet the same person will allow no such preconceptions to impede his spontaneous enjoyment of Mickey Mouse, which is a far more unrealistic creation than Chagall's violinist.

Up to now in this chapter I have used the term "work of art" in the widest possible sense to include any imaginative creation produced to give pleasure or enjoyment, without defining what a work of art is and begging the question whether a film can be a work of art. Both are matters we shall have to return to. For the moment, since it is the film we are concerned with, I propose simply to begin talking now about films rather than works of art in general. Given that one is confronted with a film, and given that one has with unprejudiced attention watched it unfold and has allowed it to make its impact, what are the questions one should then try to answer?

It might be supposed from what has just been said about the importance of understanding the artist's purpose that one's first question should be: What was the film-maker's purpose in making this film? Important and inevitable though this question is, I normally find myself beginning at the other end, with the particular rather than the general, and asking: Is this film filmic? By which I mean: Does it use the language of the motion picture, as we have studied it in the earlier chapters of this book? Does it build up its total effect by a composition of visual details, skillfully selected and welded together by means of editing? To know the answer to this question at the outset is to understand clearly the nature of the work one has to judge.

It is obviously more difficult, and more consuming of imagination, effort, time and money, to build up a scene from fifty different shots than to take it in one continuous shot. Yet the more a director desires to delve below the obvious surface of his subject, and the more he wishes to impose his own creative conception on his material (which in the end means imposing his own creative conception on the spectator), the more is he likely to compose his film of shots of detail and to rely on the relationship of shot to shot; in a word, the more is he likely to use editing. If he lacks this compulsion, he will fall back on glib, superficial and essentially non-filmic methods, such as relying on his actors and using cinematography simply to record their performance; or, in the case of a documentary, conveying his meaning mainly by the commentary and using his pictures as a more or less casual form of illustration; or, again, resorting to an indiscriminate surfeit of music to strain after effects he has failed to achieve on the screen.

If a cinematograph production is not filmic, there is no film in the proper sense to criticize, and to be clear on this point at the outset is to save misunderstanding and misdirected effort. To be confronted with a film in which the camera has been used primarily as a recording instrument is to be in the same position as a critic of gramophone discs, whose concern with art is limited exclusively to the performance of the artists they record. It is vain in such a case to seek for artistic qualities in the director's use of film technique; one can only judge whether on technical grounds it is a good filmed record or not and whether the theatrical performance or ballet (or whatever else is recorded) is good theater or good ballet.

Of course, all this is a matter of degree. Films cannot be cleanly divided into the filmic and the non-filmic; most lie somewhere between the two extremes. Yet the extent to which a film is filmic is a measure of its quality and seriousness as a work of film art, and is therefore a valuable clue to its maker's purpose. Moreover, although this aspect has been analyzed here in terms of question and answer, in practice the answer comes immediately and almost unconsciously when one knows what to look for. After a film has been running for a few minutes, such filmic quality as it has is felt as instinctively and strongly as one "feels" the plastic use of color in a painting, or the interplay of masses and proportions in a well-designed building or the theatricality of a skillfully written play.

So important is it to the full appreciation of a film or any work of art to apprehend the characteristic quality of the medium in which it is created that even to disguise its characteristics (as, for example, by smudging the lines of a pencil drawing to a pastel-like mass, or by merging a succession of different camera setups into a long, drawn-out single shot, which was Alfred Hitchcock's method in *Rope*), is to destroy much of its value as a work of art. "An essential condition of a good work of art," says Rudolf Arnheim in his book *Film*,[4] "is indeed that the special attributes of the medium employed should be clearly and cleanly laid bare." And he adds: "A simile can be found to express our meaning. The task of the graphic artist might be compared with a Chinese puzzle in which ten pieces of various shapes have to be fitted together to make a square. The satisfaction felt by one who has solved such a problem, and by those who behold the result, is not so much the pleasure given by the sight of a square (everyone has seen plenty of squares in his lifetime), but it consists in seeing the pieces which were formerly separate now joined unexpectedly to form one simple whole."

In speaking here about the filmic quality of a film being a measure of its seriousness as a work of film art, I do not mean, of course, that the film itself must be serious, but simply that the maker of it should express himself completely and conscientiously through the film medium and should not

4 Arnheim, *Film* (Faber and Faber, London, 1933), p. 44.

avoid its challenge by expressing himself through some other medium and using the film only as a means of recording the results. In fact, it is largely because they use the film medium "seriously," in this sense, that such film comedies as René Clair's *Le Million* and Buster Keaton's *The General* survive, and will long survive, as classics.

Filmic quality becomes apparent in the opening shots of a film; purpose is usually not fully revealed until the film has come to its end. Yet before one can make any valid judgment of a film, it is essential to understand what the creator of it was trying to do and what he was trying to say. Often this may be done automatically, but at other times it is difficult; the more difficult it is, the more necessary it is to do it conscientiously and without prejudice. If a work is obscure or not readily comprehensible, like Buñuel's film *Nazarin,* or Jean Vigo's *Zéro de Conduite* or Ingmar Bergman's *The Seventh Seal,* or even if it seems fradulent or unintentionally ridiculous, as cubism or surrealism or tachisme or action-painting must seem to many people, the temptation to allow unfamiliarity and prejudice to blind one's judgment is especially strong and must be resisted at all costs. Of course, it may still be decided after every consideration that the work is in fact obscure (in the sense that the author has failed to make himself intelligible) or ridiculous or even fraudulent, but before any such judgment is made, the artist on trial deserves at least to have his case heard by an open mind. If his purpose still remains unintelligible to oneself, but appears to be understood and valued by other reasonable people, it may be better to suspend judgment than to condemn; most of us, if pressed to speak honestly, would have to confess that there are works of art, and even whole forms of art, that seem to give pleasure to others and yet are beyond our appreciation, but there is no shame in that. Nearly everyone's comprehension is limited, however much he may try to extend it, and none of us is competent to judge outside it.

Occasionally an artist may define his purpose. Carol Reed

did so at the beginning of *Odd Man Out,* in the following introductory title: "This story is told against a background of political unrest in a city of Northern Ireland. It is not concerned with the struggle between the law and an illegal organization, but only with the conflicts in the hearts of the people when they become unexpectedly involved." Some critics ignored or overlooked this statement and argued that Carol Reed, in omitting to dwell on the political issues his hero had at heart, had evaded the very core of his subject, with the result that the hero, instead of appearing as a political idealist, was indistinguishable from a common gangster. For the declared purpose of the film, however, it is irrelevant whether we look on its central figure, Johnny McQueen, as idealist or gangster; either way, he is a mortally wounded man fleeing from the law, and what Carol Reed is more concerned with are the reactions of other people, ordinary people, who are suddenly and unexpectedly confronted with his plight. The film, in other words, is concerned with something deeper and more fundamental in human experience than anything that happened in Ireland at a particular moment in its history; it is concerned with human charity, and Johnny McQueen, at the climax of his struggle against his growing physical weakness, at the point where we finally recognize there is no hope for him, staggers to his feet to recite that most familiar text on charity, the thirteenth chapter of St. Paul's Epistle to the Corinthians. One may feel that the director has realized his purpose well or ill, but that criticism is misguided that ignores a purpose so clearly defined and tries instead to argue that the film should have concerned itself with something quite different.

It is unusual for the purpose to be given in this explicit form; normally the artist leaves the work to stand on its own feet, and purpose then becomes a matter of interpretation, as to which genuine differences of opinion may arise. The scene from *Brief Encounter,* for example, described on page 153, has been commented on by Dr. Roger Manvell as follows:

In the final train image when Celia Johnson, as the married woman who has just parted for the last time from her lover, rushes out to throw herself beneath the familiar express train, the rush of sound and the staccato flashing of the window lights on her agonized face become a terrifying reminder that she is too old to accept this final surrender to the headlong and insane journey of passionate romance.[5]

Dr. Manvell sees this scene, which is the climax of the film, as a moment of defeat, with Laura succumbing to the loss of her youth. For me, however, this moment when Laura confronts the full anguish of her loss and conquers it is a moment of victory. I do not see Laura forging her love affair because she is too old, but voluntarily renouncing it for a greater good; what impels her to rush toward the oncoming train is the sudden realization of the price she must pay.

There is no question here of the one view being more correct than the other. The only point I am concerned to make is that where purpose is a matter of interpretation, such differences of opinion are bound to arise. This example from *Brief Encounter* is of interest for the further reason that it illustrates the close mutual relationship, the two-way traffic as it were, between such general conceptions as that of purpose on the one hand, and single scenes or single shots on the other. One deduces the purpose, it is true from the total effect of the details, but the conception of the purpose thus formed also conditions the precise significance that one reads into the detail. Dr. Manvell and myself see the same images on the screen, but for each of us a particular shot, a particular camera setup, has a slightly different quality, and this difference has nothing at all to do with technique, but lies in the fact that we interpret the intention and purpose of the film in two different ways.

The problem of identifying purpose is somewhat complicated by the fact that an artist is usually preoccupied not

5 *Film*, revised edition, (Penguin Books, London, 1946), p. 65.

with one single purpose, but with a group of related purposes operating at various levels and of differing importance. It would not be untrue to say, for example, that one of the purposes that led Robert Flaherty to embark on the making of *Louisiana Story* was to earn money, since even an artist has to make a living; obviously, however, this has nothing to do with that special quality of *Louisiana Story* that leads many others besides myself to regard it as Flaherty's finest film.[6] We have to dig deeper. His money on this occasion came presumably from his sponsors, the Standard Oil Company, who had commissioned him to make a propaganda film that would promote public goodwill toward their undertakings. This was his ostensible purpose in making this particular film rather than any other, and up to a point it conditioned his subject: prospecting for oil and opening up a new well in the Louisiana swamps. But we have still not gone far enough. In his treatment of this subject, Flaherty was prompted by a deeper, more inward purpose, the true artistic purpose (and therefore the one that as critics we must most closely consider), which had nothing to do with earning money or with oil companies, but which was the characteristic thing he as an artist was drawn to say, not only in this film, but in many of his others. It was this deeper impulse that led him to view his subject through the eyes of a small boy, living a life as native to the swampland as that of the animals which inhabited it and startled into surprise and wonder by the unfamiliar but friendly oil men and their strange, huge, awe-inspiring machinery. It is the boy who interests Flaherty even more than the oil wells, and as we watch him we realize he is no stranger to us; we remember the little Eskimo boy Allee, who appears briefly in *Nanook of the North*, and young

---

[6] Yet it is curious how even film-makers themselves will refer to this purpose, especially when seeking to justify their work while disavowing any claim to artistic pretensions. Harry Watt, in a television broadcast (in the BBC program from London, August 8th, 1959), said that what brought him into film-making was that "I was hungry. I wanted to eat. I'm quite proud of this because one hears an awful lot of chi-chi at times about the creative urge, desire to express oneself and so on."

Michael Dirrane casting his fishing line from the clifftop in *Man of Aran,* and the youth approaching his initiation ceremonies in *Moana,* and Sabu, the hero of *Elephant Boy,* and we realize that the deeply personal thing Flaherty was concerned to express, not in *Louisiana Story* only, but throughout much of his work, was a childlike sense of mingled awe and familiarity before the wonders of nature, the mysterious experience of growing up in the world, which he found it most appropriate to convey through the eyes of a boy.

In trying to determine of any particular work the artist's innermost purpose (a purpose of which he himself may be unaware, or at least unable to put into intellectual terms), our most immediate evidence is, of course, the work itself, but it may also be necessary to compare it with his other works (as we have done here with *Louisiana Story*) or to delve into the facts of his personal life or, where time has elapsed, to familiarize ourselves with the circumstances of the period in which the work was created. Much argument has been wasted on the proposition that a work of art must always stand on its own feet and be judged by itself alone. This is based on a fallacy. The artist communicates with his audience by reference to a common background of experience and culture; when someone says he is judging a work solely on its merits, he means only that, wisely or unwisely, he is taking this common background of reference for granted. Where the critic is separated from the artist by a break in time or by any other difference of cultural or social experience, he has to try to rediscover the artist's references by a kind of intellectual detective work, which in its most professional form become a function of scholarship.

The cinema is not yet old enough, or respected enough, to have created its scholars, but they will inevitably appear as the body of significant films grows and as the older ones recede further into the past. Meanwhile, a simple illustration of how critics can be misled when they are unfamiliar with the soil from which a film springs and when they endeavor to consider it in isolation is provided by the unmerited praise given in Britain, for example, to a French or Italian or American film for the uncompromisingly realistic picture it gives of the life in its country, whereas in that same country the film is condemned for its artificiality: conversely, a British film of British life, which we in Britain recognize to be false, sometimes receives surprising praise abroad as a vivid social document. In both cases those who are not of the country and who do not have the feeling of its life in their bones mistake the appearance of realism for true realism, conventions and clichés for firsthand observation.

With the nature and purpose of the film clear in our minds, we are in a position to express, to ourselves or to others, our impression of its merits or defects by an analysis of its parts. One of the most elementary demands we are entitled to make of a film is that it should hold our attention, which means in turn that its purpose should be of value and interest, and that the film should be well constructed. The action-theme (if it is a fiction film), or the thesis or argument (if it is non-fiction), should be appropriate to the purpose. The action or exposition should be developed sufficiently but economically, without either omissions or redundancies. The opening should immediately capture our attention, the development should move logically to its climax, and the ending should be neither too abrupt nor too prolonged. The delineation of the characters should be sufficient for its end, which is to give conviction to that interlocking of motives and reactions that constitutes the plot. And the behavior, thoughts and feelings of the characters should be appropriately and vividly presented in the language of the film medium.

All these, however, are considerations of means, of mechanics and everything that we say about them must be directed toward a final assessment of the value of the film as a whole, which is at one and the same time an assessment of the maker's purpose and of the skill and success with which he has achieved it. Both factors are essential in the finale valuation, and indeed it may seem one of the injustices of criticism that a critic's judgment of a high purpose imperfectly realized is usually harsher than that of a light and frivolous purpose skillfully attained. It is the artist's aim that conditions the standards by which he is judged, not his success in achieving it.

Underlying this chapter, and indeed the whole of this book, is an assumption that some films out of the many hundreds made each year have the quality of works of art. Owing to the economic conditions under which films are made, it is usually necessary for film-makers to serve other ends: to make films ostensibly for entertainment or for propaganda. In order to criticize them as works of art, however, it is necessary to delve below their overt, proclaimed purpose or purposes and find that hidden one that the film-maker was pursuing, consciously or unconsciously, and which gives the film that rare quality that enables us to distinguish it from other entertainment films or other propaganda films. Are we right, however, to suppose that such a purpose exists and to seek for it? To put the question otherwise, one may set out deliberately to amuse and entertain people, or one may set out to persuade them to think or act in certain ways (which is the function of propaganda), but is there in addition such an activity as the creation of art, which can be purposefully pursued as an end in itself, or is this simply an illusion? Is art instead no more than entertainment or propaganda achieved with unusual distinction and skill? Or if it is truly an end in itself, what is this end, which is not simply to entertain and not simply to persuade? If art, in short, is not an accidental by-product, what is its nature and function? What, fundamentally, is the artist in the film or any other medium trying to achieve? These are questions we can no longer evade.

11 · To Delight or to Instruct?

*And therefore it is necessary for a society in which
works of art arise and are supported, to find out
whether all that professes to be art is really art;
whether (as is presupposed in our society) all that
which is art is good; and whether it is important and
worth those sacrifices which it necessitates.*
LEO TOLSTOY

Many people, eminent artists and critics among them, believe that the purpose of art is simply to give pleasure.
Others, equally expert and eminent, cannot reconcile this
view with either their conscience or their experience and
maintain that all art must by definition conduce toward
raising the moral tone of the persons receptive to it, and
thus of society in general. The Roman poet Horace, in his
Ars Poetica, tried to reconcile these two points of view;
"Omne tulit punctum qui miscuit utile dulci" ("He will win
universal applause who blends what is improving with what
is pleasing, and both delight and instruct the listener").

Although this urbane compromise is often quoted, it does
not in practice cut much ice. The division between those
who see art as a source of personal delight and those who
see it as an instrument of moral good continues to run persistently and deeply through all criticism. It has been further confused in recent times by the unprecedented importance given in our society to entertainment, which is also
designed to give pleasure, although not the same kind of
pleasure, it is assumed, as art, and which may also exercise
a good or bad influence on moral standards.

No kind of critic is so much beset by these divisions and
confusions as the film critic. When professional film critics
assume the same function as critics of painting, music, lit-

erature and drama and find fault on artistic grounds with
the films presented to them, film producers are apt to protest that their purpose is being misjudged, that they had
no aim other than to entertain and that it is as entertainment alone that their work should be judged, not as art or
as a serious criticism of life.

The critics themselves are divided on the same issue.
Some are willing to accept the role of a reporter on public
entertainment whose chief aim is to make his reports easily
readable, entertaining in their own right, in fact. Others
argue that films are so important in propagating ideas and
influencing thought and conduct whether their makers in-
tend them to do so or not, that no critic can afford to be
neutral and detached in reviewing them. Some of those who
take this view describe their attitude, in the current jargon,
as one of "commitment"; those who take the opposite view,
who reject Horace's *utile* and put their faith in *dulce*, are
"uncommitted."

Professional film critics seldom (unfortunately) make a
public declaration of their principles, but two such declarations have appeared over the last twenty-five years, and
they have a special interest because they present, in dia-
metrical opposition, the two conceptions of the critic's function just described. The first of these articles, by Mr. Alistair Cooke, was called "A Critic's Testament." [1] Mr. Cooke
had just been appointed film critic of the British Broadcast-
ting Corporation, and the article was a publication of his
first broadcast. He began as follows:

> I declare that I am a critic trying to interest a lot of peo-
> ple into seeing, a few ambitious people into making, in-
> teresting films. . . . As a critic I am without politics and
> without class. I swear I am committed to no country, no
> director, no star, no theme, no style. For a film hero I am
> prepared to take John Barrymore, George Robey, a bat-

[1] *The Listener*, October 17, 1934; republished in *Sight and Sound* (British Film
Institute, London), January-March 1953, p. 112.

tleship, Mickey Mouse or an Italian straw hat. I hope that everyone who wants to make a lot of money in films will make it, that every girl who aches to become a star overnight will become one. I hope a little more fervently that any man or woman who can make an interesting film will somehow, somewhere, be allowed to make it. My malice extends only to those who have a dull talent and continue to exploit it. . . .

Mr. Cooke then referred to war films and the arguments for and against war as an instrument for settling international quarrels. He continued:

And yet, however much I want in private to rage or protest or moralize, these actions have nothing to do with criticism. As a moralist I could be shocked. As an educationist I might lament that the subject was not elevating. . . . But I am not a moralist, an educator. . . . I am merely a critic and I have to try and decide whether Miss Harlow's smiles and pouts were performed expertly enough to entice Mr. Gable away, and whether in deserting his Texas farm for Miss Harlow he was being wicked, obvious, tactful, or just plain cynical. So if a film comes from Elstree and is full of propaganda for, let's say, social slavery, it is not for me to say that such propaganda is shocking. It is simply my job to try and describe how tellingly the propaganda has been done. . . . I have to say if the story, the direction, the acting, are likely to move you to believe for the time being in the propaganda. If they don't, the film is trivial. If they do, it's probably a good film.

On the critic's right of condemnation he added:

And there is perhaps only one occasion when he should heartily condemn. That is when he strongly dislikes a film, thinks he knows good reasons why, and is sure that the film is likely to set a fashion in dullness.

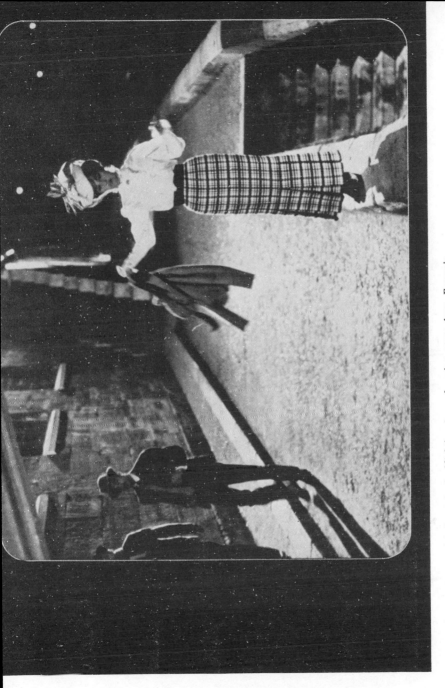

33. *Jeanne Moreau picked out by backlighting in a charming scene from François Truffaut's* JULES ET JIM *(France, 1961-2).*

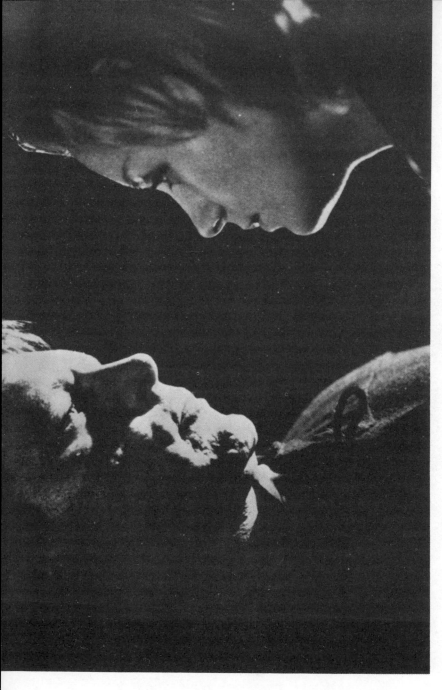

34. *An effective use of spotlight. Richard Burton and Mary Ure in Tony Richardson's* LOOK BACK IN ANGER *(Great Britain, 1959).*

This is a forthright statement of the approach to criticism that professes to avoid every kind of commitment, political, moral, social or religious, to consider only technical aspects, and in judgment to confine itself solely to whether the film is dull or interesting.

The second article, by Mr. Lindsay Anderson, was published in *Sight and Sound* under the title "Stand Up! Stand Up!" [2] It was provoked by a letter [3] from Mr. J. R. Taylor published in the same issue of *Sight and Sound*, which attacked the committed position taken up by Mr. Anderson and others in their criticism of certain films. Referring to two such films in particular, Mr. Taylor wrote:

> To me they seem bad simply because they are boring—over-long and over-leisurely in treatment for their subjects, variably acted and, most importantly, directed heavily, without imagination or individuality. The most sensational, blatantly one-sided view of things can be acceptable if handled with conviction and imagination—if it seems a true reflection of a point of view, however far that point of view may be from one's own. In this way, if we are fair, we must admit that an honest glorification of the good sides of war can be just as valid as a statement of complete disgust with the whole thing. . . . In the same way *Potemkin, The Triumph of the Will* [3] and *Mr. Smith Goes to Washington* all have a right to exist and a right to non-partisan aesthetic judgment as works of cinema.

> By all means let critics prefer committed, humanist films on contemporary subjects, but such moral judgments should be presented as what they are—personal, subjective tastes, not the be-all and end-all of criticism.

This is, in effect, a restatement of Mr. Cooke's thesis; to it Mr. Taylor added the following comment on "committed" criticism:

2 *Sight and Sound*, Autumn, 1956, p. 63.
3 *Ibid*, p. 110.
4 Miss Leni Riefenstahl's film of the Nuremberg Rally of the Nazi Party in 1936.

It lays, the less committed critic might think, far too much stress on the subject-matter of the film and far too little on the treatment. . . . The trouble with a demand for "commitment" in subject-matter is that it demands also the rejection of much that to the "irresponsible" aesthetic makes the cinema worthwhile.

To this letter Mr. Lindsay Anderson replied at length. He opened with the statement that "the essence of the matter is in the importance we attach to our principles, and the extent to which we think they are relevant to our enjoyment of art." His development of this idea led him into a wide survey, condemning the disease of a society in which the acceptance of liberal ideas had become so widely diffused that their defense had come to seem tedious and unfashionable; but we have only space and occasion here for its reference to film criticism. To begin with, Mr. Anderson, like Mr. Taylor, makes it clear that he has no doubt of the status of the cinema as an important art form; it is the only common ground between them:

It is a matter of fact, not of opinion, that the cinema is an art. This does not call for theoretical discussion—unless, of course, you enjoy that kind of intellectual exercise. If it is simply the truth that we are after, the question has already been answered, empirically. If *L'Atalante, Strike, Rashomon* and *Louisiana Story* are not works of art, then there is no way of describing them.

But he adds:

The importance of the cinema as a cultural and propagandist force is a matter of fact also. Everyone who has seen more than half-a-dozen films with his eyes open knows that if the cinema does not create the significant social movements of our time, it intimately reflects them. And that it provides a reflection just as intimate—and just as significant—of social stagnation.

He refers back to Mr. Cooke's *Critic's Testament* of twenty-five years earlier and says:

> It is fascinating to find Mr. Cooke, in 1935, expressing both the essential attitude and the characteristic tone of a number of critics today. There is the claim to a liberal standpoint, "without politics and without class," that tolerantly estimates every work on its own merits. Immediately, however, the liberalism is negated by a sort of facetious self-parody: "I hope that everyone who wants to make a lot of money in films will make it. . . ." Taken seriously, this would imply abandonment of any standards at all. But, of course, its purpose is exactly to ensure that the writer is not taken seriously; to prove that he does not take himself too seriously; to prove that he does not take himself too seriously either. Scorn of "highbrow nonsense about art and culture" is only round the corner from here, and so the pursuit of "fun." It is the "dull" talent that the critic really disapproves of: he wants to be entertained.

> . . . the denial of the critic's moral responsibility is specific: but only at the cost of sacrificing his dignity. "I am *merely* a critic." And facetiousness lends its defensive air once more with the joke about Miss Harlow's smiles and pouts. The instance of a propagandist film for "social slavery" from Elstree is similarly dishonest; the case of an anti-Semitic film from Nazi Germany would have been more awkward.

This last point brings him to Mr. Taylor:

> Just as Mr. Cooke uses an example which he knows his audience will think absurd, Mr. Taylor in his letter demands fair treatment for a film "glorifying the good side of war." (It is the film that glorifies the bad side of war that presents him with a challenge.) It is true that Mr. Taylor presents the slightly different case of the critic who has a further reason for rejecting moral issues as irrelevant—in favor of what he calls a "non-partisan

aesthetic judgment." In other words, he believes that a critic's function must be restricted to an examination of the aesthetic form of the film under discussion.

I hope I will be pardoned if I say that I find this distinction between form and content somewhat naïf. It is the essence of poetry (in any medium) that the thing said cannot be distinguished from the way of saying it. Perhaps we see here the pernicious influence of a school of "Film Appreciation" which analyses every film according to certain textbook conceptions of technique, and which is as insensitive to meaning as it is to subtleties of individual style. . . .

Effect, then, is more important than meaning. From this position it is only a step to a conception of art that actually rejects significance.

And, finally, two further quotations from the conclusion of his article:

My whole point is that criticism (film criticism included) cannot exist in a vacuum; and that writers who insist that their functions are so restricted are merely indulging in a voluntary self-emasculation. "I am not a moralist . . ." insisted Mr. Cooke, "I am merely a critic." Why should anyone be content to be a *mere* critic? A critic has his special gift, but is he any less a man than the rest of us? The moral faculty and the intellectual faculty are essential instruments to him. They are certainly no less important than the ability to write vivid and evocative reportage.

Then, after a further brief reference to the political and humanist implications of his argument, he ends as follows:

The cinema is not apart from all this; nor is it something to be denigrated or patronized. It is a vital and significant medium, and all of us who concern ourselves with it take on an equivalent responsibility. And in so far as film criticism is written here and now, and deals with an art intimately related to the society in which we live, it cannot escape its wider commitments. Essentially, in fact, there is no such thing as uncommitted criticism, any more than there is such a thing as significant art. It is merely a question of the openness with which our commitments are stated. I do not believe that we should keep quiet about them.

I have quoted from these statements at some length because they represent a dichotomy that runs through much of the critical thinking and writing of the present time, and yet which is seldom made so explicit. Unless one is prepared to accept the view that art has nothing at all to do with morality, it seems difficult to deny Mr. Anderson the strength of his position. Yet one knows very well what Mr. Taylor has tried to say: namely, that there are certain works of art that profoundly move us for reasons that have nothing to do with their expression of any particular moral or political attitude—*King Lear*, for example, the Beethoven string quarters, Michelangelo's painting on the ceiling of the Sistine Chapel or Milton's *Samson Agonistes*—and that, contrariwise, there are many worthy works inspired by political or moral convictions, most sincerely held, that are artistically feeble and therefore die after their content has ceased to be topical. This points forcibly to the conclusion that the distinguishing quality of a work of art must lie in something other than any practical moral or political ends it may have been intended to serve and that if we are to recognize art in the cinema it is this quality we must look for.

What has gone wrong is that although both sides use the word "art" (it is their only common ground, as we have noted), they use it to mean different things; they are simply at cross-purposes. Although Mr. Anderson declares emphatically that "it is matter of fact, not opinion, that the cinema is an art," and although he later says that "it is the essence of poetry (in any medium) that the thing said cannot be distinguished from the way of saying it," it is quite clear that the real stimulus to his argument is his other more lively and perhaps less academic conviction that "the importance of the cinema as a cultural and propagandist force is a matter of fact also." It is by keeping resolutely to this idea that his argument gains its force.

Mr. Taylor is talking about something else, but because he fails to define it, and indeed shows no clear realization that it is different, he not only fails to meet Mr. Anderson's case, but finds his logic leading him to such untenable positions as the equating of moral judgments with "personal subjective tastes." To unravel this tangle it is important to define what Mr. Taylor has tried to defend. What, in fact, do we mean by art, as applied to something that survives the social and political theories of the time in which it was created?

Since Tolstoy wrote that provocative and exciting mixture of common sense and wrongheadedness that he published under the title *What Is Art?* there have been countless attempts to answer the same question. The most illuminating one known to me is Professor Collingwood's *Principles of Art*.[5] Professor Collingwood's concern is to establish a theory of art, and his starting point is a recognition of what we have just observed—that our discussions about art are confused by applying the word to numerous but quite distinct activities, and talking about them all indiscriminately as though they were a single activity. His first concern, therefore, is to separate art proper from art falsely so-called. He distinguishes two main kinds of art falsely so-called; namely, amusement and what he calls "art as magic."

Amusement, or entertainment, is readily recognizable. In the form of fiction, at least, it is the use of representation to create make-believe situations that are designed to arouse

5 *The Principles of Art* by R. G. Collingwood (Oxford University Press, London, 1938).

emotion for its own sake and for the mere pleasure of having it aroused. It is not intended that the emotion shall be carried forward into the practical affairs of life. The emotion is both aroused (titillated is perhaps a better description) and satisfied within a self-contained framework.

A work of art, especially of representative art, may be composed, however, in order to arouse emotion not for its own sake, and not for its immediate satisfaction, but with the intention that it shall be carried forward into the affairs of practical life. The most clearly defined films of this kind are propaganda films and films calculated to win our support and sympathy for particular moral, social, political or religious beliefs and points of view. It is to this function of art so-called that Collingwood applies the term "art as magic," with the wish, as he says, "to rescue the word magic from . . . a meaningless term of abuse, and use it as a term with a definite meaning." [6] "The primary function of all magical arts," he says, "is to generate in the agent or agents certain emotions that are considered necessary or useful for the work of living; their secondary function is to generate in others, friends or enemies of the agents, emotions useful or detrimental to the lives of these others." [7] And again: "The function of magic is to develop and conserve morale; or to damage it." [8] Magic is associated with varous forms of representation—cave drawings, waxen images, and imitative dances, often with the dancers dressed up to represent animals, spirits and the like. Many of our arts have their primitive origins in these magical devices, and Collingwood notes that "the similarities between magic and art are strong and intimate. Magical practices invariably contain . . . as central elements, artistic activities like dances, songs, drawing or modelling." [9] He also stresses that magic in this sense, far from being outworn, primitive belief, is alive and potent in our own society, in folk art, in religious art,

6 *Ibid.*, p. 57.
7 *The Principles of Art*, p. 66.
8 *Ibid.*, p. 67.
9 *Ibid.*, p. 65.

in what he calls "the low-brow arts of the upper classes." [10] (church sermons, hymns, the instrumental music of the military band, etc.), in patriotic art (patriotic poems, school songs, statues of soldiers and statesmen), in sport and in our social ceremonies. He therefore suggests that "magic" is a suitable word, brief, accurate, and all-embracing, to describe all art so-called whose purpose is to influence us in some way in attitude, thought or action in our daily lives. When I use it here it will be in the same sense.

We have distinguished one form of art so-called, which is amusement, and another called magic. What, then, is art proper? I can only briefly present Collingwood's answer to this question, without the complex reasoning with which he supports it. First, he suggests that whereas both amusement art and art as magic are designed to arouse emotion, art proper is not intended to arouse it but to express it. To illustrate the difference by a simple example: I may deliberately provoke someone else to feel anger, and may indeed do so without feeling angry myself; on the other hand, I may feel angry myself, and express my anger to someone else, who will then understand how I feel, but will not necessarily share my anger, or feel any in himself. An artist expresses himself, and in doing so he is not addressing any particular audience; he addresses primarily himself, and only secondarily anyone who can understand.

Secondly, although art is commonly spoken of and described as though it were a craft, art proper is not a craft. A craft, Collingwood points out, is defined by several characteristics. First, there is a distinction between planning and execution (the carpenter must know exactly what size and shape his table is to be before he can begin to make it); there is a distinction between raw material and the finished product (the planks of wood and the table that is made out of them), and this distinction is also a distinction between matter and form (for one can distinguish in a table the matter, the wood, out of which it is made, and the form

[10] *Ibid.*, p. 72.

given to that matter, which is the form of a table, not the form, say, of a chair). Art proper, however, has none of the characteristics of a craft. In the making of a poem there is no distinction between means and end; the poet composes in his head, his creation is a work of the imagination. Neither is there a distinction between planning and execution; the poet often has no idea what form his poem will take until he has composed it. Similarly, a painter paints not simply what he sees, but *in order to see*; he put a great deal more into his experience of the subject than a man who merely looks at it, and the spectator who enjoys the picture shares the richer and more highly organized experience of a person who has looked at it and painted it together. There is no distinction between raw material and product; words are not the raw material of a poem, because the poet does not take certain words, as a carpenter cuts off pieces of wood, and then shuffles them in a certain order until he gets a poem. Finally, there is no distinction between form and matter because, to quote again the words of Mr. Lindsay Anderson, "it is the essence of poetry that the thing said cannot be distinguished from the way of saying it."

On the other hand, amusement art and art as magic, considered per se, in Collingwood's view are indeed forms of craft, because they represent the use of means to achieve an end that is foreseen and planned in advance. The means is representation, the depicting of people and places and objects as they appear to us all in common ("Representation, we have seen, is always a means to an end. The end is the re-evocation of certain emotions. According as these are evoked for their practical value or for their own sake, it is called magic or amusement." [11]) Skill in representation, which is commonly mistaken for art, is in fact a form of craft. Collingwood here quotes from Van Gogh:

> Tell Serret that I would be dismayed if my figures were good, tell him that I do not want them to be academically

11 *Op. cit.*, p. 57.

correct, tell him that I mean that if one were to take a photograph of a man digging, he would certainly not be digging. Tell him that I find the figures of Michelangelo admirable, although the legs are decidedly too long, the hips and thighs too large . . . true painters . . . do not paint things as they are . . . but as they . . . feel them.[12]

He might with even more force have quoted William Blake:

No man of sense ever supposes that copying from Nature is the Art of Painting; if Art is no more than this, it is no better than any other Manual Labour—anybody may do it, and the fool will often do it best because it is a work of no mind.

Professor Collingwood's definition of art proper springs from the two points that have thus been established: first, that it is a form of expression, a form of language; and secondly, that it is a creation of the imagination. Experience is what we apprehend through our senses, what comes to us through our feelings; but feelings, with the emotional charges attached to them, make their impression upon us at a level below that of consciousness. It is not until we direct our attention to a given area of feeling or impression that we become conscious of it, and in this act of consciousness what was fleeting sense impression becomes idea and as such is held lastingly in the imagination, where it becomes the material of empirical thought, or thought in its primary form.[13] In thus becoming aware of a sensum (or sense impression) we also become aware of ourselves apprehending it (which is the essence of consciousness). At the same time the sensum, which at the level of unconscious feeling or mere sentience had its own form of expression in a reaction we could not control, in emerging into consciousness as idea achieves bodily expression in a form dominated and controlled by consciousness—in other words, in lan-

---

12 Vincent van Gogh, *Letters*, ed. Philippart, 1937, p. 128. I have translated from the original French quoted by Professor Collingwood.

13 Empirical thought in turn becomes the material of intellectual thought, which Collingwood terms thought in its secondary form.

guage—and this act of expression has its own emotional charge (the aesthetic emotion).

In our ordinary, everyday communication with each other the language we normally use is secondhand (this is not Professor Collingwood's word but I take it to be his meaning). As a means of expressing feeling it has acquired more or less the form of *cliché*, and expresses not our actual feeling, but a vague generalization to which it approximates; as a means of expressing thought, it has acquired that element of symbolism (commonly agreed upon meaning) that attaches to intellectual language. If at a given moment I feel angry, this feeling of anger, by its causes and circumstances and by the way I react to them at that moment, has a special quality that makes it not quite like any anger I have felt at any other time; but if I simply say "I feel angry," I give no sense of this special quality but only a vague generalization (a description, not an expression) that embraces all the states of anger I might have felt in the past, or might feel in the future, or which, for that matter, anyone else might feel also.

Art is not secondhand language but language, as it were, at its birth. It is not cliché, not generalization; on the contrary, it particularizes and individualizes. An artist is one who by a direction of his attention becomes aware of a certain complex, a galaxy of feelings and impressions, converts them by his imagination into idea, and in so doing finds expression for them. Insofar as he is successful, he creates art, and what he creates will be an expression of that unique, individual experience that gave rise to it.

Art does not have its origin at the level of mere sensation and feeling nor, to go to the other extreme, does it have its origin in the artist's intellect, which is concerned with concepts. It originates in his nature as a thinking being, it is true, but at the level at which feeling emerges into consciousness, the level at which we dominate and control feeling by becoming aware of it as idea through the activity of the imagination.

Furthermore, each emotion has its appropriate form of

expression, and the same experience cannot be expressed in different ways. What a composer expresses in music can only be expressed in music; what a painter expresses in paint on his canvas can only be expressed in paint; and what a film-maker (one may add) expresses in film, if it is art, can only be expressed in film. Each is expressing a different kind of experience. In Professor Collingwood's words:

> If there is no such thing as an unexpressed feeling, there is no way of expressing the same feeling in two different media. . . . The emotions which we express in music can never be expressed in speech, and vice versa. Music is one order of languages and speech is another; each expresses what it does express with absolute clarity and precision; but what they express is two different types of emotion, each proper to itself.

> . . . if a person acquires the ability to express one kind of emotion and not another, the result will be that he knows the one kind to be in him, but not the other.[14]

It is, of course, quite impossible to do justice in a few paragraphs to a theory that Professor Collingwood required over 300 pages to elaborate, and the two great dangers of such intense compression are, first, that one may make the argument seem incomprehensible, and secondly, that one may even positively distort it; perhaps I have not succeeded in avoiding either. The process of artistic creation is a complicated and mysterious one and many theories of art have foundered by trying to oversimplify it. It cannot be described in simple terms. Those who are interested will no doubt read Professor Collingwood's book. To me it is clear that his theory, at least in its main outlines, is remarkably near the truth.

To begin with, it explains much that one is aware of in the appreciation of art, and it is borne out by what artists

14 *Op. cit.*, p. 245.

themselves are able to tell us of their creative activity. Henry James, for example, twenty-seven years after the first publication of his novel *The Portrait of a Lady*, wrote a preface to it for a collected edition of his works in which he sought to recall how the idea of the novel first came to him. "Trying to recover here, for recognition, the germ of my idea," he wrote, "I see that it must have consisted . . . in the sense of a single character, the character and aspect of a particular engaging young woman . . . an acquisition I had made, moreover, after a fashion not here to be retraced. Enough that I was, as seemed to me, *in complete possession of it.*" [15] But in order that this character should be put also in the possession of the reader, Henry James had to place it in a setting, construct a story, with all its character relationships and events, and he likened this laborious work to the erection of a building: ". . . this single small corner-stone, the conception of a certain young woman affronting her destiny, had begun with being all my outfit for the large building of *The Portrait of a Lady*. It came to be a square and spacious house—or at least it has seemed so to me in this going over it again; but, such as it is, it had to be put up round my young woman while she stood there in perfect isolation . . . I should clearly have to pile brick upon brick for the creation of an interest." And then he poses to himself and to us the question: If this elaborate setting was necessary to make the central character a real and vivid person to the reader, how was it that the author was himself already "in complete possession" of the character, and how had she become so real and vivid to him, before a single brick of the setting had been laid?

If the apparition was still all to be placed, how came it to be vivid?—since we puzzle such questions out, mostly, just by the business of placing them. One could answer such a question beautifully, doubtless, if one could do so subtle, if not so monstrous a thing as to write the history of the *growth of one's imagination*. One would describe then what, at a given time, had extraordinarily happened to it, and one would so, for instance, be in a position to tell, with an approach to clearness, how, under favour of occasion, it had been able to take over (*take over straight from life*) such and such a constituted animated figure or form. The figure has to that extent, as you see, *been placed—placed in the imagination that detains it, preserves, protects, enjoys it, conscious of its presence in the dusky, crowded, heterogeneous back-shop of the mind.* . . .

It is clear, particularly in the passages I have italicized, that Henry James here describes his own creative process in terms that fall exactly within Collingwood's theory. The germ of the work existed as impression in "the dusky back-shop" of his mind, that is to say, he had become conscious of it as idea held, "detained," in his imagination, and he then had to interpret it to himself (and to others, of course) by the labor of creation.

Secondly, the distinction Professor Collingwood makes between amusement art, art as magic (both art falsely so-called) and art proper strikes at the very root of the confusion that entangles so much current criticism and critical discussion. It is easy to confuse them not only because they superficially resemble each other, but even more because they can be found intermingled within the same work. Throughout his whole career as a playwright, Bernard Shaw's purpose was to influence public opinion on serious issues by presenting them in the guise of entertainment. Milton's purpose in writing *Paradise Lost* is explicitly stated in the invocation with which his poem opens:

> What in me is dark,
> Illumine! What is low, raise and support!
> That to the height of this great argument
> I may assert eternal Providence,
> And justify the ways of God to Men.

Today, Milton's theology and his conception of the cosmos

as an argument for justifying the ways of God to men has lost its force, but his poem is still valued as art proper, partly perhaps because (as Collingwood says of Dante) he has succeeded in "fusing thought itself into emotion; thinking in a certain way and then expressing how it feels to think in that way," and partly because the subject matter of his poem, drawing substance from Milton's experience, assumes a life of its own that is independent of the moral argument.[16] In fact, as we have had occasion to observe earlier, the value of all art as magic is restricted to the time, the mental climate and the social conditions that gave it birth, and any power it has to survive this time is due to those elements of art proper with which it may be combined.

The value of Professor Collingwood's distinctions is self-evident. One can recognize, for example, that in the two great political and cultural camps in which the world is split today, it is the United States of America that, in film production at least, is preeminently the world center of the trade in amusement ("there's no business like show business"), while the Soviet Union and its satellite countries are devoted almost exclusively to the use of films as magic, "to develop and conserve morale" within their own political system; in both camps the genuine artist often has a grim struggle to survive.[17] I have already described the object of the questions we must pose in criticism as the resolving of

[16] Shelley drew attention in *A Defence of Poetry* to the supremacy of Milton the artist over Milton the moralist. "Milton's Devil as a moral being," he observed, "is as far superior to his God, as one who perseveres in some purpose which he has conceived to be excellent in spite of adversity and torture, is to one who in the cold security of undoubted triumph inflicts . . . revenge. . . . And this bold neglect of a direct moral purpose is the most decisive proof of the supremacy of Milton's genius."

[17] Eisenstein is the classic case. When he failed to conform to official artistic dogmas in the Soviet Union, he ran into heavy criticism, and at least one of his films, *Bezhin Meadow*, was suppressed and has never been seen. When he went to America in 1930 he did not succeed in making a single film. He put several projects to Paramount (including a complete script adapted from Dreiser's *An American Tragedy*). Mr. Sam Goldwyn, after expressing his admiration for *Battleship Potemkin*, suggested Eistenstein might attempt "a similar subject on a slightly less ambitious scale, suitable as a vehicle for Ronald Colman" (a story for which I am indebted to Mr. Ivor Montagu, who was present), and finally, after shooting many thousands of feet for *Que Viva Mexico*, he was not allowed to complete it and was forced to return to his native land in the most extreme despair.

"a highly organized and complex structure into its basic elements" (p. 226), and it is clear that the disentangling of these elements of art so-called and art proper is one of the most important clarifications to be made. Failure to distinguish them is almost bound to lead to confusion.

To begin with, each of the three has a different purpose and therefore requires to be measured by different critical standards; an attempt to measure them by the same standards will result in nonsense. Bad art proper is art that fails to express what its author has tried to express; but bad amusement is simply amusement that fails to amuse. Amusement and art as magic are not to be criticized on aesthetic grounds as being bad or imperfect or under-developed forms of art proper; they do not fail to express, because they make no attempt to express. Therefore, if art is identified either with amusement or magic, critcism goes astray.

The case of art as magic presents a special problem, because this will naturally be judged according to the sympathy one has for the ends it seeks to serve; where these ends evoke a sympathetic response from all the members of a given society, they are likely to agree in accepting that which provokes the response as being "good" or "beautiful" or otherwise praiseworthy, and "it will be thought the mark of a good critic to insist that the common magic of the society is good art." [18] This, however, is to substitute a false critical objectivity for a true one. For example, within a Communist society, a work that effectively promotes sympathy for Communist ideas will evoke admiration; but the work of a genuine artist in such a society, whose efforts to be true to his own experience do not appear to conform to these ideas (Boris Pasternak, for example, in writing *Dr. Zhivago*), is likely by the same token to be condemned.

Another confusion of thought that may arise from a failure to distinguish art proper from art so called is to imagine that amusement is simply art at a low level, or at

[18] R. G. Collingwood, *op. cit.*, p. 93.

least something that contains within itself the germs of art, and that by pushing its development to a higher level of competence, one can eventually arrive at art proper. Or, alternatively, one may turn from amusement art and concentrate on art as magic—art with a serious purpose valuable for practical life—and suppose that by doing that with the greatest skill and to the top of one's bent, one may develop in this way an art proper. Both these, if our theory is correct, are illusions. The various kinds of art may exist side by side in the same work, but neither amusement art nor art as magic can be developed into art proper, because they are different in kind; so far as a given emotion in a given audience at a given moment is concerned, they are mutually exclusive.

The same fallacy lies at the root of the almost universal assumption that what the vulgar enjoy is amusement, whereas that which pleases more refined tastes is art; in fact, however, it is often nothing more than amusement of a different and more sophisticated kind. Many of those who enjoyed Max Ophuls' film *La Ronde* might well scorn the simpler pleasures of *Charley's Aunt*, but this would be no justification for describing the first as a work of art and the second as a mere entertainment; they are the entertainments of two different social groups.[19]

In particular, Professor Collingwood's distinctions reveal what has gone wrong in the discussion between Mr. Lindsay Anderson and Mr. Taylor. Lindsay Anderson is concerned with the effect of the cinema on society, on the practical affairs of life. As a critic he is concerned with the effects films have and the implications they carry, whether these results come unintentionally from films made for amusement, or intentionally from films made with an ulterior motive; as film-maker, he is concerned to be associated with

19 "If the gigantic ramp by which the trade in genteel amusement passes itself off as art were once for all exposed, the critics could either come out frankly as the advertisement writers which many of them are, or stop bothering about sham art and concentrate, as some of them already do, on the real thing." (R. G. Collingwood, *op. cit.*, p. 91.)

films that deliberately promote liberal ideals, that is, with films falling under our definition of art as magic. It is true that he writes of the essence of poetry as being that the thing said cannot be distinguished from the way of saying it, which is a concept belonging to art proper, but this is no more than a contribution to the general confusion; his whole argument makes it clear that his real interest is in "the importance of the cinema as a cultural and propagandist force." With this many readers will sympathize; Collingwood certainly did:

> . . . magic is a thing which every community must have, and in a civilization that is rotten with amusement, the more magic we produce the better. If we were talking about the moral regeneration of our world, I should urge the deliberate creation of a system of magic, using as its vehicles such things as the theatre and the profession of letters, as one indispensable kind of means to that end.[20]

Mr. Anderson was certainly talking about "the moral regeneration of our world." Mr. Taylor's purpose, on the other hand, was to advance the claims of what we can now recognize as art proper, but unfortunately he failed to clarify to himself or his readers what he meant by this, with the result that both he and Mr. Anderson supposed themselves to be taking different sides on the same question, although in truth we were each arguing a different question. It was doubtless as a result of Mr. Taylor's desire somehow to get at Lindsay Anderson across the gulf that he was led into the false position of suggesting that art had nothing to do with morality. This position is untenable. The morality of art as magic is to be measured in terms of the ideas it propagates or the attitudes it is meant to induce. The moral value of art proper requires to be measured in a different way.

If any art might be supposed to have nothing to do with morals, it would be the nonrepresentational art of music. Yet Sir Donald Tovey has this to say of Beethoven:

20 R. G. Collingwood, *op. cit.*, p. 278.

Beethoven is a complete artist. If the term is rightly understood, he is one of the completest that ever lived ... he was eminently a man who held himself responsible. .... To put the matter in unfashionable terms, Beethoven's music is edifying. There is nothing inartistic in that ... Beethoven's sense of duty was to preach; and, whatever may be found in commentaries on Beethoven, there is in his own works even less of a doctrine from which revolt is possible than there is in Shakespeare's. .... His music is, in fact, a supremely masterly and hopeful criticism of life. The difficulties and dangers of demonstrating this arise mainly from the fact that music can only be descibed in terms of music.[21]

It is apparent that Sir Donald Tovey was not using the word "edifying" here in its commonly accepted sense of conducive to particular moral precepts or beliefs (as hymns in church, for example, may be said to be edifying), because he adds that "music can only be described in terms of music." We come nearer to his meaning by considering the words of J. W. N. Sullivan in trying to describe precisely the same quality in Beethoven:

His morality may perhaps be summed up as consisting of unfaltering courage in being true to his own experience. ... That note of authenticity that we find in all Beethoven's greatest music is incompatible with anything less than complete sincerity on the part of the man.[22]

Here again, Professor Collingwood's theory is illuminating. Art proper, he had told us, is the result of a man becoming conscious of a part of the total sensuous-emotional field of experience available to him and simultaneously expressing it successfully, that is to say, truthfully, in language appropriate to it. But it is possible for such a man to

<hr />

[21] *Beethoven* by Donald Francis Tovey, ed. Hubert J. Foss (Oxford University Press, London, 1944), pp. 1-2.
[22] *Beethoven: His Spiritual Development* by J. W. N. Sullivan (Cape, London, 1927).

take fright at that which his consciousness recognizes and at the idea to which it gives rise in his imagination; [23] "in the latter case, certain feelings are not ignored, they are disowned; the conscious self disclaims responsibility for them, and thus tries to escape being dominated by them without the trouble of dominating them." [24] This Collingwood terms "the corrupt consciousness," and it forms a vital part in his theory; he identifies it with that disowning of experiences that psychologists call repression, with what Spinoza called "inadequate ideas of affections," and what Plato called "the lie in the soul." It is not a pretense belonging to the region below consciousness (since consciouness is involved in it) or belonging to the region of consciousness (since a man cannot literally tell himself a lie) ; it is a malpractice of the conscious act itself, the act by which feeling is converted into conscious idea. It is a condition against which all artists must wage a constant war, and in this they may be more or less successful. Since consciousness is the very foundation of our knowledge of ourselves, and since it provides the only facts upon which intellect can build, "in so far as consciousness is corrupted, the very wells of truth are poisoned. Intellect can build nothing firm. Moral ideals are castles in the air. Political and economic systems are mere cobwebs. Even common sanity and bodily health are no longer secure."

So, in the closing words of his book, Professor Collingwood gives us the key to the morality of art proper:

> The artist must prophesy not in the sense that he tells things to come, but in the sense that he tells his audience, at the risk of their displeasure, the secrets of their own hearts. His business as an artist is to speak out, to make a clean breast. But what he has to utter is not, as the in-

---

[23] Or, I would myself add, he may shrink from the sheer labor of identifying and interpreting what his consciousness reveals to him, and because of laziness and a slipshod disregard for the truth, he substitutes something else in its place; either way, he escapes from the reality of his experience.

[24] R. G. Collingwood, *op. cit.*, p. 224.

dividualistic theory of art would have us think, his own
secrets. As spokesman of his community, the secrets he
must utter are theirs. The reason why they need him is
that no community altogether knows its own heart; and
by failing in this knowledge a community deceives itself
on the one subject concerning which ignorance means
death. For the evils which come from that ignorance the
poet as prophet suggests no remedy, because he has already given one. The remedy is the poem itself. Art is
the community's medicine for the worst disease of the
mind, the corruption of the consciousness.[25]

This approximates very closely to the terms in which
Tovey and Sullivan refer to the morality of Beethoven's
music; and to balance these observations about an artist by
reflections made by an artist himself on his own work, one
need go no further than the preface of Henry James from
which I have already quoted. Speaking of the subject of a
novel, he refers to "the one measure of the worth of a given
subject, the question about it that, rightly answered, disposes of all others—is it valid, in a word, is it genuine, is it
sincere, the result of some direct impression or perception
of life?" And he adds.

There is, I think, no more nutritive or suggestive truth in
this connection than that of the perfect dependence of
the "moral" sense of a work of art on the amount of felt
life concerned in producing it. The question comes back
thus, obviously, to the kind and the degree of the artist's
prime sensibility, which is the soil out of which his subject springs. The quality and capacity of that soil, its
ability to "grow" with due freshness and straightness
any vision of life, represents, strongly or weakly, the
projected morality. That elements is but another name
for the more or less close connection of the subject with
some mark made on the intelligence, with some sincere
experience.

25 R. G. Collingwood, *op. cit.*, p. 336.

There is nothing very new in all this: for a final testimony we may turn to Shelley, writing a hundred years earlier:

Ethical science arranges the elements which poetry has created, and propounds schemes and proposes examples of civil and domestic life: nor is it for want of admirable doctrines that men hate, and despise, and censure, and deceive, and subjugate one another.

But poetry acts in another and diviner manner. It awakens and enlarges the mind itself by rendering it the receptacle of a thousand unapprehended combinations of thought. . . . The great instrument of moral good is the imagination; and poetry administers to the effect by acting upon the cause. Poetry enlarges the circumference of the imagination. . . . Poetry strengthens the faculty which is the organ of the moral stature of man, in the same manner as exercise strengthens a limb. A poet therefore would do ill to embody his own conceptions of right and wrong, which are usually those of his place and time, in his poetical creations, which participate in neither. By this assumption of the inferior office of interpreting the effect, in which perhaps after all he might acquit himself but imperfectly, he would resign a glory in a participation in the cause.[26]

Films can indubitably be amusement; during the last fifty years they have provided the material of the biggest amusement industry the world has ever known. Equally they can be magic of an extraordinarily potent kind. But can they be art proper? The answer to this question depends on two considerations.

Amusement and art as magic, being forms of craft, can be created by teams of people working in cooperation; for either purpose the pooling of ideas in a script conference such as was described in the earlier pages of this book may

[26] *A Defence of Poetry*, 1821.

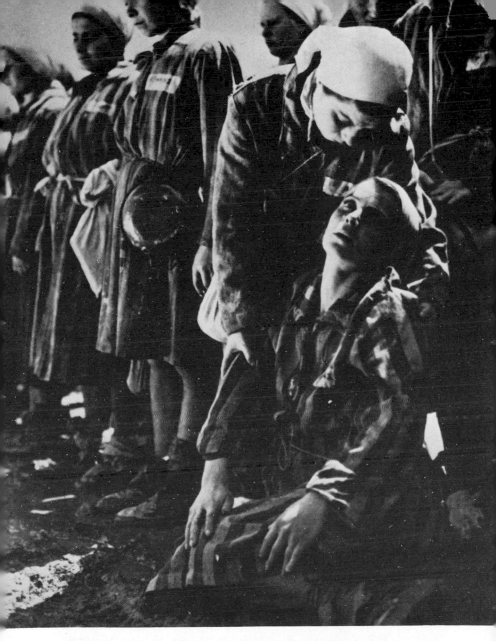

35. *The film industries of Eastern Europe have sought to fortify national morale by realistic reminders of past conflict and suffering. A concentration camp scene from Wanda Jakubowska's* THE LAST STAGE *(Poland, 1948).*

36. *Vittorio de Sica, as director, has been passionately concerned with the suffering an indifferent society can inflict on the individual.* (Above): MIRACOLO A MILANO *(Italy, 1950), in which he used fantasy to portray the plight of the homeless.* (Below): UMBERTO D. *(Italy, 1952), a deeply felt study of the problem of old age.*

well be fruitful. Art proper, however, by its very nature, can only be the expression of the experience and vision of a single man, the creative artist. The first consideration therefore is the purely practical one as to whether it is possible for individuals to win such power, authority and independence as to be able to use the complicated and expensive resources of the film medium to express their personal vision and their personal experience. The examples of Charles Chaplin (in *The Gold Rush, Modern Times, The Great Dictator* and *Monsieur Verdoux*), of Carl Dreyer (in *The Passion of Joan of Arc*), of Eisenstein (in *Battleship Potemkin, Alexander Nevsky* and *Ivan the Terrible*), of Dovjenko (in *Earth*), of Jean Vigo (in *L'Atalante*), of Buñuel (in *L'Age d'Or* and *Viridiana*), of Flaherty (in *Louisiana Story*), of Vittorio de Sica (in *Bicycle Thief* and *Umberto D.*), of Ingmar Bergman (in *The Seventh Seal* and *Wild Strawberries*) and many others show that this achievement, though rare, is possible.

Even though directors may gain the opportunity to make the films they want to make, however, no one will concede that what they make can ever be a work of art who views them on the assumption that the film as a medium is incapable of artistic use; and there is no doubt that many people, even among those who enjoy films as an entertainment, would not allow the film the same place in their consideration as music or literature or painting. Therefore the second question we have to face is whether the film medium contains within itself such resources and potentialities as to lend itself to the creation of art proper; it is one we shall consider in the final chapter.

12 · The Film as an Art

There is this difference between a story and a poem, that a story is a catalogue of detached facts, which have no other connection than time, place, circumstance, cause and effect; the other is the creation of actions according to the unchangeable forms of human nature, as existing in the mind of the Creator, which is itself the image of all other minds. The one is partial, and applies only to a definite period of time, and a certain combination of events which can never again recur; the other is universal, and contains within itself the germ of a relation to whatever motives or actions have place in the possible varieties of human nature. Time, which destroys the beauty and use of the story of particular facts, stripped of the poetry which should invest them, augments that of poetry, and for ever develops new and wonderful applications of the eternal truth which it contains.
PERCY BYSSHE SHELLEY

If in the phrase "art of the film" the word art is used to mean craft or skill (as when we talk of the art of the potter or the art of dressmaking), it cannot, on the evidence we have considered, be questioned; for it is clear that a considerable degree of skill and not one but many crafts have to be employed to make even the most indifferent film. As a craft, the film may be designed for the self-contained activity of amusement and entertainment; or it may be designed to provoke emotion and thought that are meant to be carried forward in some way into the affairs of practical life, so that it has a social influence; or it may be used to do both of these things together.

Can we go further than this, however, and say that it also has the attributes of a language which can be used, in favorable circumstances, by a single individual—the creative artist, Yeats's "solitary man"—to express his own personal experience, to become conscious indeed of that experience by expressing it as filmic idea, so that something is communicated to us, the spectators, that could not be communicated in any other way, so that we can say of it, as we may say of poetry, "that the thing said cannot be distinguished from the way of saying it"? If we cannot, then we are being deluded if we regard *Earth, La Notte, Rashomon* and *Louisiana Story* as works of art, and all film criticism that is based on the supposition that fine films can be considered in the same terms as fine drama or music or painting is simply pretentious nonsense.

There is no doubt that many people, otherwise intelligent and sensitive, who may even enjoy certain films as entertainment, are nevertheless more than a little contemptuous of it as a medium and would not seriously entertain any consideration of it as an art in the fullest sense. This is not surprising when the entertainment film industry itself treats its medium so contemptuously and not only turns out vast quantities of ephemeral rubbish, but presents it, good and bad alike, round and round in mechanical sequence so that members of the audience may enter or leave at any point, a system which would not be tolerated in the theater or concert hall. This example justifies the skeptics in an attitude that has its roots in a lack of understanding of the nature of the film medium. They regard the film as being essentially photographic, able only to record what already exists outside itself; they consider its nature to be purely mechanical and belittle the film as canned theater. While conceding that by editing it is possible to juggle with various fragments of recording and place them in certain relationships, they would argue that the creative possibilities of mere assembly are nevertheless extremely limited. The film offers no artist (they would add) the possibility of being able to create out of the void a pure work of the imagination as Cézanne did when he first stood before his naked canvas, or Michelangelo before the shapeless marble block, or Shakespeare with the blank sheet of paper in front of him. But what precisely is meant here by a "pure work of the imagination"? Does any artist in fact, create out of the void, out of nothingness?

In 1927 there appeared a book by the American scholar John Livingston Lowes, called *The Road to Xanadu: A Study in the Ways of the Imagination*.[1] It is concerned with an examination of the sources that went to the making of two of Coleridge's best-known poems, "The Rime of the Ancient Mariner" and "Kubla Khan," the first composed in the normal way, the second conceived in Coleridge's unconscious mind while he was under the influence of opium. Simply as a study of sources, it is one of the most fascinating of detective stories; but the author's interest lay not so much with the sources themselves as with the light they threw on the workings of the creative imagination.

Coleridge was a voracious reader and in all his reading was constantly on the watch for illustrations, images and phrases that might suggest ideas for his poems. He was in the habit of making notes of any such fragments that struck his fancy, and where a book contained references to other books, he would regularly obtain these also. By good fortune one of Coleridge's notebooks has been preserved in the British Museum in the form of "a small manuscript volume of ninety leaves . . . partly in pencil, partly in ink and always with most admired disorder." Aided by this notebook, Livingston Lowes was able to trace and reread many of the books Coleridge must have read between the years 1795 and 1798, "the years which lead up to and include the magnificent flowering of Coleridge's genius on which his renown as a poet rest," and the results are of quite extraordinary interest.

There is no space here to present even a summary of Livingston Lowes' long and elaborate argument, pursued through 434 pages of text and nearly as great a quantity of notes. A brief résumé of a single fragment must suffice. In Coleridge's poem the ancient mariner is describing how his ship became becalmed in tropical seas, "as idle as a painted

[1] Houghton Mifflin Co., Boston, 1927; also Constable, London.

ship upon a painted ocean"; his companions have all died of thirst, and he alone lives:

> The moving Moon went up the sky,
> And nowhere did abide;
> Softly she was going up,
> And a star or two beside—
>
> Her beams bemocked the sultry main,
> Like April hoar-frost spread;
> But where the ship's huge shadow lay,
> The charméd water burnt alway
> A still and awful red.
>
> Beyond the shadow of the ship,
> I watched the water-snakes:
> They moved in tracks of shining white,
> And when they reared, the elfish light
> Fell off in hoary flakes.
>
> Within the shadow of the ship
> I watched their rich attire:
> Blue, glossy green, and velvet black,
> They coiled and swam; and every track
> Was a flash of golden fire.

These lovely lines are simple and clear enough. Here, surely, is the creative imagination at work. But did Coleridge fashion them wholly from the void, conceive them and bring them to birth entirely within his own brain? To concentrate on the last two stanzas only, and to condense almost to the point of crudity, here is a collection of passages Coleridge certainly read at the period of his writing the poem, several of which he actually marked down in his notebook:

(a) Not only the Wake of a Ship produces this Light, but Fishes also in swimming leave behind 'em a *lumi-*

nous Track. . . . I have sometimes seen a great many Fishes *playing in the Sea,* which have made *a kind of artificial Fire in the Water,* that was very pleasant to look on. (Extract from a letter written by Father Bourzes on "Luminous Appearances in the Wakes of Ships at Sea," taken from *Letters of the Missionary Jesuits,* and quoted in *Philosophical Tansactions of the Royal Society* (Abridged), Vol. V, p. 213.)

(b) *During a calm,* on the morning of the 2nd, some parts of the sea seemed *covered with a kind of slime;* and some small sea animals were *swimming about.* The most conspicuous of which, were of the gelatinous kind, almost globular; and another sort smaller, *that had a white or shining appearance.* . . . Sometimes they . . . assum (ed) various tints of *blue* . . . which were frequently mixed with a ruby, or opaline *redness;* and glowed with a strength sufficient to illuminate the vessel and water. . . . But, with candle light, the colour was, chiefly, a beautiful, pale *green,* tinged with a *burnished gloss;* and in the dark, it had a faint appearance of *glowing fire.* They proved to be . . . probably, an animal which has a share in producing some sorts of *that luicd appearance, often observed near ships at sea, in the night.* (Captain James Cook, *Voyage to the Pacific Ocean,* II 257.)

(c) What a most beautiful creature is this fish before me, gliding to and fro, and figuring in the still clear waters, with his orient attendants and associates. The whole fish is of a pale gold (or *burnished brass*) colour . . . the scales are . . . powdered with *red,* russet, silver, *blue* and *green* specks [while at the gills is] a little spatula . . . encircled with silver, and *velvet black.* (Bartram, describing "the yellow bream or sunfish" in his *Travels,* pp. 153-4.)

(d) . . . an instance whereof he [Hawkins] sheweth in
the Queenes Nauie, in the yeere of our Lord 1590,
at the Asores many moenths becalmed, the Sea
thereby being replenished with seuerall sorts of gel-
lies and formes of Serpents, Adders, and *Snakes,
Greene,* Yellow, *Blacke, White,* and some partie-
coloured, *whereof many had life,* being a yard and a
halfe, or two yards long. *And they could hardly draw
a Bucket of Water, cleare of some corruption withall.*
(*Purchas his Pilgrimage,* 1617 folio, quoting from
the *Observations of Sir Richard Hawkins, Knight, in
his Voyage into the South Sea.*)

(e) In the Sea we saw . . . Abundance of Water-Snakes
of several Sorts and Sizes—This day we saw two
Water-Snakes—The Snake swam away . . . very fast,
keeping his Head above Water. (Captain William
Dampier, *New Voyage Round the World.*)

(f) As we sailed we saw Multitudes of Grampusses every
Day; as also Water-Snakes of divers Colours—We
saw likewise multitudes of Fish. . . . Also Water-
Snakes of divers Colours, (*The History of the Bu-
oaniers of America,* II, 1 ff.)

(g) [The dolphin] *playing in the sea* (*in mari ludens*),
moves curvingly in manifold circles and coils (in
varios se vertat *gyros et spiras*), part of it being
hidden by the waves, part of it *rearing* (*exserta*)
above the surface of the water.

In the dog-days, when the sea lies unruffled by the
winds, the sea-serpent is wont to emerge, *arched into
all sorts of coils* (*in varia spiras sinuatus*), of which
some project from the water, while the rest are hidden under it. (Leemius, *De Lapponibus Finmarchiae,*
Copenhagen, 1767; pp. 307, 332.)

(h) But now, beneath the lofty vessel's stern,

> A shoal of sportive dolphins they discern,
> Beaming from *burnished* scales refulgent rays,
> Till all the *glowing* ocean seems to blaze:
> In *curling wreaths* they wanton on the tide,
> Now bound aloft, now downward swiftly glide;
> Awhile beneath the waves their *tracks* remain.
> And burn in silver streams along the liquid plain. . . .
>
> Now to the north, from Afric's burning shore,
> A troop of porpoises their course explore;
> In curling wreaths they gambol on the tide,
> Now bound aloft, now down the billows glide:
> Their tracks awhile the *hoary* wave retain,
> That *burn* in sparkling trails along the main.
> (Falconer, *The Shipwreck,* Canto II, 11. 63-70, 213-18·)

No one who compares the words Livingston Lowes has italicized in these passages, both with each other and with the last two of the four stanzas quoted from Coleridge, can fail to perceive the links; and a glance at the last four lines in each of Falconer's stanzas even suggests one possible source for Coleridge's own verse form with its balanced repetitions. What has happened is clear; the fragments of imagery that had struck Coleridge in his reading and had been held fast by his extraordinarily tenacious memory had sunk into the depths of his unconscious mind, where they had merged into a new whole that had had no previous existence. As Livingstone Lowes himself puts it:

> Those, then, at last, are the raw materials. The result is all of them and none of them—it is a new creation. The fishes which Father Bourzes saw in tropical seas and Bartram in a little lake in Florida, and the luminous blue and green protozoa which Captain Cook observed in the Pacific, and the many-hued ribbon-like creatures that Sir Richard Hawkins marvelled at off the Azores, and Dampier's water-snakes in the South Seas, and Leemius's coiling, rearing marine serpents of the North, and Fal-

coner's gambolling porpoises and dolphins—all of them
or some of them—have leapt together like scattered dust
at the trumpet of the resurrection, and been fused by a
flash of imaginative vision into the elfin creatures of a
hoary deep that never was and that will always be. The
shaping spirit of the imagination must have materials on
which to work, and a memory steeped in travel-lore was
this time the reservoir on which it drew.[2]

That the separate elements were not consciously combined is made abundantly clear. Livingston Lowes applies
the same analysis to "Kubla Khan," which was dreamt by
Coleridge while asleep under the influence of opium, and the
surviving fragment of which he wrote down from memory
when he awoke, and the results are even more striking.
Lowes also records an experience of his own when he tried
to trace a striking observation he remembered having read
in *The Autocrat of the Breakfast Table* thirty years earlier.
He found the right place in the book, but the sentence that
confronted him there fell disappointingly short of his recollection; in turning over the pages, however, he discovered
that the missing part of what he expected to find was in another place; evidently the two halves had fused in his unconscious mind and emerged in his memory as a single
whole. He suggests that this is a common experience, and
goes on to say:

Now that, to compare small things with great, is a
process which, it would seem, goes on with peculiar intensity in a poet's mind, and which in Coleridge's case apparently went on incessantly. One after another vivid
bits from what *he* read dropped into that deep well. And
there, below the level of conscious mental processes, they
set up their obscure and powerful reactions. Up above, on
the stream of consciousness (which is all that we commonly take into account) they had floated separate and
remote; here in the well they lived a strangely intimate

2 *The Road to Xanadu*, p. 53.

and simultaneous life. I am speaking in parables, I know, for there seems to be no other way; but the thing itself, however phrased, is, I believe, in its essentials, true. Facts which sank at intervals out of conscious recollection drew together beneath the surface through almost chemical affinities of common elements, as my trivial elements from *The Autocrat* swarm together and coalesced. And there in Coleridge's unconscious mind . . . there in the dark moved the phantasms of the fishes and animalculae and serpentine forms of his vicarious voyagings, thrusting out tentacles of association, and interweaving beyond disengagement. Father Bourzes's playing fishes "made a kind of artificial Fire in the Water"; Captain Cook's protozoa "in the dark . . . had a faint appearance of glowing fire". And about the common element of fire the other trails of fish and animalculae alike converged, and blended into a *tertium quid* endowed with the qualities of both.[3]

The implication behind Livingston Lowes' argument is that it is in precisely this way that every creative artist works. Coleridge's work lends itself to analysis to a degree probably unique, simply because he drew largely upon books for his raw material and left clues to his reading that enable these books to be identified. In the case of other artists it would be far more difficult, in most cases impossible, to trace the origins from which their creations sprang, but there can be no doubt that in their case also, "the shaping spirit of the imagination must have materials upon which to work." In a memorable passage in his *Craft of Fiction*, Percy Lubbock describes the creative mind of Tolstoy the novelist, "surveying the free and formless expanse of the world of life." He continues:

And Tolstoy, with the help of some secret of his own, which is his genius, does not hesitate for an instant. His hand is plunged into the scene, he lifts out of it great fragments, right and left, ragged masses of life torn from

3 *The Road to Xanadu*, p. 58.

37. *A meticulous attention to detail, observed both realistically and sardonically, is an outstanding characteristic of Erich von Stroheim's masterpiece,* GREED *(USA, 1923). The wife was Zasu Pitts, the husband Gibson Gowland.*

38. India's entertainment film industry is large, but highly localized. Satyajit Ray, by his single-minded devotion to the film as a form of art and expression, is one of the few Indian directors to have achieved world-wide appreciation. Smaran Ghosal and Karuna Banerjee are shown here in a scene from APARAJITO (1956), the second part of Ray's trilogy of life in Bengal.

their setting; he selects. And upon these trophies he sets to work with the full force of his imagination; he detects their significance, he disengages and throws aside whatever is accidental and meaningless; he remakes them in conditions that are never known in life, conditions in which a thing is free to grow according to its own law, expressing itself unhindered; he liberates and completes. And then, upon all this new life—so like the old and yet so different, *more* like the old, as one may say, than the old had ever had the chance of being—upon all this life that is now so much more intensely living than before, Tolstoy directs the skill of his art; he distributes it in a single embracing design: he orders and disposes. . . .

Instead of a continuous, endless scene, in which the eye is caught in a thousand directions at once, with nothing to hold it to a fixed centre, the landscape that opens before the critic is whole and single; it has passed through an imagination, it has shed its irrelevance and is compact with its own meaning.[4]

And if we turn from Tolstoy to an artist of a very different kind working in another medium altogether, to Henry Moore, the sculptor of abstract forms, we find him saying: "In my sculpture I do not draw directly upon memory or observation of a particular object, but rather use whatever comes up from my general fund of knowledge of natural forms." And to this he adds: "The observation of nature is part of an artist's life, it enlarges his form knowledge, keeps him fresh and from working only by formula, and feeds inspiration."[5]

The artist nourishes his imagination by observing life (primarily, of course, in terms of his chosen medium, the sculptor being especially sensitive to solid shapes, the painter to forms and colors) ; the fragments of observation sink into his unconscious mind where they are free to form

4 Percy Lubbock, *The Craft of Fiction* (Cape, London), pp. 18-19.
5 *Henry Moore: with an Introduction by Herbert Read* (Lund, Humphries, London, 1944).

with each other relationships of a completeness and complexity that would be beyond the power of conscious brainwork alone to achieve; in the moment of inspiration the artist becomes aware of such a pattern of relationships and must then labor to externalize it in a work of art that will make it apparent to others. This is perhaps a crude description of a psychological process that is highly complicated and incompletely understood, but it appears near enough to the truth to serve our purpose.

The language of poets, Shelley observed, "is vitally metaphorical; that is, it marks the apprehended relations of things and perpetuates their apprehension." [6] Is this not precisely what the film-maker is enabled to do, within the sphere of his own medium, by means of editing? "To the film director," says Pudovkin, "each shot of the finished film subserves the same purpose as the word to the poet. . . . Editing is the basic creative force, by power of which the soulless photographs (the separate shots) are engineered into living, cinematographic form . . . editing is the creative force of filmic reality, and . . . nature provides only the raw material with which it works. That precisely is the relationship between reality and the film." [7]

And Eisenstein writes ten years later: "The basic fact was true, and remains true to this day, that the juxtaposition of two separate shots by splicing them together, resembles, not so much a simple sum of one shot plus another shot—as it does a *creation*. It resembles a creation—rather than a sum of its parts—from the circumstance that in every such juxtaposition the *result is qualitatively* distinguishable from each element viewed separately." [8]

It may be argued that the resemblance here suggested is nothing more than a superficial one, and that there can be no fundamental kinship between the dark and complex workings of the unconscious mind and the conscious and physical

6 *A Defence of Poetry.*
7 *Film Technique*, pp. xiv-xvi.
8 *The Film Sense*, p. 18.

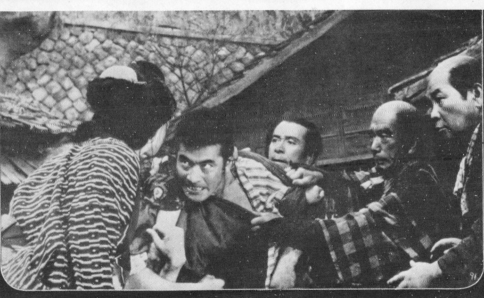

39. *Two aspects of the Japanese film.* (Above): *Beauty and tenderness, from* UGETSU MONOGATARI *(1953), directed by Kenji Mizoguchi (the actors are Mitsuko Mito and Machiko Kyo).* (Below): *Conflict and violence from* DONZOKO *(1957), directed by Akira Kurosawa, with Toshiro Mifune.*

40. *The talented Swedish director Ingmar Bergman has been give a creative freedom almost unique in the history of the cinema.* (Above): *A medieval dance of death from his allegory* THE SEVENTH SEAL *(1957).* (Below): *The late Victor Sjostrom in a scene from* WILD STRAWBERRIES.

business of joining one filmstrip to another. Writing words on paper, however, or applying paint to canvas, is equally a physical process, consciously performed. What we have to look to are the operations of the mind that precede conscious creation; and editing, as we have already seen, is ideally conceived in the mind of the scriptwriter before a foot of film has been shot. Fundamentally, it is a treatment of, an approach to, reality. When the scriptwriter gives himself up to thought, visualizing the white screen before him, he is in precisely the same position as Cézanne before his canvas; and when, with his mind's eye, he sees a succession of visual images pass, he is as much under the spell of the imagination, and as able to profit by it, as any creative artist. If this fact is not more obvious, it is only because it is obscured by the vast and elaborate machinery of production through which the original ideas have to find their way onto the final projection print. [9]

There is nothing very surprising or original in all this. There is no difference in kind, after all, between the workings of the artist's mind and the workings of our own, merely a difference in degree. We are conscious of the world around us not merely by the impressions we receive through our senses, but by the relationships we perceive to exist between them. We are all ruled by an instinct to discern and create such relationships. Percy Lubbock, in the book from which I have already quoted, remarks how in reading a

[9] The following observation of Miss Margaret Kennedy, while not perhaps strictly germane, is not wholly irrelevant:

"Most story tellers still prefer to say what they have to say in some other medium, in spite of the possibilities offered to them by the screen.

"And why is this?

"It is because the conditions of screen-story telling are, at present, so discouraging to any genuine artist. The screen composer has no place in the scheme of things, no means of carrying his vision of life and truth safely through this dogfight of technicians. Nor has he any position in the cutting-room, where the emphasis, which is the true soul of his story, will be determined.

"A picture must be a group production, just as operas, symphonies and plays are group productions. But no group production can ever be classed as a great work of art unless it has the stamp of one predominating, creative mind. This single signature, in screen art, is at present the signature of the director. And while this is the case, no screen Keats is ever likely to supply scripts."

(Margaret Kennedy, *The Mechanised Muse*, pp. 48-9.)

novel we each create our own image of it, giving particular importance to some portions and scarcely remembering others; and he goes on to say:

Creation of this kind we practice every day; we are continually piecing together our fragmentary evidence about the people around us and moulding their images in thought. It is the way in which we make our world; partially, imperfectly, very much at haphazard, but still perpetually, everybody deals with his experience like an artist. And his talent, such as it may be, for rounding and detaching his experiencing of a man or woman, so that the thing stands clear in his thought and takes the light on every side—this can never lie idle, it is exercised every hour of the day.[10]

The only difference between one individual and another lies in the complexity of the relationships they are capable of apprehending. The mind of an uncivilized man, for example, can only appreciate relationships of the simplest kind. The French traveler, Gontran de Poncins, tells this story of the Eskimos among whom he lived:

I remember that one day an Eskimo came into the Post with a troubled look on his face. Gibson and I stood before him and waited for him to speak. As no word came from him, Gibson asked him after a time what the matter was. Standing in the middle of the room, the Eskimo raised his eyes vaguely to the ceiling, pointed to his chest, and said, *"Hamane"* (here). That was where a pain was, we assumed. He remained standing, and it was clear that he had more to say, for he would wave a hand and let it fall; he would open his month, bring up the hand once more, and again his hand would drop. Finally, he began to speak, lost the thread of his thought, and wandered in a mental labyrinth. Men like ourselves have some control over our thoughts: this primitive man had none. He began

10 *The Craft of Fiction,* p. 7.

in the middle, pronouncing directly the most important word in his mind. Then he went back to the beginning of a phrase and started afresh. I remembered what a missionary had said to me about the Eskimo: "He thinks; then he stops thinking; then he thinks again. But he cannot pursue a train of thought from beginning to end." A word would come forth from this Eskimo. Then nothing. Suddenly images would flow through his mind, but so many that he could not reduce this chaos to order. Disconnected words would tumble out of his mouth as if he was afraid that unless he pronounced all of them simultaneously, they would leave him and never return. Then silence again.[11]

Civilization and culture develop with the growth of man's power to subjugate the apparent chaos of the universe to order. To a large extent, of course, he exercises his power consciously and deliberately, concentrating on the objective aspects of experience that are common to us all and drawing those deductions that are the basis of science and philosophy. The artist, on the other hand, is concerned not merely with the deductions conscious reasoning can draw from experience, but with his reaction to experience as a complete human being.

And what has all this to do with the film? It has everything to do with it if, when we talk of the art of the film, we mean anything at all and are not merely deluding ourselves with a high-sounding phrase. To begin with, it disposes of the argument that the film cannot be an art on the grounds that all one can do in it is to arrange fragments of moving image and fragments of sound in a certain order and thus create certain relationships; for it is precisely in this business of ordering and arranging elements taken from life that creation in any art consists. The only questions that remain are: How varied and how complex are the relationships that can be represented? How far is the medium

11 *Kabloona* (Cape, London, 1941), p. 169.

capable of presenting the most subtle perceptions of the great creative artist? A child who is asked to sew brightly colored pieces of material onto a square of hessian will place them in an arrangement he finds pleasing, and the result is a form of self-expression, but a limited one. The elements with which a musical composer works are not quite so simple, but they are simple enough: at any given moment of time he can control his sounds only in turns of pitch, harmony (the harmony of a single chord), loudness and duration; but by continually varying these elements from one instant to the next, he can create patterns of the most complex and satisfying kind—complex, that is to say, in the sense of being charged with significance.

The case of the film is not dissimilar from that of music. The visual unit of the film, the single shot, offers within itself a certain choice of viewpoint, of lighting and of duration, as we have seen, but alone its expressive possibilities are severely limited. With a series of shots following each other in succession, however, it is quite another story; the Soviet directors in their silent films gave some indication of the powerful and complex effects that can be obtained in passing from one shot to another, and the range has since been extended by the addition of sound, bringing with it not only unlimited potentialities of its own, but also making possible new and exactly calculated relationships between visual images on the one hand, and sound on the other.

It is impossible to conceive of anything the eye might behold or the ear hear, in actuality or in imagination, that could not be represented in the medium of the film. From the poles to the equator, from the Grand Canyon to the minutest flaw in a piece of steel, from the whistling flight of a bullet to the slow growth of a flower, from the flicker of thought across an almost impassive face to the frenzied ravings of a madman, there is no point in space, no degree of magnitude or speed of movement within the apprehension of man that is also not within the reach of the film. Nor is this all; in the treatment of its material it has similar freedom. It can treat it naturalistically and objectively on the one hand, or entirely subjectively on the other, with a realism in either extreme impossible in any other medium; or it can establish a point of view anywhere between these two extremes. It might have been supposed, on the evidence of the disastrous experiments that have been made in the past with superimposed angels with wings and halos, and "dream balloons" and other such trickery, that there is at least one kind of experience that lies beyond the film's scope, namely, the dream and the vision; but Jean Vigo and others have convincingly demonstrated that by concentrating, once more, on editing, on the relationship of shots in succession, and by replacing the matter-of-fact logic of everyday life with the free associations of the dream state, it is possible to represent that state with a disconcerting vividness.

The color film and television have opened up new possibilities that are still being explored; the three-dimensional film is also within reach. Such developments will enrich the film with new resources, although it appears unlikely that they will lead to any fundamental innovations in technique. The addition of color, for example, has not been nearly comparable in importance to the addition of sound. Much of the interest of television will lie in its ability to enable us to see events in the making, but events in the making are in their nature unforeseeable and uncontrollable—in that lies their fascination; the more television producers endeavor, therefore, to use their medium creatively, the more they are likely to use both cinematograph film and the technique of the film, because for creative work control over the raw material of life is essential, and this is afforded in greatest measure by film recording. As for the three-dimensional film, some have expressed the fear that it will lead to the loss of our present freedom in editing, on the grounds that the illusion of actuality will be so vivid as to make rapid and continual changes of viewpoint acutely disturbing. Personally, I have no such fears; on the contrary, I believe that, by adding a new dimension to movement, it will enable the film-maker to achieve patterns of movement even richer and more exciting than is now possible.

To what extent are these resources being used? That the film can tell a story in a manner to lull disbelief and maintain suspense is fully evident. But the interest in a story, which E. M. Forster calls "the lowest and simplest of literary organisms," [12] is an extremely elementary one: it is merely an interest in what is going to happen next; and when one knows that, interest immediately dies. The great majority of films, including many above the average, concern themselves with nothing more than the telling of a story, which is why one finds no interest in seeing them a second time.

As the story develops in complexity, however, the question "what?" begins to give ground to the question "why?" To the mere succession of events are added links of cause and effect; events cast their shadows forward; what is shown happening here is a direct result of something else that happened there; a plan dimly revealed at the beginning is seen working itself out with growing clearness toward the end; in short, the plot (if we may use a well-known cliché in a slightly new sense) thickens. The question "why?" then comes to be directed not only toward what happens, but toward those who do and suffer, the participants in the action. Why is it that he or she does thus or reacts thus? Considerations of motive and reaction are inevitably linked with character, and as we ask more of the story, so we force the characters to reveal themselves more clearly and more credibly, transforming themselves from performing puppets into thinking, feeling, living beings. We call upon them to express themselves more fully; and in doing so, we both develop the complexity of the pattern of their relationships, and made greater play with the resources of medium, straining more and more toward its limits.

The highest point that has been reached by the art of fiction in complexity, richness and significance is represented

12 *Aspects of the Novel*, p. 43.

by the plays of Shakespeare, notably by his greater tragedies. Using, then, the highest standard available to us, let
us, without flinching or compromise, face this question: Is
the film medium, so far as we can analyze its possibilities,
capable of development to Shakespearean levels? I have no
doubt in my mind that it is capable of such development. As
we have already seen, in the formal use of movement, in
particular, lie poetic resources that have so far been tapped
hardly at all. I am well aware that this is a high claim.
"Now that I have finished *Deserter*," wrote Pudovkin in
1933, "I am sure that sound film is potentially the art of the
future . . . it is a synthesis of each and every element—the
oral, the visual, the philosophical; it is our opportunity to
translate the world in all its lines and shadows into a new
art form that has succeeded and will supersede all the older
arts, for it is the supreme medium in which we can express
today and tomorrow." [13] To this I add the words of Eisenstein: "The perspectives of the possibilities of the film are
unlimited. And I am firmly convinced that we have barely
touched these possibilities." [14]

The most significant development of the last fifteen years
has not been any new technical innovation, comparable to
those made by Eisenstein and Griffith. It has been the emergence of directors, such as Vigo, Buñuel, De Sica, Bergman,
Ray, Antonioni, who have taken the technical possibilities of
the cinema for granted and have subordinated them to personal expression of a quality not realized by any of their
predecessors. It is in their hands, and the hands of others
like them, that the future of the cinema lies; their achievement encourages one to hope that this future will far out-
shine the past.

13 *Film Technique* (1933 ed.), p. 173.
14 *The Film Sense*, p. 8.

APPENDICES

Appendix I

SELECT BIBLIOGRAPHY

GENERAL

DAVY, Charles, editor, *Footnotes to the Film*. London, Lovat Dickson, 1938. Articles by Alfred Hitchcock, Robert Donat, Basil Wright, Graham Greene, Alberto Cavalcanti, John Betjeman, Maurice Jaubert, John Grierson, Alexander Korda, Basil Dean, Maurice Kann, Elizabeth Bowen, Sidney L. Bernstein, Alistair Cooke, Forsyth Hardy, Charles Davy.

MANVELL, Roger, *Film*. London, Penguin, 1944; Revised 1946; Further revised 1950.

SELDES, Gilbert, *Movies for the Millions*. London, Batsford, 1937.

SPENCER, D. A., and WALEY, H. D., *The Cinema Today*. London, Oxford University Press, 1939; New edition 1956.

EARLY ORIGINS

HOPWOOD, Henry V. and FOSTER, Norman, *Living Pictures*. London, Longmans, 1915. A detailed survey of the technical developments between approximately 1830 and 1897, which culminated in the invention of cinematography.

QUIGLEY, Martin, *Magic Shadows: The Story of the Origin of Motion Pictures*. London, Quigley, 1948; New edition 1960.

HISTORY

BARDECHE, Maurice, and BRASILLACH, Robert, *History of the Film*. London, Allen & Unwin, 1938.

FULTON, A. R., *Motion Pictures; the Development of an Art from Silent Days to the Age of Television*. Norman (Oklahoma, USA), University of Oklahoma Press, 1960.

JACOBS, Lewis, *The Rise of the American Film*. New York, Harcourt Brace, 1939.

KNIGHT, Arthur, *The Liveliest Art: A Panoramic History of the Movies*. New York, Macmillan, 1957; paperback edition, London, Muller, 1959.

KRACAUER, Siegfried, *From Caligari to Hitler*. London, Dennis Dobson, 1947. A detailed study of the German film.

LEYDA, Jay, *Kino: A History of the Russian and Soviet Films*. London, Allen & Unwin, 1960.

Low, Rachael, and MANVELL, Roger, *The History of the British Film*. 3 volumes. London, Allen & Unwin, 1948-49. Volume I, 1896-1906; Volume II, 1906-14; Volume III, 1914-18.

ROTHA, Paul, *The Film Till Now*. London, Cape, 1930; new and revised edition, Vision Press, 1948; second revised edition in collaboration with Richard Griffith, Vision Press, 1959.

AESTHETICS, CRITICISM, TECHNIQUE

ARNHEIM, Rudolf, *Film as Art*. London, Faber and Faber, 1958.

BALAZS, Bela, *Theory of the Film:* Character and Growth of a New Art. London, Dennis Dobson, 1952.

EISENSTEIN, Sergei, *Film Form*. New York, Harcourt Brace, 1947.

EISENSTEIN, Sergei, *The Film Sense*. London, Faber and Faber, 1943; New edition 1958.

EISENSTEIN, Sergei, *Notes of a Film Director*. London, Lawrence and Wishart, 1959.

NICOLL, Allardyce, *Film and Theatre*. London, Harrap, 1936.

NILSEN, Vladimir, *The Cinema as a Graphic Art*. London, Newnes, 1936.

NIZHNY, Vladimir, *Lessons with Eisenstein*. London, Allen and Unwin, 1962.

PUDOVKIN, Vsevolod, *Film Acting*. London, Newnes, 1935.

PUDOVKIN, Vsevolod, *Film Technique*. London, Newnes, 1933.

PUDOVKIN, Vsevolod, *Film Technique and Film Acting*. London, Vision Press, 1959.

PRODUCTION

ANDERSON, Lindsay, *Making a Film*. London, Allen & Unwin, 1952.

CARRICK, Edward, *Designing for Films*. London, Studio, 1949.

NAUMBERG, Nancy, editor, *We Make the Movies*. London, Faber and Faber, 1938. Articles by Jesse Lasky, Samuel Marx, Sidney Howard, John Cromwell, Clem Beauchamp, Hans Dreier, Robert Edward Lee, Phil Friedman, Bette Davis, Paul Muni, John Arnold, Nathan Levinson, Anne Bauchens, Max Steiner, Lansing C. Holden and Walt Disney.

POLITICAL AND ECONOMIC PLANNING, *The British Film Industry*. London, P.E.P., 1952; Supplement, 1958.

REISZ, Karel, *The Technique of Film Editing*. London, Focal Press, 1957.

SPOTTISWOODE, Raymond, *The Film and Its Techniques*. London, Faber and Faber, 1951.

SCRIPTWRITING

BLUESTONE, George, *Novels into Film*. Baltimore, Johns Hopkins

Press, 1957. The aesthetics of film adaptation and scriptwriting, with a detailed analysis of seven films.

MARGRAVE, Seton, *Successful Film Writing, as Illustrated by "The Ghost Goes West."* London, Methuen, 1936.

LAWSON, John Howard, *The Theory and Technique of Play and Screenwriting.* New York, Putnam, 1949; paperback edition, Hill and Wang, 1960.

MUSIC

EISLER, Hans, *Composing for the Films.* London, Dennis Dobson, 1951.

LONDON, Kurt, *Film Music.* London, Faber and Faber, 1936.

MANVELL, Roger, and HUNTLEY, John, *The Technique of Film Music.* London, Focal Press, 1957.

ANIMATION, CARTOON AND EXPERIMENTAL FILMS

FEILD, Robert D., *The Art of Walt Disney.* London, Collins, 1944. A comprehensive and fully illustrated survey of the work of the Walt Disney Studios.

HALAS, John, and MANVELL, Roger, *The Technique of Film Animation.* London, Focal Press, 1959.

MANVELL, Roger, editor, *Experiment in the Film.* London, Grey Walls, 1949. Articles on experimental and avant-garde films throughout the world.

DOCUMENTARY FILMS

HARDY, Forsyth, *Grierson on Documentary.* London, W. H. Allen, 1946. A selection of John Grierson's writings from 1930 to 1954.

ROTHA, Paul, *Documentary Film.* London, Faber and Faber, 1936. Second edition 1939; third edition, in collaboration with Sinclair Road and Richard Griffith, 1952.

Appendix II

GLOSSARY

"A" Certificate (n.). Certificate awarded by the British Board of Film Censors to a film to denote that it may not be seen by children under sixteen unaccompanied by a parent or guardian.

"A" Picture (n.). 1. Film designed by its producer to be shown as a first feature in a commercial cinema program. 2. Film that has been given an "A" Certificate by the British Board of Film Censors.

Absolute Film (n.). Film of moving visual patterns having no representational significance.

Abstract Film (n.). Film in which the relationship between the shots is entirely formal and non-representational; an absolute film (q.v.).

Accelerated Motion (n.). Means whereby movement in a shot is represented as taking place at a greater speed than it did in reality; the opposite of slow motion (q.v.).

Acetate (n.). Abbreviation for *Amyl Acetate;* hence, film cement; (adj.) made of cellulose acetate (q.v.).

Acetic Acid (n.). Colorless corrosive liquid with pungent smell used as an ingredient in the cement for joining acetate film.

Acetone (n.). Colorless liquid solvent with pleasant smell, used as one of the constituents of film cement.

Action Negative (n.). See *Mute Negative.*

Action Still (n.). Still of a scene as it actually appears in the completed film (to be distinguished from *Art Still* and *Production Still*).

Action-Theme (n.). Central action of a fiction film expressed in the briefest possible form.

Actuality (n.). Recording of an actual event without acting, special posing or reconstruction.

Adapt (v.). To alter a story, novel or play for the purpose of filming.

Additive Process (n.). Any process of color cinematography dependent on two or more basic colors being juxtaposed on the film in such a way that when projected they mingle in various proportions on the screen.

Adult Certificate (n.). See *"A" Certificate.*

Advance (n.). In the projection print of a sound film the extent to which any point on the sound track lies ahead of its corresponding picture so that as the film passes first through the picture head of

the projector and then through the sound head, the parts of the
film (i.e. picture and sound, respectively) being reproduced in each
head at the same moment shall appear to be in synchronization.
(For standard 35-mm. film the advance is normally 20 frames.)

Ampex (n.). Trade name for a system of recording a television picture and its accompanying sound electronically onto a form of magnetic tape.

Amplitude (n.). Characteristic of a sound wave that determines its
loudness.

Amyl Acetate (n.). Liquid with smell of pear drops used as a constituent of film cement.

Anaglyph (n.). Two pictures of a stereoscopic pair, each printed in a
color complementary to the other and superimposed on the same
photographic print, so that when viewed through a pair of spec-
tacles with one eyepiece of the one complementary color and the
other of the other (the anaglyphoscope), the pictures combine to
give a three-dimensional appearance.

Anamorphic (adj.). A lens system that, by laterally compressing the
wide-screen picture within the dimensions of the frame during
shooting, and contrariwise extending this laterally compressed
image during projection so that it undistortedly fills the full width
of the screen, enables wide-screen pictures to be taken and projected
by the use of standard film.

Angle (n.). See *Camera Angle*.

Animate (v.). To arrange and photograph static drawings of objects
so that when the photographs are shown cinematographically they
will produce the illusion of movement.

Animator (n.). Artist who makes the separate drawings necessary to
give the appearance of movement to any part of a cartoon or diagram film.

Answer Print (n.). The first combined print of a color film to be approved by the producer as reaching the standard he requires in all
subsequent prints.

Aperture (n.). Opening in front of camera through which light passes
to the sensitive negative film; the size of such opening expressed
as a fraction of the focal length of the lens being used.

Arc (Lamp) (n.). High-powered source of illumination used for projectors and studio lights, consisting of a luminous electrical discharge across a gap between two carbon rods.

Art Director (n.). Technician responsible for designing and supervising the construction of the studio sets and (sometimes) the costumes for a film.

Art Still (n.). Specially posed portrait photograph of a film actor.

Aspect Ratio (n.). The relationship, expressed as a proportion or ratio, between the width and height of a projected cinematograph picture and of the screen that it exactly fills. Thus the aspect ratio of a square picture would be 1:1, that of a standard sound-film picture is 1.37:1, and that of the Cinemascope wide-screen 2.34:1, etc.

Assemble (v.). To carry out the first process in film editing, namely, to collect together the required shots and join them in correct order, thus producing what is known as the rough cut.

Assistant Director (n.). Director's factotum who is responsible for the smooth running of the detailed arrangements associated with shooting.

Associate Producer (n.). Assistant to whom the chief producer of a large studio entrusts the production of a certain film or films to be made by that studio.

"B" Picture (n.). Film designed by its producer to serve as a second or supporting feature in a commercial cinema program.

BW Print (n.). A black-and-white positive projection print of a film, of the maximum contrast suitable for projection.

Baby Spotlight (n.). Small type of spotlight used in studio lighting.

Back Lighting (n.). Lighting directed onto the subject of a shot from a point behind it (the front being regarded as the side facing the camera).

Back Projection (n.). Projection of a film onto a translucent screen from a projector behind the screen (the front being defined as the surface facing the spectator). This method is used (a) in the course of production, to provide a moving background for actors working in the studio; (b) in ordinary cinemas where for any reason normal front projection is not possible; (c) in school classrooms and lecture rooms as a method of daylight projection, in which case it is frequently described as "rear projection."

Background Film (n.). Type of educational film that can help to provide students with a general background of knowledge of a given subject, as distinct from a classroom or lesson film treating its subject more didactically.

Background Music (n.). Subdued music accompanying speech, dialogue or other recorded sound.

Backing (n.). Any flat background, either in the form of a large photograph or painting, or quite plain, in front of which actors are filmed.

Base (n.). See *Support*.

Beater Movement (n.). Action by which a film is pulled through the gate of the projector by means of a roller beating down intermittently on the lower loop, instead of by means of a claw engaging the sprocket holes.

Big Close-up (n.). Shot taken with the camera nearer (or apparently nearer) to the subject than would be necessary for a close-up; in relation to a human subject, a shot of part of the face only.

Blimp (n.). Soundproof cover in which the camera is enclosed to prevent the noise of its mechanism from being picked up by the recording microphone during shooting.

Blind Booking (n.). Booking of a film for exhibition before it has been made or shown to the film trade.

Block Booking (n.). Booking of a film or films on conditions that require the exhibitor at the same time to book other films, usually of inferior quality.

Bloop (n.). Small opaque patch over a splice in a positive sound track designed to smother any intrusive noise the splice might otherwise produce. (The bloop may be produced by painting it onto the positive track, by cementing on a specially prepared blooping patch, by punching a triangular hole in the negative from which the positive is to be printed or by fogging the film during printing.)

Blow Up (v.). To make a standard 35-mm. film by enlargement from a substandard original; the opposite of *Reduce*.

Blurb (n.). Fulsome praise of a film prepared for purposes of publicity.

Booking (n.). Arrangement between a renter and an exhibitor, whereby the renter undertakes to hire a film or films to the exhibitor on an agreed date and for an agreed period.

Booking Contract (n.). Statement of the details of a booking and of its terms and conditions that, when signed by exhibitor and renter, legalizes the booking agreement so made between them.

Boom (n.). Cranelike device for suspending the recording microphone in mid-air and moving it from one position to another during shooting.

Booth (n.). Soundproof cabin designed to house the sound recordist and his apparatus.

Breakdown (n.). Analysis of film script in terms of materials, personnel, time, etc., prepared for costing purposes.

Breathing (n.). The intermittent loss of sharp focus in a projected image when the film is not held flat in the gate of the projector. This may be due to inadequate pressure between the plates of the projection gate or to buckling of the film.

Bridging Shot (n.). Shot inserted in the editing of a scene to cover a jump in time or other break in continuity.

Bridging Title (n.). See *Continuity Title*.

Broad[side] (n.). Floodlight used to illuminate a studio set.

Buckling (n.). Curling and unevenness found in a film that has been exposed to excessive strain or heat, or which has shrunk unevenly.

Camera (n.). Apparatus for securing photographic images on cinematograph film.

Camera Angle (n.). Angle of view subtended at the lens by the portion of the subject included within the picture area; camera viewpoint (q.v.).

Cameraman (n.). Technician responsible for the lighting and photography of a film.

Camera Viewpoint (n.). Position of camera in relation to the subject being photographed, especially as compared with the view of a person seeing it from a normal distance at eye level (e.g. low viewpoint, high viewpoint, distant viewpoint, etc.); see also *Setup*.

Cartoon Film (n.). Film of animated drawings.

Cast (n.). All the actors appearing in a film; a list of the actors or principal actors.

Casting Director (n.). Official in a studio responsible for maintaining records of actors who might be suitable for parts in the studio's films.

Cel[1] (n.). Rectangular sheet of transparent celluloid carrying one section of a drawing required in the making of an animated cartoon, the complete drawing usually being composed of several such cells placed one on top of the other, each of which can be replaced by its successor independently of the others.

Celluloid (n.). See *Cellulose Nitrate*.

Cellulose Acetate (n.). Flexible transparent plastic used since 1950 in the making of cinematograph film, and always used for all substandard film, because of its slow combustibility.

Cellulose Nitrate (n.). Flexible transparent plastic, known also as celluloid, used before 1951 for the manufacture of standard cinematograph film, despite its high inflammability, because of its resistance to wear and tear.

Cement (n.). Cellulose solvent used for joining cinematograph film. (Cement for nitrate film may be made by mixing 2 parts of amyl acetate with 3 parts of acetone; for acetate film, 2 parts of glacial acetic acid are added.)

Censor (n.). Official who examines films to suppress what he considers to be immoral, seditious or otherwise unfit for public exhibition.

Changeover (n.). Transition made from one reel on one projector to the next reel on a second projector during the continuous projection of a multireel film program.

Changeover Cue (n.). Small spot or other mark made in the top right-hand corner of certain frames near the end of a reel to give the projectionist a signal for the changeover.

Channel (n.). A single electronic recording and reproducing system that may be combined with, or alternated with, other similar systems; thus in re-recording, a channel is that part of the apparatus that will reproduce the impulses carried on one track or tape for the purpose of combining them with the impulses from other tapes or tracks being simultaneously reproduced on other channels of the apparatus: in broadcasting, a channel is the output of an individual television station, selected as an alternative to the output of other such stations.

Cheat Shot (n.). Shot in which the part of the subject or action is excluded from view in order to make the part that is recorded appear different from what it actually is (e.g., the shot of a man falling from the top of a building into a net spread six feet below, but with the net out of view in order to suggest that he has fallen a great distance).

Chief (n.). The head projectionist in a cinema.

Cinema (n.). Building or hall especially designed for the showing of films to the public; the production and exhibition of films in general.

Cinema Manager (n.). Person responsible for management of cinema.

Cinemascope (n.). A proprietary system of wide-screen projection involving the use of anamorphic lenses (see *Anamorphic, Wide Screen*).

Cinerama (n.). A proprietary development of cinematography that, by the use of three films simultaneously running through three projectors, makes possible the projection of a moving picture so wide that it extends in a broad arc from the extreme left to the extreme right of the spectator's field of vision.

Cine-Magazine (n.). Short film composed of several diverse items of topical or general interest, after the manner of a printed magazine.

Cinematograph Projector (n.). Device for producing the illusion of moving pictures by the projection onto a screen in rapid succession of a series of static photographs carried on a perforated ribbon of transparent material.

Circuit (n.). Group of cinemas owned by one company.

Circuit Release (n.). A film made available for showing throughout the cinemas of one particular circuit.

Clapper (n.). Pair of boards hinged at one end that are banged together in view of the camera at the beginning of a take to enable the sound cutting print and the picture cutting print to be synchronized in editing. (The bang appears as a pronounced fluctuation in the sound track, and this is related to the first frame in the picture print showing the boards in contact. The clapper is frequently a part of the number board.)

Clapper Boy (n.). Junior technician who works the clapper.

Claw (n.). Tongue of metal linked with the intermittent of camera or projector that engages with the perforations in the film and pulls it through the gate so as to withdraw one frame from the gate aperture and move the next one into it.

Clip (n.). A short section taken from a complete film, either to be shown for its own sake as a quotation or illustration, or to be incorporated into another film or into a television program.

Closed Circuit (n.). A television system in which the transmission signals are not broadcast but are fed to the receiver by cable, so that the system can be used for demonstration, testing, monitoring, etc.

Close Medium Shot (n.). Shot between a close-up and a medium shot; of a human subject, from knees to head.

Close-up (n.). Shot taken with the camera actually or apparently very close to the subject; in relation to a human subject, a shot of the face only.

Color Filter (n.). Transparent colored glass placed in front of the camera lens to alter the tone relationships of a picture.

Combined Print (n.). Positive print of a film carrying both sound and picture.

Commentary (n.). Descriptive talk accompanying a film.

Condenser (n.). 1 (Electrical). Device for holding or "storing" static electricity used in sound recording and reproducing equipment. 2 (Optical). Lens or system of lenses designed to concentrate rays of light from a luminant onto a given object as, for example, in a film projector to concentrate light on the film frame to be projected, or in a studio spotlight for concentrating light on the area to be illuminated.

Console (n.). Form of re-recording apparatus.

Contact Print (n.). A print made from a master film (usually, of course, a negative) by the process of running the two lengths of film in contact with each other through the printer (as opposed to an optical print—for example, a reduction print—which is made through the intermediation of a lens system).

Continuity (n.). Smoothness of transition from one part of a film to the next; the carrying of the spectator's attention from one shot to another without any displeasing breaks or discrepancies.

Continuity Girl (n.). Technician responsible for recording the details of every take during shooting in order to ensure that no discrepancies occur to disturb continuity when the shots are joined together in their proper order.

Continuity Title (n.). Title designed to bridge a break in the pictorial continuity.

Contrast (n.). Range of the tonal scale between the darkest and lightest parts of a photograph, it being said to have high contrast when this range is restricted, with very few halftones, and low contrast when it is very wide, with a great number of halftones.

Crane Shot (n.). Moving shot taken by the camera on a specially constructed crane.

Credit Film (n.). Title placed normally at the beginning of a film, but sometimes at the end, recording the names of players, technicians or organizations concerned in its production.

Creeping Title (n.). Title that moves slowly upward on the screen as it is being read.

Cross-cut (v.). To intermingle the shots of two or more scenes in the course of editing so that fragments of each scene will be presented to the spectator's attention alternately (see *Parallel Development*).

Crossover (n.). See *Changeover*.

Crowd Artist (n.). Person who is hired by the day to appear as one of a group or crowd in a film.

Cut 1. (n.). Transition between two shots linked together by a simple join, giving the impression during projection that the first shot is suddenly and instantaneously displaced by the second. 2. (v.). To trim and join shots together in the process of editing, hence often used synonymously with *edit* (q.v.); to terminate a shot, as when used in the imperative tense as an instruction by director to cameraman to stop the camera at the end of a take.

Cutter (n.). Technician who carries out the more mechanical operations of editing, especially the trimming and joining of the film pieces.

Cutting Print (n.). The particular positive print that the editor assembles and on which he works.

Cyclic Film (n.). Short, educational or demonstration film having its ends joined together in the form of an endless band, which can be run uninterruptedly through a projector to give a continuous repetition of its subject.

Dailies (pl. n.). See *Rushes*.

Daylight Projection (n.). Projection of films in daylight instead of in a darkened auditorium, usually achieved by back projection onto a translucent screen.

Depth of Focus (n.). Extent to which a lens will clearly focus near and distant objects at the same time.

Develop (v.). To bring out the latent photographic image on exposed film by treating it with certain chemicals that reduce the silver salts affected by light to metallic silver; this appears as a black deposit.

Diagram Film (n.). Film of animated diagrams.

Differential Focus (n.). Method by which main item of interest in a shot is photographed in sharp focus, the remainder of the subject being out of focus.

Diffuser (n.). Screen made of silk, gelatin, frosted glass or other suitable material which is placed in front of a studio lamp to soften and diffuse its light; similar device placed in front of camera lens to soften the outline of the picture.

Diffusion Disc (n.). See *Diffuser*.

Dissolve (n.). See *Mix*.

Distance Shot (n.). Shot of a subject actually or apparently at a great distance from the camera.

Distributor (n.). See *Renter*.

Director (n.). In the narrowest sense, the technician responsible for the shooting of a film, including supervision of the work of actors, cameramen, etc., but because this also normally involves cooperation with scriptwriters and editor, the director usually becomes the dominant creative mind in the production unit and the individual most responsible for the character and success of the completed film.

Director of Photography (n.). Title sometimes conferred on the chief cameraman.

Documentary (n.). Type of nonfiction film utilizing material, either actual or reconstructed, drawn from real life, and based on a sociological theme or having a sociological reference.

Dolly (n.). Vehicle on which camera and cameraman can be wheeled about during the taking of a shot.

Dolly Shot (n.). Shot taken while the camera is in motion on a truck or dolly.

Double (n.). One employed to substitute for a film actor in scenes of exceptional risk or danger.

Double-Feature Program (n.). Program containing two feature films.

Dub (v.). To re-record the sound track of a film, substituting for the speech of the language originally used a spoken translation in some other language; to re-record (q.v.).

Dunning Process (n.). Device for combining the performance of an actor in a studio with a background filmed elsewhere. (A yellow-toned positive print of the background scene is threaded into the camera in front of a panchromatic negative, and the actors, lit with a yellow light, perform in front of a brightly lit purple-blue backing; since the blue is complementary to the yellow, wherever blue light from the backing meets the yellow-toned film, it is absorbed in proportion to the density of the yellow, and a print of the yellow image is thus recorded in reverse on the negative; wherever the actors move in front of the backing, however, they prevent blue light from reaching the film, their own yellow-lit figures recording in its place.)

Dupe (v.). To print a duplicate negative from an existing positive.

Dupe Negative (n.). Negative of a film that is not the original negative; negative made from a positive print.

Duping Print (n.). Special soft print (lavender or fine grain) made from an original negative so that a dupe negative can subsequently be made from it.

Edit (v.). To assemble a complete film from its various component shots and sound tracks.

Editola (n.). Trade name of instrument designed for same purpose as Moviola (q.v.).

Effects Track (n.). Sound track of sound effects other than speech and music.

Emulsion (n.). Gelatin, containing silver bromide or silver chloride in suspension, with which cinematograph film is coated in order to make it sensitive to the action of light.

Establishing Shot (n.). Long shot introduced at the beginning of a scene to establish the interrelationship of details to be shown subsequently in nearer shots.

Exciter Lamp (n.). Lamp in sound head of projector that shines through the sound track on to the photo electric cell.

Exhibitor (n.). One who arranges the showing of films to the public; owner of a cinema or cinema circuit.

Expose (v.). To uncover light-sensitive film to the action of light.

Exposure (n.). Length of time a single frame of film in the camera is exposed to the action of light in shooting.

Exposure Meter (n.). Instrument for gauging the amount of exposure to be given to a film to secure the best result under any given lighting conditions.

Exterior (n.). Representation of an outdoor scene.

Extra (n.). Actor hired by the day to appear in a film, who has no lines to speak.

Fader (n.). Device to enable the projectionist to control the volume of sound reproduction of his projectors.

Fade-in. 1. (n.). Beginning of a shot that starts in darkness and gradually lightens up to full brightness. 2. (v.). To bring up sound volume gradually from inaudibility to full strength.

Fade-out (n. and v.). Opposite of *Fade-in*.

Fan (n.). Uncritical enthusiast.

Feature Film (n.). Film of 3,000 feet (of standard film) or more in length.

Feature Player (n.). Actor contracted by studio for a week at the minimum.

Feed Spool (n.). Spool from which film is fed into the mechanism of a film projector.

Fill-up (n.). Film added to a program merely to fill it out to a desired length.

Film. 1 (n.). Perforated ribbon of celluloid or other transparent flexible material, coated with photographic emulsion, which is used in cinematography; a complete cinematographic production; the art of representation in the medium of cinematography. 2 (v.t. and i.) To make a film (of); to shoot.

Film Appreciation (n.). Encouragement and development of criticism and discrimination among filmgoers, especially by organized courses of instruction.

Film Society (n.). Any group of people who are associated together as members of a private, non-profit-making association for the purpose of viewing films of their choice.

Filter (n.). See *Color Filter*.

Fine-grain Print (n.). See *Duping Print*.

First Feature (n.). More important feature film in a double-feature program, the other being known as the second feature.

First-run Cinema (n.). Cinema that can afford to have the first showing of a film on its general release. (When a film has circulated in the first-run cinemas it goes to the second-run and then to the third-run, the hiring terms being reduced at each stage.)

Fix (v.). To render that portion of sensitized film that has not been affected by light during exposure insensitive to further exposure after developing, usually by immersion in a solution of "hypo" (sodium thiosulphate); the hypo reacts with the unaffected silver bromide to produce a soluble double salt, silver sodium thiosulphate, which then has to be washed away.

Flashback (n.). Repetition in a film of a brief extract from an earlier scene, either as a reminder to the audience or to indicate the recollection of one of the characters.

Flash Pan (n.) A transition between two camera setups by means of a very rapid pan (real or apparent) from the one to the other.

Flicker (n.). Any disturbance of the smooth and steady movement of a cinematograph picture on the screen.

Floating Release (n.). A film made freely available to any cinema which wishes to book it, as distinct from a circuit release (q.v.).

Floor (n.). Part of studio where shooting is in progress.

Floor Secretary (n.). Continuity girl (q.v.).

Focal Length (n.). Distance from the optical center of a lens to the principal focus.

Focus (v.). To adjust a lens so that it produces a sharply defined image, e.g., on the negative film in the case of a camera, or on the screen in the case of a projector, such an image being then described as *in focus*.

Focus Puller (n.). Member of the camera crew responsible for adjusting the camera lens.

Follow-Focus (n.). Device for keeping the lens of a camera in focus as the camera is moved toward, or away from, the subject.

Footage (n.). Length of a film measured in feet.

Foreground Miniature (n.). Miniature model of part of a studio set used for purposes of economy when it is not essential for the whole set to be constructed full size, the model being placed at a short distance in front of the camera in such a position that it will appear to be in the same scale as the more distant full-size portion of the set and to merge with it to form a complete whole.

Frame (n.). One single transparent photograph of the series printed on a length of cinematograph film. (When the film is so adjusted in the projector that each frame is moved exactly into the projector aperture, it is said to be *in frame*.)

Frame Line (n.). Dividing line that separates one frame from the next.

Frequency (n.). Number of vibrations per second that will produce a sound of a given musical pitch.

Full Shot (n.). Close medium shot (q.v.).

Gaffer (n.). Chief electrician.

Gag (n.). Joke or comic action or situation inserted into a film.

Gate (n.). That part of camera or projector in which each frame is held during exposure or projection.

Gauge (n.). The width of a film, normally expressed in millimeters (as 35 mm., 16 mm., etc.).

General Release (n.). Release of a film for distribution to cinemas in general.

Ghost (n.). See *Travel Ghost*.

Glass Shot (n.). Shot of action in a setting only part of which is constructed full size, the remainder being painted or photographed in miniature on a sheet of glass suspended a short distance in front of the camera in such a position that the miniature will appear to be in the same scale as, and to merge with, the more distant full-size set seen through the clear part of the glass.

Gobo (n.). Black adjustable screen used to keep rays of light from camera.

Grade (v.). To measure the accidental variations in overall density of the shots and scenes in a negative film (which arise from the fact that they have been shot at different times and under different lighting conditions), and to mark them correspondingly with indicators designed to regulate the light of a printer automatically in such a way as to produce projection prints that are of even density throughout.

Grain (n.). Particles of silver salts held in suspension in photographic emulsion.

Green Film (n.). Film immediately after it has been printed and processed, and which has not been waxed or otherwise treated or run on a projector.

Ground Noise (n.). Noise reproduced through the loudspeakers due to the interruption of the sound-reproducing beam by grain, scratches, dust, etc., on the film; the residual noise of a sound-amplifying system when no sound is being picked up from a sound track; see also *Unmodulated Track*.

Guide Track (n.). Sound track recorded during shooting not for use in the finished film, but as a guide in post-synchronization (q.v.).

"H" Certificate (n.). Special certificate at one time attached by the British Board of Film Censors to horrific films (q.v.).

Halation (n.). Spread of the light parts of the photographic image due to reflection or dispersal of light.

Horrific Film (n.). Extreme type of horror film.

Horror Film (n.). Fiction film designed to play on the emotions of horror and terror.

Impressionism (n.). Building up of a general impression in a film by joining together a series of shots of subjects that in actuality are disconnected in space or time or both.

Incandescent Lamp (n.). Lamp consisting of a wire filament supported in a vacuum or a gas within an hermetically sealed glass bulb, so that the filament when heated by an electric current glows with intense brightness.

Infrared (adj.). Relating to electromagnetic rays similar to those of light but of comparatively long wavelength lying beyond the red portion of the spectrum and therefore invisible. (Infrared photography can be used to photograph objects through mist or cloud or in a darkened room.)

Inkie (n.). Abbreviation for *Incandescent Lamp*.

Insurance Print (n.). See *Protective Master*.

Intercut (v.). See *Cross-cut*.

Interest Film (n.). Film that deals with a nonfictional subject in a popular manner.

Interior (n.). Set representing the interior of a room or building; a shot or scene taken on such a set.

Intermediate Positive/Negative (n.). A positive film made from a negative for the purpose of making a second negative therefrom, or a negative film made from a positive for the purpose of producing a second positive.

Intermittent Movement (n.). Mechanism in film camera, printer or projector, whereby the frames on a length of film are successively brought into position for exposure or illumination, held there the necessary length of time, and then moved on again; the jerky movement thus imparted to the film.

Jump Cut (n.). Cut that breaks continuity of time by jumping forward from one part of an action to another obviously separated from the first by an interval of time.

Join (v. and n.). See *Splice*.

Kinematograph (n.). Alternate form of *Cinematograph*.

Kinescope (n.). A proprietary form of telerecording; a cinematograph film record of a television program made by photographing direct from the cathode-ray tube of a television receiver.

Kinetoscope (n.). Peep-show machine for showing moving photographs carried on an endless band of perforated celluloid film 50 feet in length, invented by Thomas Edison in 1891, and the direct source of all commercially successful developments of the cinematograph.

Laboratory (n.). Place where cinematograph film is processed and printed.

Lace-up (v.). See *Thread-up*.

Lap Dissolve (n.). See *Mix (optical)*.

Lavender Print (n.). See *Duping Print*.

Lead, Leader, Leader Strip (n.). Length of film joined to the beginning of a reel for threading through the camera, projector, etc.

Lens (n.). Transparent refracting medium, usually glass, bounded by two surfaces, one curved and the other flat or curved, for concentrating or dispersing light rays according to certain optical laws.

Lens Turret (n.). Revolving device on camera carrying two or more lenses, any one of which can quickly be turned into position for shooting.

Library Shot (n.). Shot used in a film, but not recorded especially for it: shot taken from a library or store of shots kept in the hope that they may at some time be useful.

License (n.). In Britain, permit that every cinema is obliged under the Cinematograph Act of 1909 to obtain annually from the local authority; permit that every renter of films for public exhibition is obliged under the Films Acts of 1938 to 1960 to obtain from the Board of Trade.

Load (v.). To place a roll of unexposed film into a camera ready for shooting.

Loader Boy (n.). Member of camera crew responsible for loading the camera.

Location (n.). Any place away from the studio where shots for a film are taken.

Long Shot (n.). Shot actually or apparently taken with the camera a considerable distance away from the subject.

Loop (n.). Bend of slack film left above and below the gate in threading a film camera or projector in order to prevent the intermittent action straining and tearing the film.

Loop Film (n.). See *Cyclic Film.*

Lot (n.). Piece of land outside or near the studio building, and belonging to the studio, that can be used for shooting.

Magazine (n.). Box or container in cinematograph camera or projector for holding the roll or spool of film.

Magnetic Tape (n.). A plastic tape coated with ferric oxide powder that, on being run through a variable magnetic field, can be made to register in a permanent form the impulses necessary for the reproduction of electronically produced sounds and pictures.

Magnetic Track (n.). The sound track of a film recorded on magnetic tape, either separate from the picture film, or (in the case of striped film) on the picture film itself. (See *Optical Track, Striped Film.*)

Main Title (n.). Title at the beginning of a film that gives its name.

Maltese Cross (n.). A mechanical device for producing the intermittent movement of film through a cinematograph camera or projector.

Manager (n.). See *Cinema Manager, Studio Manager.*

Married Print (n.). See *Combined Print.*

Mask (n.). Shield placed before a camera lens to cut off some portion of the camera's field of view. (An example is the mask that covers the whole field of view save for an aperture in the shape of a keyhole or telescope eyepiece or the like.)

Master Shot (n.). Single shot occasionally taken of an entire piece of dramatic action in order to facilitate the assembly of the component shots of which it will finally be composed.

Matt (n.). See *Traveling Matt.*

Medium Shot (n.). Shot taken with the camera apparently nearer to the subject than for a long shot, but not so near as for a close-up; in relation to the human subject a shot of the human figure from the knees upward.

Microfilm (n.). Film used for recording printed or written documents, successive pages of the original being photographed on successive frames of the film, so that the frames can subsequently be projected one by one for perusal.

Microphone (n.). Instrument for picking up sound vibrations and converting them into electrical impulses, used in sound-film recording.

Mid-Shot (n.). See *Medium Shot*.

Miniature Shot (n.). See *Model Shot, Foreground Miniature*.

Mix (v. and n.). 1 (Optical). Gradual merging of the end of one shot into the beginning of the next, produced by the superimposition of a fade-out onto a fade-in of equal length. 2 (Sound). To combine the sounds of several sound tracks for the purpose of re-recording them onto a new track.

Mixer (n.). One who mixes sound tracks for the purpose of recording; the apparatus on which sound tracks are mixed.

Model (n.). Miniature replica of a film set made by the art department for purposes of experiment or discussion before the set is finally built full size on the studio floor; a miniature model made to be used in the actual shooting of a film in such a way as to give the illusion of being a full-size construction.

Model Shot (n.). Shot in which models are used (as where small model ships floating in a studio tank are photographed so as to give the illusion of real ships at sea).

Monitor (v.). To reproduce on special apparatus, as the audience is intended to see or hear it, the whole or some constituent part of a radio or television program while it is being recorded or broadcast, or of a film as it is being shot or projected, either to check its quality or content, or to act as a guide for actors or technicians involved in the production; (adj.) descriptive of any apparatus used in monitoring, e.g., monitor speaker, monitor screen, etc.

Montage (n.). Combination in a film of both the picture and sound elements regarded fundamentally as a creative art process; editing regarded as a treatment of reality; the combination in art of representations of fragments of nature to form an imaginative whole that has no counterpart in nature; (in United States) an impressionistic assembly of short shots designed to bridge a lapse of time in a film narrative by briefly indicating the passage of events within it.

Motion Picture (n.). Cinematograph film (especially in United States).

Motivation (n.). Provision of an appropriate cause for a given event, whether in the action (as when a character is delineated as jealous in order to supply the motive for which he subsequently kills his wife) or in the editing (as when the shot of a church tower from below is preceded by a shot of a man looking up at it).

Movie (n.). Film (especially in United States).

Moviola (n.). Trade name of an American instrument in common use in studio cutting rooms that will reproduce the picture of a film in miniature and the sound; and hence (by popular usage) any viewing instrument of a similar kind.

Multiplane Camera (n.). Camera used in making of cartoon films for photographing drawings in several planes to create the illusion of depth.

Multiple Exposure (n.). Two or more exposures made on the same series of film frames.

Mute Negative (n.). Picture negative of a sound film without the sound track.

Mute Print (n.). Positive film print of the picture part of a sound film without the sound track.

Musical (n.). Type of light-entertainment film containing a considerable portion of music and dancing; the film equivalent of a musical comedy.

Narratage (n.). Method whereby one of the characters in a fiction film is depicted as telling the story of the film.

Negative (n. and adj.). Cinematograph film in which the natural tone values of the picture are inverted, and which constitutes a master copy from which a large number of positive prints can be made (see *Positive*).

Newsreel (n.). Actuality film of current events.

N.G. Take (n.). See *Out-take*.

Nigger (n.). Form of screen used in studio lighting.

Nitrate (adj.). Made of cellulose nitrate (q.v.).

Nonflam (adj.). Nonflammable; slow burning; made of cellulose acetate.

Nontheatrical (adj.). Pertaining to film shows (especially on substandard film) that are not presented for public entertainment in ordinary cinemas.

Number Board (n.). Board momentarily held before the camera and photographed at the beginning of a take, recording the title of the film, the number of the scene (i.e. shot) and the number of the take, in order to facilitate identification during editing. (Number board and clapper are usually combined in one unit.)

Observation Port (n.). Aperture in cinema projection box through which the projectionist can observe the auditorium and screen.

Operator (n.). Member of camera crew who operates the camera; film projectionist.

Optical (n.). Any device carried out by the optical department of a laboratory, requiring the use of the optical printer, such as a fade, dissolve, wipe or other special effect.

Optical Printer (n.). Apparatus for enabling images from one film
to be photographed onto another film by means of a lens, used in
making reduction prints and for special effects and trick work.

Optical Track (n.). A sound track produced by the action of a variable light source on a light-sensitive photographic emulsion. (See
Magnetic Track.)

Orthochromatic Film (n.). Photographic film coated with an emulsion
more sensitive to green and yellow light than an ordinary emulsion,
and thus giving a truer rendering of light and shade. (Orthochromatic film was originally so called to distinguish it from the
less sensitive emulsions previously in use; nowadays the term is
used chiefly to distinguish it from the *more* sensitive panchromatic
film, q.v.)

Out-take (n.). Take that is not used in the finished production; often
described also as *N.G. Take.*

Overlay (n.). One soundtrack superimposed on another in re-recording; in television, one camera image combined with another during
transmission, after the manner of a traveling matt (q.v.).

Pan (adj.). Abbreviation of *Panchromatic.*

Pan (v.). To rotate the camera horizontally in taking a shot.

Panchromatic Film (n.). Photographic film sensitive to all colors.

Parallel Development (n.). Device of narrative construction in which
the development of two pieces of action is represented simultaneously by showing first a fragment of one, and then a fragment of
the other, and so on alternately (see *Cross-cut*).

Patron (n.). Name given to cinemagoer by those on the exhibition
side of the film industry.

Perforation (n.). See *Sprocket Hole.*

Persistence of Vision (n.). Tendency of a visual impression to remain
on the retina of the eye for a brief space of time (approximately
one tenth of a second) after the actual light stimulus is removed.

Phase (n.). When the shutter of a camera or projector is moving in
correct relationship to the intermittent movement of the film, so
that it intercepts the light at precisely the moment that the film
begins to move and allows the light to pass again at precisely the
moment the film reaches its next stationary position, they are said
to be in *phase;* when this is not the case, they are said to be *out of
phase.*

Photoelectric Cell (n.). Device for converting variations of light into
corresponding variations of electrical current.

Photogenic (n.). Of a character that lends itself to the making of
good photographs, used especially of persons in a film.

Photographic Track (n.). See *Optical Track.*

Picture Head (n.). That part of the projector mechanism designed to project the picture frames on the screen (as distinct from the sound head, q.v.).

Playback (n.). Reproduction of a sound track in a studio during shooting to enable action or additional sound or both to be synchronized with it.

Plot-Theme (n.). See *Action-theme*.

Positive (adj. and n.). Cinematograph film in which the tone values of the picture correspond to those of the actual scene it represents, the dark parts of the scene appearing dark in the picture, and the light parts appearing light.

Post-Synchronization (n.). Recording and adding sound to a picture after the picture itself has been shot.

Premiere (n.). First exhibition of a film to the public, usually restricted to a single cinema.

Prerelease (n.). Special showing of a film given before the general release.

Prescore (v.). Compose and/or record music for a film before the picture has been shot.

Preview (n.). Special showing given to a film before its premiere or general release to test audience reactions to it.

Print (n.). Positive copy of a film.

Process (v.). To develop and fix exposed film.

Process Shot (n.). Shot in which some special process is used, such as the Dunning or Schufftan process, use of models, etc.

Producer (n.). One who is in charge of all the work involved in the making of a film, or in the work of a film studio, and who bears the ultimate responsibility for its commercial success or failure.

Production Manager (n.). Official in studio responsible for supervising and coordinating expenditure of the various specialist departments engaged in the making of the studio's films.

Production Still (n.). Still photograph that shows any aspect of production work done on a film.

Projection Box (n.). Room, normally behind the rear wall of a cinema auditorium, where the projectors are housed and operated.

Projection Head (n.). See *Picture Head*.

Projectionist (n.). One who operates a projector, or is competent to do so.

Projection Theater (n.). Small private cinema or projection room in a film studio or film company's offices.

Projector (n.). See *Cinematograph Projector*.

Properties (n. pl.). Any articles used in the shooting of a scene in a film such as furniture, etc., which are not actually part of the set construction, and which do not fall under the heading of costumes.

Property Manager (n.). One who is responsible for obtaining, and who looks after, the properties in a film studio.

Props (colloqu.). See *Properties*.

Protective Master (n.). A master copy of a film (e.g., a fine-grain duplicating positive in the case of a black-and-white film, or separation positives in the case of color film) from which a new duplicate negative or negatives can be printed, which is made as an insurance against deterioration or loss of the original negative or working negatives.

Puff (n.). Exaggerated praise written for publicity purposes; a highly favorable criticism of a film.

Puppet Film (n.). Film made by cinematographic animation of puppet figures.

Quick Cutting (n.). Cutting and joining together shots so short that they follow each other in rapid succession on the screen.

Quickie (n.). Abbreviation for *quota quickie*, a type of film made quickly and cheaply (usually by foreign interests) to meet the legal requirements (but normally to defeat the real object) of the Quota Act, in operation in Britain from 1927 to 1937. (The second Quota Act of 1938 was designed to eliminate the quota quickie by basing quota value on production cost.)

Quota (n.). Minimum percentage of British film that a renter is compelled by law to rent, or an exhibitor to show, during a given year.

Rack (v.). To adjust the relative positions of film and gate in a projector by means of a knob or other device, in order to put the film in frame.

Rain (n.). The mesh of fine scratches that constant projection imposes on a film, which, especially when filled with dirt, appear on the screen as a fine rain pouring downward across the projected picture.

Raw Stock (n.). Sensitized film that has not been exposed or processed.

Reaction Shot (n.). A shot showing the reaction of a character in a film to something said or done in the immediately preceding shot.

Realist Film (n.). Type of nonfiction film utilizing material either actual or reconstructed, drawn from real life.

Rear Projection (n.). See *Back Projection*.

Reconstruction (n.). Lifelike reproduction of an actual scene or event for the purpose of filming.

Record (v.). To secure by mechanical means a permanent impression, on either cinematograph film, wax disc or other suitable medium, of sounds of any kind in such a way that they can subsequently be reproduced at will.

Reduce (v.). To make a substandard copy of a film from a standard original (opposite of *Blow-up*).

Reduction Print (n.). A print of narrower gauge than the master copy from which it is made (for example, a 16-mm. print made from a 35-mm. negative), so called because the size of the image has to be reduced optically in printing to the size of the frame on the smaller gauge.

Reduction Process (n.). Process of making a reduction print.

Reel (n.). Roll of film, or the amount of film, that can be wound onto a standard-size spool. (The British standard spool will carry 1,000 feet of film, although a 2,000-foot spool is now in use on most projectors, and is standard in the United States. The 16-mm. equivalent of the 1,000-foot reel is 400 feet.)

Reissue 1. (v.) To put a film into distribution again after it has once been generally released and withdrawn from circulation. 2. (n.). A film so reissued.

Relational Editing (n.). Editing of shots to suggest associations of idea.

Release (v.). To make a film available for hire to exhibitors.

Release Print (n.). Print designed for general showing.

Release Script (n.). Script of film made after it has been completed as a detailed record of its contents.

Renter (n.). One who buys the distribution rights of a film from a producer for a given period in order to be able to hire it out to exhibitors.

Reproducer (n.). Loudspeaker.

Re-record (v.). To make a sound record by electrical means from one or more other sound records; especially to make in this way a single combined sound track from the several component tracks (such as dialogue, music, sound effects, etc.) of a film.

Retake (n.). Repetition of a take.

Reversal Film (n.). Film made for use in cameras (usually substandard) which, when processed, becomes a positive print ready for projection.

Rewind (v.). To wind a reel of film back again after projection so that it is once more ready for projection.

Rewind, Rewinder (n.). Apparatus for rewinding film.

Rough Cut (n.). First assembly of a film that the editor makes by roughly trimming the selected takes and joining them together in the order planned in the script, and which he can then proceed to polish by more exact cutting and rearrangement.

Running Time (n.). Length of time a film will run when projected at its correct speed.

Rushes (n. pl.). Prints of takes that are made immediately after a day's shooting so that they can be viewed by the director and his associates on the following day.

Safety Film (n.). Film of slow combustibility, especially film containing a high proportion of cellulose acetate.

Scene (n.). Series of actions or shots in a film narrative forming a single unit by reason of their essential continuity in time; a piece of continuous action; an abbreviation for script scene (q.v.).

Scenario (n.). Film story cast in the form of sequences and scenes; a production script.

Scenario Editor (n.). Manager of studio department responsible for finding and adapting stories suitable for filming by the studio.

Scenarist (n.). See *Writer*.

Schufftan Process (n.). Method of shooting action on a set, only part of which is constructed in full size, the remainder being constructed in miniature and photographed in a mirror. (The mirror is placed between the camera and the full-size set at such an angle that the view of the model is reflected into the camera, portions of the mirror backing that must be removed to reveal the full-size portions being then scraped away.)

Scout (n.). See *Talent Scout*.

Scraper (n.). Tool used to remove emulsion from film in making a join.

Scratch Print (n.). A print that has been deliberately scratched to prevent it being used for projection, as in the case of shots or sequences that a production library supplies on approval to a customer prior to purchase.

Screen (n.). Diffusive reflecting surface, usually made of opaque white material, on which projected images can be thrown.

Screen Shape (n.). See *Aspect Ratio*.

Script (n.). Written record of the scenes, shots and/or dialogue of a film prepared for the purposes of production.

Script Scene (n.). Shot (q.v.). (Script scene is a term used by scriptwriters, and probably derives from the early practice of taking each scene of a film in one shot.)

Second Feature (n.). Less important of the two feature films in a double-feature program.

Second-run Cinema (n.). See *First-run Cinema*.

Separation Positives (n.). Black-and-white positive prints each copied through an appropriate filter from one of the constituent bands of a color negative (e.g., in the case of Technicolor from the magenta, cyan and yellow) and from which a new color negative can be made if necessary; they are normally made to serve the purpose of protective masters (q.v.).

Sequence (n.). Main division of a film; succession of shots or scenes concerned with the development of one subject or idea; in a story film a succession of scenes that together form a single stage in the development of the narrative.

Serial Film (n.). Film divided into parts designed to be shown successively at different times; film designed to be shown in installments.

Set (n.). Specially constructed artificial setting for a film scene or shot.

Setup (n.). Mutual relationship of subject and camera when latter is in position for the taking of a given shot.

Shoot (v.). To take pictures with a cinematograph camera.

Shooting Schedule (n.). Film script in which the shots are arranged not in the order in which they will finally appear, but in the most convenient order for shooting.

Shooting Script (n.). Completed film script divided into script scenes and containing all necessary technical instructions for shooting.

Short (n.). Any film less than 3,000 feet (of standard film) in length.

Shot (n.). Fragment of moving picture that has been taken, either actually or apparently, in one uninterrupted running of the camera.

Shutter (n.). That part of the mechanism of camera or projector that cuts off light during the instant when the film is moving between the exposure or projection of one frame and the next.

Silent Film (n.). Film planned and produced for exhibition without recorded and mechanically synchronized sound.

Silhouette Film (n.). Film made by cinematographic animation of silhouettes.

Slapstick (n.). Knockabout comedy.

Slow Cutting (n.). Cutting and joining of shots so lengthy that they follow each other in slow succession on the screen.

Slow Motion (n. and adj.). Means by which movement in a shot is represented as taking place more slowly than it did in reality; the opposite of accelerated motion. (Slow motion is achieved by running the camera abnormally fast during shooting, accelerated motion by running it abnormally slowly.)

Sneak Preview (n.). Unadvertised preview.

Soft Focus (adj.). Soft and slightly hazy effect obtained by shooting slightly out of focus.

Soft Print (n.). Print of low contrast, especially suitable for duping (q.v.) purposes.

Sound Camera (n.). Apparatus in which electrical vibrations corresponding to original sound waves are converted into light vibrations and so photographed onto film.

Sound Channel (n.). Complete single-recording equipment; part of sound-film reproducer or re-recorder capable of taking one sound track.

Sound Head (n.). That part of the projector mechanism in which the variations of the sound track are projected onto a photoelectric cell and so converted into electrical impulses, subsequently to be amplified and conveyed to the loudspeakers behind the screen.

Sound Track (n.). Narrow path normally running along one side of the frames of cinematograph sound film, in which the sound is recorded in the form of a photographic trace varying in its light transmission.

Speaker (n.). Loudspeaker, normally situated behind the screen, from which sound is produced in projection of a sound film.

Special Effect (n.). Any effect introduced into a film after shooting and during laboratory processing, e.g., mix, wipe, etc.

Speed (n.). 1 (Of cutting). Rate at which shots follow each other on the screen, determined by their length. 2 (Of emulsion). Rapidity with which a photographic emulsion reacts to incidence of light. 3 (Of lens). Amount of light transmission of the lens. 4 (Projection speed). Speed at which film passes through the projector, the two normal speeds being 16 frames per second for silent film, and 24 frames per second for sound film.

Splice (v. and n.). To join film; a film join.

Split-Screen Process (n.). Process used in making a shot of an actor playing a dual role. (The shot is made in two phases. In the first, part of the frame area is masked, the actor playing his first role in such a position as to register on the exposed portion of the film. In the second, *exactly* this exposed part is masked, and the actor plays his second role so as to register in the remaining portion, now exposed. The two combined give the desired effect.) See also *Traveling Matt*.

Spot (n.). Abbreviation for *Spotlight*.

Spotlight (n.). Lamp capable of projecting narrow beam of bright light onto a small area, used in studio and stage lighting.

Sprocket Hole (n.). Small hole punched at regular intervals along cinematograph film to engage with the sprocket teeth in camera, projector, etc.

Sprocket Tooth (n.). Tooth projecting from sprocket wheel (q.v.).

Sprocket Wheel (n.). Roller in camera, projector, etc., made with projecting teeth on one or both rims, which engage with the sprocket holes of the film and move it forward.

Squeezed Print (n.). A print of a film the pictures on which have been laterally compressed by the anamorphic process (q.v.).

Stage (n.). Part of studio building designed for shooting or recording of sound.

Standard Film (n.). Cinematograph film 35 mm. wide.

Stand-in (n.). One who takes the place of a star during the arranging of lights, adjusting of camera and other lengthy preparations that precede the rehearsal and taking of a shot.

Star (n.). Actor or actress whose appearance in the principal role of a film is regarded as one of the main requisites for its commercial success.

Star System (n.). System of film production that depends primarily for its success on exploitation of film stars.

Static (n.). Fogging of film due to the discharge of static electricity.

Stereophonic (adj.). Descriptive of sound coming from two or more loudspeakers simultaneously, each reproducing an individual recording and so positioned as to combine to give the listener the impression that he can hear the constituent parts of the total sound effect coming from the several directions of which he would be aware if he could hear the sound in reality.

Stereoscopic Film (n.). Film that when projected on the screen, presents a stereoscopic or three-dimensional effect.

Still (n.). Photograph of a scene from a film or of a film personality or of some aspect of production.

Stock (n.). See *Raw Stock*.

Stock Shot (n.). See *Library Shot*.

Stop-Action Camera (n.). Automatically operated camera for exposing successive frames of film at regular but lengthy intervals, as in shooting growth of a plant in accelerated motion (see *Time-Lapse Cinematography*).

Stop-Action Photography (n.). Procedure of stopping the camera and arresting the action at a given moment during the taking of a shot, rearranging some part of the scene, and then continuing with the shooting as before, the result being to present on the screen the illusion of a magic transformation (for example, if the rearrangement consists in removing a pumpkin and putting in its place a coach, nothing else being altered, the pumpkin will appear in the finished film to change suddenly into the coach); see also *Time-Lapse Cinematography*.

Stop-Motion Photography (n.). See *Stop-action Photography*.

Stripe (n.). A narrow band of ferric-oxide coating running along the sound-track area of a cinematograph film to enable the sound of the film to be recorded and reproduced magnetically instead of photographically.

Studio (n.). Premises used by a production company for making films.

Studio Manager (n.). Official responsible for running of a film studio, employment of its work people, etc.

Substandard Film (n.). Any cinematograph film of a width less than 35 mm.

Subtitle (n.). Title inserted in a film to elucidate or advance the action or argument.

Subtractive Process (n.). Any process of color cinematography in which two or more basic colors are mingled in various proportions by superimposition on the film.

Superimpose (v.). To print two shots, one on top of the other on the same length of film, so that when projected on the screen each can be seen through the other.

Support (n.). Flexible durable transparent material (normally, but not necessarily, cellulose) that is coated with photographic emulsion to make cinematograph film.

Supporting Program (n.). Films shown in a program as an accompaniment to the main or feature film.

Synchronize (v.). To adjust the sound track of a film to the picture in editing so that whenever the source of a reproduced sound is shown visually on the screen, the time relationship between sound and picture appears natural; to secure in projection the relationship between the sound and picture of a film intended by its makers. (A film so synchronized is colloquially described as *in sync.*; and contrariwise as *out of sync.*)

Sync. (n.). See *Synchronize.*

Synopsis (n.). Brief summary of a story considered suitable for filming and prepared as the first stage in the writing of the scenario; a summary of the story of a finished film, prepared for publicity purposes.

Take (n.). Single recording of a shot made during production. (Usually several takes of a shot are made, the best one being selected for inclusion in the completed film.)

Take-up Spool (n.). Spool on which film is taken up after it has passed through the projector mechanism.

Talent Scout (n.). Person employed to search for potential actors for a film production company.

Tape (n.). See *Magnetic Tape.*

Technician (n.). Skilled worker in any branch of film production.

Technicolor (n.). A proprietary color process involving the production in a special camera of three separate negatives during shooting, registering the blue, green and red elements of the scene, respectively, and the making of color prints by means of matrices made (through intermediary separation positives) from these negatives.

Technirama (n.). A wide-screen color process controlled by the Technicolor Company.

Telecine Projector (n.). Apparatus enabling cinematograph films to be transmitted on television.

Telephoto Lens (n.). Lens of great focal length capable of producing enlarged photographs of objects at a distance.

Teleprompter (n.). A device for displaying close to the camera the words a television performer has to speak so that he can be prompted while seeming to continue to look directly at the camera.

Telerecording (n.). A cinematograph film of a television program made by photographing it directly from the cathode-ray tube of a television receiver.

Tempo (n.). Impression of speed that a film makes on the spectator, either by the succession of incidents or of shots, or by the rate of movement shown or the rhythm of the sound.

Theater (n.). See *Projection Theater*.

Theme (n.). Subject, central idea.

Theme Song (n.). Song occupying a prominent place in the action of a film.

Thread (v.). To lace the first few feet of a reel of film through a projector or other film mechanism in order that the film can be run through it.

Thread Up (v.). To thread film from the feed spool through the various appropriate parts of any film mechanism (camera, printer, editing viewer, projector) to the take-up spool preparatory to operating the mechanism.

Three-D (adj.). Three-dimensional (see *Stereoscopic*).

Three-Dimensional Film (n.). See *Stereoscopic Film*.

Throw (n.). Distance from film projector to screen.

Tilt (v.). To turn the film camera up or down in shooting so that the axis of the lens rotates through a vertical plane.

Time-lapse Cinematography (n.). Extreme form of accelerated-motion cinematography (q.v.) whereby, in order to secure a moving picture of an extremely slow process—such as the growth of a plant—the film is exposed, frame by frame, at a considerable time interval.

Tint (v.). To color film with a dye. (In the days of the silent film shots and scenes were thus tinted different colors for emotional and dramatic effect.)

Title (n.). Any written or printed statement introduced into a film for its own sake and not merely as a part of a picture.

Todd A-O (n.). A wide-screen process dependent on the use of special film 65 mm. in width.

Tone (v.). To obtain color effects by treating a monochrome print with chemicals.

Topical (n.). Newsreel.

Track (n.). Sound track (q.v.).

Tracking Shot (n.). Shot taken with the camera moving sideways, forward or backward.

Trade Show (n.). Exhibition of a film to members of the film trade that every distributor is legally compelled to give before he can take bookings on it.

Trailer (n.). Very short film of two or three minutes' duration shown for publicity purposes or for making a series of announcements; especially, such a film composed of extracts from a longer film and shown beforehand to advertise it.

Transit Case (n.). Traveling case for reels of 35-mm. film made of metal lined with wood to meet the requirements of railway and shipping companies.

Travel Ghost (n.). Upward or downward overspilling of the lighter portions of the screen image due to the projection shutter being out of phase (q.v.).

Traveling Matt (n.). Film that is run through a film printer together with the film to be printed in order to mask a portion of it and prevent that portion from printing. (The traveling matt process is used to mask an area that does not remain static but moves and changes with the rest of the picture. For example, where an actor is to be shown in two roles, A and B, simultaneously, he plays A on the set, and B against a plain blue backing. The negative of B is processed and then duped several times, the contrast being increased with each duping until a silhouette effect is obtained. A print is then made from the negative of A, with the silhouette used as a traveling matt to mask the area occupied by the figure of B. Finally, a new negative is made by combining this masked print with the first print of B.)

Travelogue (n.). Actuality film of life and scenes in other countries; travel film.

Treatment (n.). Stage in the development of a film story from its original synopsis form to the final shooting script.

Trick Film (n.). Film that depends mainly on the representation, through special manipulation of the technical processes of production, of situations and events that would in reality be impossible, such as a cyclist riding up the side of a house, or a magic horse flying through the air.

Trim (v.). Cut film preparatory to making a join.

Trolley (n.). Wheeled vehicle on which the camera can be moved in taking a shot.

Trucking Shot (n.). Shot taken with the camera in movement on a truck or trolley.

Two-Shot (n.). Close shot of two persons with the camera as near as possible while still keeping them both in the shot.

"U" Certificate (n.). Certificate awarded to a film by the British

Board of Film Censors to denote that it is suitable for universal exhibition to unaccompanied children as well as to adults.

Unmodulated Track (n.). Sound track that has no modulations and is therefore incapable of producing sound other than ground noise.

Variable Area Track (n.). Opaque sound track traversed along its length by one or more lines of clear film, its light transmission varying as the width of the lines varies.

Variable Density Track (n.). Sound track composed of a series of transverse bands of different densities.

Variable Width Track (n.). See *Variable Area Track*.

Variable Focus Lens (n.). Lens whose focal length can be altered during shooting, as, for example, by mechanism to change distance between front and rear components of the lens.

Vault (n.). Film store for inflammable film, of such construction and dimensions as to comply with the regulations of the local authority or (where part of a film factory) of the Home Office in Britain.

Velocitator (n.). A form of dolly (q.v.) incorporating a small crane for the camera and seats for the technicians operating it.

Video Tape (n.). 35-mm. magnetic tape used in the Ampex apparatus (q.v.).

Viewpoint (n.). See *Camera Viewpoint*.

Vignette (n.). Mask placed before camera lens to produce a picture in which only the center part is visible in a diffused oval, circle, etc.

Vision Mixer (n.). Television technician responsible under the producer for switching transmission from one camera to another, from camera to film, etc.

Vista-Vision (n.). A proprietary system of wide-screen cinematography depending on the use of an image whose horizontal axis runs parallel to the length of the film instead of across it.

Visual (n.). Shot, or other single visual component of a film (*visuals* is sometimes used by pretentious theorists as a counterpart to *sounds*, but the term appears to have no precise meaning).

Wax (v.). To apply a thin coating of wax to the edge of newly processed film to enable it to run more easily on the projector.

Western (n.). Film of adventure among cowboys in the "Wild West" of America, which usually has its climax in a pursuit on horseback.

Whip Over (n.). See *Flash Pan*.

Wide Screen (n.). Descriptive of a cinematograph picture of exaggerated width, as produced, for example, by the CinemaScope, Technirama, Todd A-O, Vista-Vision and other similar proprietary processes. (See also *Aspect Ratio*.)

Wild Track (n.). Sound track recorded quite independently of any picture with which it may subsequently be combined.

Wipe (n.). Form of transition from one shot to another in which a margin moves across the screen to eliminate the first shot and reveal the second.

Wipe Off (v.). To remove the recording from a magnetic tape so that it is in a condition to take a new recording.

Writer (n.). Technician who writes script of a film, or any part of it.

"X" Certificate (n.). A certificate allotted by the British Board of Film Censors to denote that a film is in their opinion unsuitable to be shown to children under sixteen, irrespective of whether they are accompanied by parents or other responsible adults.

Zip Pan (n.). See *Flash Pan*.

Zoom Lens (n.). Lens of variable focal length. (The name presumably derives from the fact that when the focus is quickly increased during shooting, the effect on the screen is a rapid change from distant shot to near shot, giving the impression that the camera has "zoomed," or swung, toward the subject.)

INDEX